Herberg, From Marxism to Judaism

FOR MY PARENTS
Rabbi William and Bella Dalin
With Love and Gratitude

FROM MARXISM TO JUDAISM:

THE COLLECTED ESSAYS OF WILL HERBERG

Edited with an Introduction by
David G. Dalin

Maurice Greenberg Center for Judaic Studies
University of Hartford

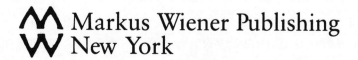

Markus Wiener Publishing
New York

MASTERWORKS OF MODERN JEWISH WRITING SERIES
is issued in conjunction with the Center for the Study of the
American Jewish Experience, Hebrew Union College–Jewish
Institute of Religion, Cincinnati.

Cover Design: Cheryl Mirkin

Copy Editing: Daniel Marcus

Library of Congress Cataloging-in-Publication Data

Herberg, Will.
  From Marxism to Judaism : selected essays / by Will Herberg :
edited with an introduction by David G. Dalin.
    p.   cm.—(Masterworks of modern Jewish writing)
  ISBN 0-910129-91-6 :
  1. Judaism—20th century. 2. Antisemitism. 3. United States-
-Religion—1945– 4. Church and state—United States. I. Dalin,
David G. II. Title. III. Series.
  BM565.H33   1989
  296—dc19   88-34200
                                                                   CIP

Printed in the United States of America.

Acknowledgments

I would like to thank Professor Donald G. Jones, of Drew University, the legal executor of the Will Herberg Estate, for his permission to reprint all of the Herberg essays included in this volume.

My thanks also go, individually, to the publishers of the following essays for their permission to reprint them:

"Will Herberg in Retrospect"—Reprinted in slightly abridged form from *Commentary*, July 1988, by permission; all rights reserved.

"The Crisis of Socialism"—Reprinted from *Jewish Frontier*, September 1944, by permission.

"From Marxism to Judaism"—Reprinted from *Commentary*, January 1947, by permission; all rights reserved.

"Christian Apologist to the Secular World"—Reprinted from *Union Seminary Quarterly Review*, May 1956, by permission.

"Has Judaism Still Power to Speak: A Religion for an Age of Crisis"—Reprinted from *Commentary*, May 1949, by permission; all rights reserved.

"Rosenzweig's 'Judaism of Personal Existence': A Third Way Between Orthodoxy and Modernism"—

Commentary, April 1950, by permission; all rights reserved.

"The Religion of Americans and American Religion"—Excerpt from *Protestant-Catholic-Jew: An Essay in American Religious Sociology,* by Will Herberg. Reprinted by permission of Doubleday, a division of Bantam, Doubleday, Dell Publishing Group, Inc. Copyright © 1955, 1960 by Will Herberg.

"America's Civil Religion: What It Is and Whence It Comes,"—Reprinted from Russell E. Richey and Donald G. Jones (edited) *American Civil Religion,* 1974, by permission.

CONTENTS

Preface

William F. Buckley, Jr.

Will Herberg was a scholar of promethean accomplishments. That isn't something people tend to care very much about, in weighing whether to acquaint themselves with a dead man's thoughts. But he was a rare individual: passionate, patient, exuberant, proud, humble. He had found his own way, having traversed many ideological and philosophical worlds. The voyage, and the character, made his informed writings intensively interesting. He was my colleague at National Review for a few happy and productive years, and I pity those who were not acquainted with his wisdom and with his personality. Any posthumous effort to do so is worth while.

May, 1988

Will Herberg in Retrospect

DAVID G. DALIN

Very few people today remember who Will Herberg was. If his name is recognized at all, it is probably as the author of *Protestant-Catholic-Jew* (1955), a popular evocation of America's "triple melting pot" whose thesis has become a part of the sociological language of our time. Yet Herberg, who died in 1977, was undeniably one of the most interesting Jewish intellectuals of the last half-century, and one, moreover, whose journey from Marxism to Judaism, and from the political Left to the political Right, resonates with peculiar aptness today.

Herberg was born in 1901, in the same Russian village in which his father had been born before him. By the time his family arrived in the United States, in 1904, Herberg's parents, whom he would later describe as "passionate atheists," were already committed to the faith that mankind's salvation lay in socialism. Curiously, both his father, who died when Herberg was ten, and his mother held the American public-school system in "contempt." Although he attended Brooklyn's Public School 72 and Boys' High, Herberg's real education took place at his parents' kitchen table. A precocious and versatile student, by the time he was a teen-ager Herberg had learned Greek, Latin, French, German, and Russian. Graduating from high school in 1918, he later attended CCNY and Columbia University, where he studied philosophy and history, apparently without ever completing the course work for an academic degree.

Herberg inherited and acted upon his parents' commitments. Entering the Communist movement while still a teen-ager, he subsequently brought to radical politics a theoretical erudition that, through his contributions to left-wing journals in the 20's and early 30's, helped to elevate the intellectual standards of American Marxism. While less prolific than Max Eastman or the novelist John Dos Passos, Herberg was perhaps the most "catholic" of Marxist polemicists, writing regularly on an amazingly diverse number of topics, from Edmund Wilson's views of proletarian literature, to Sidney Hook's explication of Marx on revolution, to the relationship between Freudian psychoanalysis and Communist thought.

Herberg's attachment to Communism was no mere affectation; so earnestly did he embrace the Marxist "faith" that he even sought to square it with Einstein's theory of relativity. Indeed, perhaps his boldest contribution to the radical thought of the period lay in his effort to reconcile Marxism with, on the one hand, the new Einsteinian cosmology, which had gone virtually unnoticed among radical writers in America, and, on the other hand, with Freudianism. For Herberg, both Marxism and the theory of relativity were "scientifically true," and as for Freudianism he wrote in the 30's that the "world of socialism—to which nothing human is alien and which cherishes every genuine manifestation of the human spirit—lays a wreath of homage on the grave of Sigmund Freud."

In the 1920's Herberg's allegiances within the Communist movement lay with the group headed by Jay Lovestone, followers and supporters of Bukharin, who were eventually to be ousted from the party by Stalin in 1929. At that point Herberg became a staff member and editor of the Lovestonite paper, *Workers Age,* many of whose contributors would later become bitter anti-Stalinists. As the 1930's progressed, however, Herberg found himself increasingly disenchanted not just with the party but with Marxism itself. There were the usual milestones along the path: the Stalinist purges, the Communist betrayal of the Popular Front during the Spanish Civil War, the Russian invasion of Finland, and especially the Stalin-Hitler nonaggression pact of 1939. For Herberg, as for many of his generation, this last dispelled any remaining belief that "only a socialist government can defeat totalitarianism."

But his final break with orthodox Marxism represented more than just a change in political loyalties. As he would confess years later, Marxism had been, to him and to others like him, "a religion, an ethic, and a theology; a vast all-embracing doctrine of man and the universe, a passionate faith with meaning." Not that Herberg was about to abandon the values that had first attracted him to revolutionary activity. Rather, "My discovery was that I could no longer find basis and support for these ideals in the materialistic religion of Marxism. . . ." Something else was wanted to replace the failed god of Marxism and to fill the inner spiritual void which had left Herberg "deprived of the commitment and understanding that alone made life livable." It was then he chanced to read Reinhold Niebuhr's *Moral Man and Immoral Society,* a book that was profoundly to change the course of his life.

More than any other American thinker of the 1930's and 1940's, Niebuhr related theology to politics through a realistic assessment of human nature that seemed, and not just to

Will Herberg alone, inescapably relevant in a time of the breakdown of the Communist faith. In the writings of Niebuhr, Herberg discovered a compelling theological position from which to derive his own post-Marxist, but still essentially liberal, faith. "Humanly speaking," he would later write, Niebuhr's work "converted me, for in some manner I cannot describe, I felt my whole being, and not merely my thinking, shifted to a new center. . . . What impressed me most profoundly was the paradoxical combination of realism and radicalism that Niebuhr's 'prophetic' faith made possible. . . . Here, in short, was a 'social idealism' without illusions, in comparison with which even the most 'advanced' Marxism appeared confused, inconsistent, and hopelessly illusion-ridden."

So thoroughly did Herberg fall under the spell of Niebuhr's thought that by the time he met him personally—Niebuhr was then teaching at Union Theological Seminary in New York—he was contemplating becoming a Christian. After several discussions with Niebuhr, Herberg did in fact declare his intention to convert, but Niebuhr counseled him instead to explore his own religious tradition first, and directed him across the street to the Jewish Theological Seminary. There, Herberg undertook instruction in Hebrew and Jewish thought.

Herberg was inspired by what he learned. In Judaism he found, after years of searching, a faith that encouraged social action without falling into the trap of utopianism—and also, more importantly, a religious edifice that satisfied his own hunger for orthodoxy. Throughout the 1940's, while earning a living as the educational director of the International Ladies Garment Workers Union, Herberg met regularly with rabbis and students at the Seminary and at his own home, developing and explicating his emerging theology of Judaism. "In those early days," says one of those students, "when the naturalistic theology so brilliantly expounded by Professor Mordecai Kaplan was the main intellectual influence in Jewish religious circles, we were fascinated by Herberg's espousal of the orthodox ideas of a supernatural God, Messiah, and Torah, expounded with fervor and yet interpreted in a new way."

Out of these intellectual encounters, and out of several essays published in COMMENTARY and elsewhere in the late 1940's, came Herberg's first major work, *Judaism and Modern Man,* an interpretation of Judaism in the light of existentialist philosophy which appeared in 1951 and was highly praised by Jewish scholars. (Niebuhr himself believed that the book "may well become a milestone in the religious thought of America.") Although *Judaism and Modern Man* made Herberg's reputation as a theologian, it did not lead to the academic position that he then actively sought for himself. After 1948, when his duties with the ILGWU diminished, he offered courses on a part-time basis at the New School for Social Research, served briefly as the editor of the new quarterly journal *Judaism,* but earned much of his income from free-lance articles and reviews and from lectures on college campuses and to synagogue and church groups far and wide. At least some of his energies were also devoted to the research and writing of *Protestant-Catholic-Jew* which, upon its publication in 1955, brought Herberg the recognition he had long sought and a full-time academic appointment at Drew University, a Methodist institution in New Jersey, where he would teach until his retirement in 1976.

When Herberg published *Judaism and Modern Man,* he still considered himself very much a liberal, albeit of the fervently anti-Communist variety. Throughout the first half of the 1950's he continued to publish regularly in the *New Republic, New Leader,* COMMENTARY, and *Christian Century.* As the decade wore on, however, Herberg began increasingly to identify himself with political conservatism. He became part of that remarkable group of ex-Communists and ex-Trotskyists around William F. Buckley, Jr.'s *National Review,* a group that included James Burnham, Willmoore Kendall, Frank Meyer, Freda Utley, Max Eastman, and Whittaker Chambers. As religion editor of *National Review,* and as a frequent contributor to other conservative journals like *Intercollegiate Review* and *Modern Age,* Herberg spent the ensuing years calling repeatedly for a reassessment of the prevailing liberal consensus concerning church-state separation, and more generally, for a positive role for religion in American life.

II

B y the time of his death in March 1977, Will Herberg was nowhere near so well known as he had been fifteen or twenty years earlier. The grip over American intellectual life that the Left had achieved in the 60's was only just beginning to show perceptible signs of loosening, while the neoconservative movement, which Herberg (despite his negative attitude toward Zionism and Israel) in many ways presaged, was still in the process of consolidation. Added to this was the fact that Herberg was not easily classifiable as a thinker. A Jewish theologian, a sociologist of American religion, a political conservative—he eluded the usual categories. Today, although *Protestant-Catholic-Jew* is still considered, among those who know it, a classic work in American religious sociology, and although some historians (like George H. Nash) regard Herberg as an important architect of conservative thought in the postwar period, in general his influence and his legacy remain opaque.

To properly reassess his intellectual leg one needs to turn back to the work. In an article in COMMENTARY in January 1947, "From Marxism to Judaism," Herberg had called for "a great theological reconstruction" of Judaism, arising from the thought of such contemporary Catholic and Protestant figures as Jacques Maritain, Karl Barth, and Reinhold Niebuhr. *Judaism and Modern Man* represents Herberg's own attempt to pursue this task of theological reconstruction by offering a new existentialist interpretation of historical Judaism as it is embodied in the biblical-rabbinic tradition. While the book deals systematically with God and man, reason and revelation, social ethics, the meaning of Torah, and the destiny of Israel, Herberg meant it to be more than a "neutral, objective handbook on the Jewish religion"; it was, in his own words, also "a confession of faith and declaration of total commitment" on the part of one "whose trust in the idols of modernity has broken down and who is now ready to listen to the message of faith."

At the time, Herberg's existentialist approach struck a responsive chord among many, within the Jewish community and beyond, who were searching for "enlightened" forms of spiritual inspiration. *Judaism and Modern Man* was greeted with enthusiasm by respected Jewish reviewers; Rabbi Milton Steinberg went so far as to say that Herberg had written "the book of the generation on the Jewish religion." Others, however, were less enthusiastic; and with reason.

For one thing, Herberg's theology seemed in crucial respects to owe more to Christianity than to Judaism. Thus, in *Judaism and Modern Man,* which he described as "avowedly Niebuhrian in temper and thought," Herberg sought to formulate a "new Jewish theology" predicated upon a less optimistic image of man, upon a greater recognition of human sinfulness and human limitations. Elsewhere he wrote appreciatively of Niebuhr's rediscovery of the classical doctrine of "original sin, which is one of the great facts of human life . . . at the root of man's existentialist plight." Yet the doctrine of original sin as a theological category is neither inherent in nor central to Judaism. Even though one may discover, as Herberg does, passages from the Talmud that in isolation convey the impression of a sin-preoccupied culture, the overall emphasis of traditional Judaism is far from the theological pessimism to which Herberg, following Niebuhr and Paul Tillich, subscribes. As a result, whatever vogue it may have enjoyed at the time of publication, *Judaism and Modern Man* has had little to say over the years to Jews in search of fresh formulations of their faith.

Moreover, those within the Jewish community who might have been attracted to the element of affirmation in Herberg were put off by his antipathetic views on Zionism and the state of Israel. Central to Herberg's understanding is the notion that Jewish nationalism represents "the most radical perversion of the idea of Israel," an idea that he connects instead with the "unperformed task" of redemption that the Jews are called upon to fulfill in the world. Ironically, this denigration of Jewish nationalism has more in common with the anti-Zionist ideology of classical Reform Judaism, which Herberg disdained, than with the neo-Orthodox religious thought of Martin Buber and Franz Rosenzweig to which he so often paid homage. To compound the irony, this same concept of the "unperformed task," of a special Jewish "mission" to the nations, served then and continues to serve as the rationale behind much of the Jewish political and theological radicalism of our time—the very sort of radicalism Will Herberg had come profoundly to reject.

Whatever the reason, the state of Israel never played the role in Herberg's religious thought that it did in that of Emil Fackenheim, Abraham Joshua Heschel, Mordecai Kaplan, and other postwar theologians. Quite the contrary: "For the state of Israel, however highly we may regard it," maintained Herberg, "is, after all, but another community of this world. . . ." That he did not deem it necessary to revise these views even after the Six-Day War of 1967 remains one of the more curious facets of his intellectual career, and another wedge between him and otherwise sympathetic readers.

Herberg's theological writings, finally, had little impact within the secular world of which he had once been a part and to which he continued to address his appeals. His call in COMMENTARY for "a great theological reconstruction" met with a positively inhospitable reception among his fellow Jewish ex-Marxists at *Partisan Review* and Dwight Macdonald's magazine *Politics*. These were, for the most part, cultural modernists who had—to put it mildly—little interest in theological reflection and much less in personal affirmation of religious belief.

To these secular critics, like Irving Howe, Herberg's commitments bespoke a "new failure of nerve," and his call for a religious revival represented "an escape from the responsibilities of political life and the uncertainties of worldly experience." Sidney Hook and Daniel Bell also attacked Herberg's belief that democracy rests on "religio-philosophical" truths about man's fallibility, or that religion might offer a bulwark against totalitarianism. His "defeatist" retreat to religion found little support among most of the contributors to *Partisan Review*'s 1950 symposium on "Religion and the Intellectuals," and not surprisingly, the appearance of *Judaism and Modern Man* the following year went unnoticed in *Partisan Review* and other important journals of the secular Left.

H erberg's most famous book remains, unquestionably, the 1955 *Protestant-Catholic-Jew*. In writing it he sought to account for a paradox. On the one hand, no culture had ever been so thoroughly committed to materialist consumption as was postwar America, a place where people lived as if religious teachings and spiritual values were nonexistent. On the other hand, all around one saw signs of religious revival, at least on a superficial level. There was the spectacular rise of Billy Graham; the addition of the phrase "under God" to the Pledge of Allegiance; the printing of "In God We Trust" on certain postage stamps. President Eisenhower had unexpectedly opened his inaugural address with a prayer, and had given a nationally broadcast speech on the need for religious faith. The best-selling book in America in 1953 and 1954 was *The Power of Positive Thinking,* by the Reverend Norman Vincent Peale. Church construction was booming, and church membership rising dramatically.

American Jews, too, seemed to be participating in this national religious revival. Postwar synagogue building eclipsed anything that had been seen in the 1920's and 1930's. New congregations sprang up all over the United States. The American-born children of Jews who had never thought about their Jewishness, or who had done so only to reject it, suddenly found themselves joining and even organizing synagogues in small towns and suburbia.

To Herberg, all this suggested the formation of a society in which religious affiliation, rather than class or ethnicity, had become the primary social determinant. In order "to belong" in American society, one had to belong to a religious community. Moreover, contrary to established sociological belief, America was not one melting pot, but rather a triple melting pot; to be an American in the 1950's meant to be identified with one of the "three great religions of democracy": Protestantism, Catholicism, Judaism.

There is much that was, and is, striking in this thesis—not least, in retrospect, Herberg's daring elevation of Judaism to coequal status in the national drama with the two great branches of Christianity. Indeed, one cannot help feeling that Herberg's saying so helped in some measure to make it so: published on the heels of celebrations in 1954 of 300 years of Jewish settlement in North America, *Protestant-Catholic-*

Jew served as a kind of "scientific" legitimation of the arrival of American Jews as partners on the national religious scene, bolstering Jewish self-respect and altering for the better the perceptions of American Jews held by their non-Jewish neighbors.

Nevertheless, Herberg's analysis is open to serious question. His claims about the eclipse of ethnicity, for example, were hardly borne out by developments of the next two decades. "The perpetuation of ethnic differences in any serious way is altogether out of line with the logic of American reality," he wrote in 1955, yet only a few years later Nathan Glazer and Daniel P. Moynihan were demonstrating, in *Beyond the Melting Pot,* the falsity of Herberg's statement. Or again, for the sake of his overall analysis Herberg dismissed the fundamentalist Protestant "fringe" sects in the United States—"they become very minor denominations, hardly affecting the total picture"—despite the fact that during the 1950's close to ten million American Protestants were defining themselves as evangelical Christians and even as Herberg was writing new evangelical sects were arising and older ones were undergoing revitalization. Less than five years after the publication of *Protestant-Catholic-Jew,* the sociologist Seymour Martin Lipset could note that such fundamentalist sects were "far stronger today than at any time in the 20th century," and that the much-heralded growth in church membership was taking place precisely among these "fringe sects," rather than within the traditional Protestant "mainline" denominations in which Herberg placed so much stock.

III

If one tries to account for the peculiar lack of resonance of Will Herberg's name today, these and other weaknesses in his work both as a theologian and as a sociologist must figure prominently. But to stop with those weaknesses is to miss what was fresh and even compelling about Herberg's views at the time, and what still recommends them today. The glue that held it all together was Herberg's emerging political conservatism.

The touchstone of Herberg's conservatism was a political historicism rooted in the conception of natural law as formulated by Edmund Burke (whom Herberg had begun to read at the suggestion of Niebuhr). Burkean conservatism regards traditional religion as the very basis of political culture, without which the maintenance of social order is an impossibility; drawing upon this view, Herberg argued for the necessity of religion as a "civilizing force," one that would enable the American body politic to survive as a moral entity in the postwar world.

It was Herberg's neo-Burkean approach to matters of religion and state that led to his close association with *National Review,* and in particular to the conviction, shared with Whittaker Chambers, that the struggle between Soviet Communism and the free world was, in fact, the struggle of atheism against religion. At home, of course, the problem was not so much Communism as secular liberalism, and as the religion editor of *National Review* Herberg took it as his special task to criticize systematically the established liberal consensus on issues of church and state; in so doing, he made probably his most significant contribution to postwar conservative thought.

The position Herberg espoused was predicated on the argument that the authors of the Constitution never intended to erect a "wall of separation." The "establishment-of-religion" clause of the First Amendment had been profoundly misunderstood: although the Founding Fathers did not want to favor any single religion, they were not against helping all religions, or all religion, equally. "Neither in the minds of the Founding Fathers nor in the thinking of the American people through the 19th and into the 20th century," wrote Herberg, "did the doctrine of the First Amendment ever imply an ironclad ban forbidding the government to take account of religion or to support its various activities." In the last few years this argument has been advanced with greater confidence than it once was; it is worth recalling that, outside of the legal community, Herberg was one of the first American intellectuals to articulate it.

Herberg was especially vocal in his criticism of liberal American Jews and their insistence that religion be kept rigidly distinct from public life. Jewish survival, in the liberal reading, was most secure where the wall separating religion and state was strongest, and maintaining the wall meant maintaining a steadfast opposition to any and all religious symbols or practices in public institutions. In several articles published during the 1950's and 1960's, Herberg urged the liberal Jewish "establishment" to reassess this position. "The American Jew must have sufficient confidence in the capacity of democracy to preserve its pluralistic . . . character without any *absolute* wall of separation between religion and public life," he wrote in 1952. And a decade or so later, frustrated by liberal Jewish support for the 1963 Supreme Court decisions banning the Lord's Prayer and Bible reading in the public schools, he entered a plea for a restoration of religion to a place of honor in American public life:

> Within the meaning of our political tradition and political practice, the promotion [of religion] has been, and continues to be, a part of the very legitimate "secular" purpose of the state. Whatever the "neutrality" of the state in matters of religion may be, it cannot be a neutrality between religion and no-religion, any more than . . . it could be a neutrality between morality and no-morality, . . . [both religion and morality being] as necessary to "good government" as "national prosperity."

"The traditional symbols of the divine presence in our public life," Herberg warned, "ought not to be tampered with."

Needless to say, the warning went generally unheeded within the Jewish community. Some Jewish leaders publicly dissociated themselves from Herberg's views; in the words of one liberal critic, Herberg was "certainly the most stupid Jew I've ever heard of." It has taken another two decades—which happened to be the politically and religiously fateful ones of the 60's and 70's—for Herberg's critique of the secularizing tendencies of American Jewish liberalism to find wider echoes in the internal politics of the Jewish community (where, today, the influence of the Orthodox is anyway more strongly felt).

Of course much has intervened to make this argument a more respectable one, perhaps above all the willingness of many Americans of all denominations and walks of life to assert the link between public morality and religious belief. From a self-consciously Jewish standpoint, such figures as Irving Kristol, Murray Friedman, Milton Himmelfarb, and the late Seymour Siegel have argued forcefully that an American political culture uninformed by religious beliefs and institutions itself poses a danger to the position and the security of Jews. If even today this view can hardly be said to represent the mainstream Jewish consensus, which for the most part remains committed to the old doctrine of separatism, at least it commands greater intellectual force and weight than ever before. In this it owes something, however unrecognized and unacknowledged, to the example of Will Herberg.

The publication of this collection of essays affords me a welcome opportunity to publicly acknowledge my thanks to a number of people. I owe a special debt of gratitude to Neal Kozodoy, who first suggested that I consider writing an article about Will Herberg for *Commentary*. I remain grateful for his continuing encouragement, and numerous constructive suggestions, throughout the writing and revising of this article, which was originally published in the July 1988 issue of *Commentary* and which here reappears (in slightly abridged form) as the introductory essay to this volume.

I also owe a special debt of gratitude to my good friend, Jonathan D. Sarna, for inviting me to edit this collection of Herberg's essays as part of the Masterworks of Jewish Writing Series of which he is the general editor, and for his many excellent suggestions concerning the editing of this collection. I am delighted to have this opportunity to publicly acknowledge my gratitude for his continuing advice, encouragement and friendship.

I would like to thank Markus Wiener, the publisher of this volume, for his close reading of the entire manuscript, and for his valuable suggestions and corrections.

My deepest thanks also go to my wife Hilary who has spent countless hours, hearing and reading my ideas about Will Herberg, his life and thought. She has always been both a patient listener and a most loving critic.

Finally, I owe an immeasurable debt of gratitude to my parents, Rabbi William and Bella Dalin. Words alone cannot begin to express my thanks to them for their continuing love, encouragement, and support, in all that I have done, over the years. This book is dedicated to them, with love and gratitude.

Hartford, Dec. 1988

Part I

FROM MARXISM
TO JUDAISM

—1—

The Crisis of Socialism

(1947)

For what shall it profit a man, if he shall gain the whole world and lose his own soul?—MARK 8:36

In the course of a century and a half, modern socialism has weathered many a storm. At first sight it might appear that the crisis in which socialism finds itself today is merely another of these incidents, though admittedly the worst to date. But such an estimate would, in my opinion, be a grave error. The present crisis is not just a passing phase of a forward-moving cycle of growth. The present crisis is the expression of a profound moral bankruptcy, of an inner collapse, from which there is no way out except by making a new beginning in a new direction.

Until the Bolshevik revolution and the rise of fascist totalitarianism, socialism was regarded by men of good will as a great and noble ideal unfortunately unrealizable in this sinful world. The moral worth of the ideal was freely admitted; what was questioned was the possibility of ever attaining it. Socialists were arraigned by their opponents as well-meaning visionaries who were misleading the ignorant masses with their far-fetched utopian schemes.

Opposition of this kind the socialists could take and thrive upon. Charges of utopianism meant very little to them except as a spur to speed the day of victory and thus refute the skepticism of their opponents. As long as they themselves believed, passionately and unquestioningly, in the moral worth of their goal, as long as they found it generally acknowledged by all decent people, there were no difficulties they could not surmount, no persecutions they could not sustain.

How different is the picture today! No one today will accuse socialists or communists of advocating far-fetched utopian schemes. On the contrary, the trouble with socialism, we are told, is that it is only too practicable, only too real: "Look at Russia if you want to see it in operation. There you have your socialism, but there you have also the most ruthless dictatorship, the most grinding slavery, that mankind has experienced in centuries. That is what socialism leads to."

In other words, what is now being challenged is not the practicability but the *moral* worth of the socialist goal. And it is being questioned not merely by the opponents of socialism but by every honest, thinking socialist.

Here we have the full measure of the depth and gravity of the present crisis of socialism. Socialism, the socialism with which Europe and America have been familiar for decades, is bankrupt: it has lost faith in its own ultimate worth. Party Communists, of course, have no such qualms; they glory in their degradation. But the socialist of integrity stands confused, demoralized, incapable of effective thought or action. How can he be sure that in working for his socialist goal he is not really preparing the way for a Hitler or laying the foundations for a Stalin? If he is at all honest with himself he must confess that the totalitarian collectivism on which the Russian and German regimes are erected bears an uncomfortable affinity to certain aspects of his own socialist faith.

I

Socialism arose in the modern world as a protest against bourgeois society for enslaving man by turning him into a thing, an instrument, a mere depersonalized adjunct of the machine. It held forth the vision of a social order in which "the free development of each will lead to the free development of all."[1] It called for a revolutionary transformation of the economic system, for the replacement of private capitalism by socialism, in order to liberate man and allow him to develop to the full the powers and capacities of his personality. It saw clearly that as long as the workers are kept in economic insecurity and subjection, they cannot be free in any sense. Economic collectivism it regarded as necessary only in order to provide the basis for freedom and genuine personality under modern industrial conditions. This theme runs through most of Marx's writings, particularly his early works; it is clearly formulated in his draft preamble of the French Socialist program, thus summarized by Engels:[2]

> The worker is free only when he is the owner of his own instruments of labor. This ownership can assume either the individual or the collective form. Since individual ownership is being abolished from day to day through economic development, there remains only the form of collective ownership. . . .

The point is clear. Collectivism has no *intrinsic* value. It is not desirable on its own account. It is desirable only because it helps to assure freedom. Freedom is the aim, the goal, the supreme value. Collectivism is, in the economic sphere, the means whereby that end may best be achieved.

From the very beginning, however, another very different conception has made itself felt in socialist thought, a conception which converted collectivism from a means into an end-in-itself. In this view, collectivism is not merely an economic device to promote freedom. It is a metaphysical principle, a quasi-religious dogma, a kind of higher existence transcending individual isolation and selfishness. The group, the community, the collectivity, is the true person; individual man is merely a poor, miserable fragment, an insignificant cell of the great social organism. In the ideal society of the future man will lose all sense of personality and will be absorbed into the group economically, socially and spiritually. His life will be collective life, his thoughts collective thoughts, his feelings and aspirations the feelings and aspirations of the collectivity. In fact, a distinguished Marxist scholar once wrote that in the future communist society no guarantee of freedom of thought would be necessary since in that blessed state all men would naturally think and feel alike on all questions!

To illustrate this conception of socialism I quote not from a German, not from a Russian, but from a Briton. In his work *Socialism and Government*, Ramsay MacDonald wrote:[3]

> In the eyes of the state (MacDonald is here speaking of the socialist state) the individual is not an end in himself but the means to "that far-off divine event to which the whole creation moves" . . . The state represents the political personality of the whole. . . . It thinks and feels for the whole.

This is totalitarianism, of course; we would not be surprised to encounter it in the spoutings of some Nazi demagogue or prophet. Yet this was actually put forward by the spokesman of a democratic socialist movement as a basic principle of modern socialist theory and met with but little opposition from those in socialist ranks. It is true that MacDonald's work was widely criticized, especially on the Continent, for its non-Marxist views on matters economic and political, but its flagrant totalitarianism evoked virtually no comment. Very similar sentiments, though couched in a different terminology, may in fact be found in the quite orthodox writings of Marxists throughout Europe and America. They all argue as if collectivism were of itself sufficient to establish the kingdom of heaven on earth, as if indeed the two were really identical.

These two conceptions of socialism are quite irreconcilable in principle. But in actual socialist thought and feeling the conflict has rarely come to the surface. Socialists have continued to use libertarian language while actually thinking in terms of the totalitarian engulfment of the individual in the community. And when I say socialists I mean socialists of all varieties, socialists of the Right, Center and Left—and with the socialists I would include most liberals and anarchists, although the last-named naturally prefer to worship the great Leviathan under the style of Society rather than the State.

Totalitarian socialism—and I do not hesitate to use this term for the conception that exalts collectivism into an end-in-itself and source of value—finds its inspiration in the Platonic Republic, in Hegelian and neo-Hegelian adoration of the Whole, in the regimented utopias of Fourier and Saint-Simon and in 19th century "organic" sociology. But its ultimate triumph is largely due to the fact that it early fell in with certain underlying trends in modern society as well as with the institutional and political needs of the socialist movement itself.

Very clearly, the totalitarian-collectivist element in socialism has been strengthened through the rapid replacement of small-scale individual enterprise by large-scale "collective" economics. In our epoch, when the economic pattern becomes the paradigm of all social life, the diminishing significance of the individual in economics inevitably tends to rob him of his importance in the entire scheme of things. The individual worker is nothing but a cog in the great industrial mechanism of mass-production; the individual stockholder is little more than an obscure cell in a great corporate organism. What standing then can individual man expect to have in the cosmos? What worth or significance can he lay claim to in comparison with the group, the collectivity? It becomes rather absurd to make the enhancement of his puny personality the goal of our striving. It becomes worse than absurd; it becomes "anti-social" and "individualistic"—a most grievous sin in "socialist" eyes.

The exaltation of the collectivity at the expense of the individual personality has been greatly accelerated by the repercussions of the democratic upsurge of the past century. Modern democracy is a concept pervaded with a radical ambiguity. On the one hand, it means civil and political liberty, protection of the rights of man and the citizen, decisive participation of the "common man" in the selection and control of his rulers. But on the other hand, it may be taken to mean the mass-state, the deification of the masses as the source of all right and authority ("the voice of the people is the voice of God"), the destruction of all barriers to the violence of collective passion and prejudice. According to the former view, the freedom of the individual is the very cornerstone of democracy; according to the latter, it is a blasphemous defiance of the deified People. It is this latter conception that totalitarian rulers have in mind when they speak of their regimes as "true democracies," as "democracies in a higher sense." In fact, the mass-state, rooted as it is in the dread of responsibility so characteristic of the mass mind, is the natural basis of the plebiscitary dictatorships afflicting the modern world.

The cult of the collectivity, which in Plato and Hegel is frankly aristocratic, has thus been brought into accord with the modern democratic temper by making the People (the masses, the folk, the race, society, etc.) the object of its worship. In this form the collectivist *mystique* has become the very core of contemporary "social-mindedness."

The anti-personalist direction of modern socialism is fostered by still another fundamental tendency of our age—the spread of bureaucracy and the bureaucratic spirit to every field of social life. How well calculated the "organic" concept, according to which society is everything and the individual nothing, is to serve as the philosophy of bureaucracy may be seen from the following quotation, again from Mac-Donald's *Socialism and Government:*

> In the socialist state, all political functions must be specialized . . . and cannot be diffused throughout the whole of the community. What we need is the professional politician. . . . The work of the organic nervous system is paralleled in society by political functions; the function of the nervous system is to coordinate the body to which it belongs and enable it to respond to impressions and experiences received at any point. It may also originate movements itself. Evidently, the individualist cannot admit any such differentiated organ in society. But the socialist, on the other hand, sees its necessity. Some organ must enable other organs and the mass of society to communicate impressions and experiences to a receiving center, must carry from that center impulses leading to action, must originate on its own initiative organic movements calculated to bring some benefit or pleasure to the organism. This is the socialist view of the political organ on its legis-

lative and administrative sides. It gathers up experience, carries it to a center which decides corresponding movements and then carries back to the parts affected the impulse to action.

The domination of society by permanent officials, professional administrators, "managers," is thus proclaimed to be as inherent in the nature of things, as natural and as desirable as the regulation of the human body by the nervous system!

Corporate industrialism, mass democracy and the trend to bureaucracy all combine to sustain and promote the totalitarian-collectivist bias of modern socialism. And the practical exigencies of socialism as a militant movement work in the same direction. Close organization, discipline and solidarity are certainly indispensable to a movement fighting for power in the world of today, but no less certainly do they tend to curtail individual freedom and exalt the authority of the group and its leaders. Organization makes for bureaucracy; discipline for authoritarianism; solidarity for the submergence of the individual in the mass—in every case the tendency runs counter to the goals that socialism sets out to achieve.

Here we come to the very heart of the problem. The crisis in socialism is a moral crisis in which everything turns on the relation of means to ends. Socialism is caught in the grip of an ever-present and inescapable dilemma, which in one form or another reappears on every level of socialist thought and action. Perhaps the difficulty can best be formulated along the following lines. Means instituted to achieve a goal, no matter how effective they may be in serving their intended purpose, have a way of turning around and working in the other direction as well, creating conditions and releasing forces that run counter to the original aim and tend to defeat it. If I were to use a much abused terminology, I would say that the relation between means and ends is dialectical, not only in the important sense that they act and react upon each other but in the still more important sense that their relation is one of tension and conflict so that any balance between them must necessarily be uneasy and precarious.

Thus, to repeat a previous point in another form, economic collectivism possesses not simply a positive libertarian but also a negative totalitarian potential. It harbors within itself two sets of forces, those making for freedom and those making for slavery. Attempt to throw one set into action, and you inevitably release the other as well.

On an even more elementary level, the first step in the realization of any social goal is organization. But organization too has this double potential. Without organization nothing can be accomplished. Yet, the very act of organization, as I have already suggested, sets in motion processes that threaten the goal, if that goal is the socialist goal of freedom. For organization, even the simplest, necessarily creates two categories, the leaders and the led, never quite interchangeable and therefore never quite on a par in power and privilege. Here we have in embryo—and how fast the embryo grows!—the authoritarian hierarchy that finds its culmination in the totalitarian leadership principle or in the initiative-killing drill-yard discipline that characterized German social-democracy and contributed so materially to its downfall. You cannot have the advantages of organization without its dangers.

Under modern conditions, social goals are hardly to be achieved without the exertion of political power. It is one of the enduring teachings of Marx that to be effective the socialist movement must be in some sense a political movement, preoccupied with the acquisition and employment of power. But does it need much argument to prove that preoccupation with power tends to vitiate the very ends for which power is sought? The conditions under which power is acquired, the ways in which it is used, the effect it has on the organizations and people who habitually exercise it, are hardly such as to encourage the moral idealism that must animate a new socialist order. Power is a two-edged sword that may maim and destroy its wielder. And yet can socialism abjure the struggle for power?

The struggle for power in the present-day world is a mass struggle, the clash of the massed forces of society. In order to rouse the masses to fighting pitch, socialism is led to cultivate hatred, fanaticism and intolerance as militant virtues; to stir up envy, suspicion and ill will among men. In the interest of the class struggle it is tempted to exploit the dark demonic passions of the human soul. And to what end? In order to gain the power to inaugurate upon earth the kingdom of human solidarity and good will! Was ever a social movement caught in so fatal a contradiction? Hatred has an inexorable logic of its own, a logic of destruction and self-destruction. And yet can the struggle for power be waged in a spirit of humanity and love?

Such are the dilemmas that arise at every turn, at every level of theory and practice, wherever means are used to realize ends. The great defect of traditional socialism, it seems to me, has been its utter failure to grasp this problem in its full amplitude or even to recognize that there is a problem at all. Socialism has never really understood the ambivalent, contradictory relation of means to ends. Socialists have generally tended to take for granted that once appropriate means are set into motion, everything will take care of itself. If such means are applied with vigor, intelligence and determination, under not unfavorable external conditions, the goal will be reached and no untoward by-products need be feared, except accidentally and incidentally. Today we know only too well how dangerously naive this notion is.

But the difficulty exists whether it is recognized or

not. How has socialism in fact dealt with it? By systematically sacrificing ends to means whenever the two come into conflict. The dilemma is resolved by the device of suppressing one of its members—the principal one at that—under cover of a few pious phrases and scholastic formulas. Initiated in this way, the process moves inexorably on: ends give way to means, means of a higher order give way to those of a lower— the moral level of the movement sinking uninterruptedly all the while.

Freedom is sacrificed to collectivism. Individual initiative and autonomy to effective organization. Intellectual independence to the regimentation of discipline. Organizational democracy to bureaucracy and efficient leadership. Moral principles to practical necessity. And everything to power politics . . . all with the best of intentions, of course, all in the name of the very highest ideals.

Let me make it quite clear that I am not making this criticism in a spirit of self-righteous perfectionism. I know very well that although collectivism, organization and power gravely imperil the values that give meaning to socialism, socialism cannot do without them if it is to be more than an idle dream. What I am here condemning is not the attempt to adjust principles to practical needs, for without some such attempt, however difficult and unsatisfactory, life itself is impossible. What I am condemning is the irresponsible refusal to face the moral issues involved in such conflict and adjustment. It is the easy, untroubled conscience that I find so disturbing: I cannot help seeing how neatly it plays into the hands of power-mad politicians.

Why has socialism been unable to resist this corruption? I venture to say it is because it has lacked the resources of an adequate ethic. Modern socialism—particularly Marxism—has been rather scornful of ethics and ethical systems, priding itself on its alleged scientific character which presumably enables it to dispense with moral imperatives. It has preferred an extreme moral relativism according to which good and evil are constituted by shifting class interest. Whatever serves the "interest of the proletariat" is good; whatever runs counter to that interest is evil. Everything, literally everything, is permitted if only it promotes the "proletarian class struggle." If we recall how inevitably the interest of the proletariat is identified with the interest of the "party of the proletariat" and the triumph of the party, we can see what the upshot of such an attitude must necessarily be. Party interest—power for the party and its leaders—becomes the ultimate, indeed the only criterion of right and wrong. Bolshevik amoralism is simply the culmination, brutally frank and consistent, of the ethical relativism that in one way or another is common to all schools of modern socialism.

A genuine ethic is simply the expression, perhaps even the foundation, of one's basic orientation to man and the universe. In attempting to do without an ethic transcending interest, therefore, modern socialism has also attempted to do without religion. Culturally socialism was the heir of bourgeois rationalism and materialism; politically it found itself in desperate conflict with the church, which until quite recently was undeniably a bulwark of reaction. In any case, modern socialism has developed largely outside the orbit of traditional religion. Its attitude has varied from the rancorous hatred of early Bolshevik "militant atheism" to the diplomatic evasion of European social-democracy, but with the significant exception of Great Britain, it has never felt the urge to look to our religious heritage for inspiration and spiritual sustenance.

Is socialism then without a faith? By no means; no great social movement is possible without some faith. Although it has turned its back on Judaism and Christianity, socialism has not dispensed with religion as such. It has simply replaced these historical faiths with a religion of its own. This religion is the neo-Hegelian creed of Dialectical Materialism under a number of variant forms in which God—the "great force not ourselves making for righteousness" (i.e., victory)—appears as the Dialectic, Progress, History, Social Evolution, Economic Necessity, etc. Indeed, it is primarily as a theology that Dialectical Materialism is of interest in the history of ideas. This is hardly the place to attempt to assess its permanent contributions to philosophy, which may turn out to be by no means inconsiderable, but it is clear that it is essentially a type of hylozoistic pantheism: all is matter hierarchically organized, but matter endowed with the principle of activity, with "life"; the All is God. As such, Dialectical Materialism is subject to all the objections to pantheism and hylozoism and to not a few more on its own account. But what is more important in our connection is not its philosophical soundness but its theological function. As a theology it serves to "justify God's ways to man"; to vindicate the aims and to idealize the activities of the movement; above all, to secure its values by guaranteeing the ultimate triumph of its cause.

Dialectical Materialism reveals the hidden god of the socialist religion to whom the true believer may confidently look for ultimate victory despite passing difficulties and defeats. But an invisible god is generally too abstract and remote for the uses of everyday life and so this god has been brought down to earth in a form that modern man can readily understand and worship—the great god Power. The Dialectic prescribes the course of World History and "Weltgeschichte ist Weltgericht." Only World History can decide who is right, only ultimate success can vindicate the justice of our cause. Whatever has to be done to assure its triumph will be justified in the outcome. In fact, the only true moral agent is power, for only power can gain a hearing before the court of World History. Ultimate Might makes Ultimate Right.

Thus neatly do the ethics and the religion of Power supplement each other.

From the Judaeo-Christian standpoint, of course, the cult of Power is a particularly detestable form of idolatry; it is devil worship in its modern form. How strange that socialism, which drew its original inspiration from the social humanitarianism that is but a secularized version of the Judaeo-Christian ethic of love, should have reached the point where it bows in adoration before the Enemy of God and Man. Surely the most illuminating commentary on the fate that has overtaken socialism is to be found in Dostoevsky's profound parable, The Legend of the Grand Inquisitor, in *The Brothers Karamazov*. It is the Grand Inquisitor, the guardian of the people and the defender of the faith, who feels compelled to send the returning Christ to the stake!

II

If my analysis of what has happened to socialism is at all valid, it must have some bearing on what the socialism of the future can do to avoid the same appalling fate. I think the following remarks on the subject may be ventured.

1. Socialism must be perfectly clear as to its ultimate goal and must never permit its vision of that goal to be obscured for any reason whatsoever. The aim of socialism is to create such economic and social conditions as will secure and enhance the freedom of the individual. The only consistent alternative to this view is the conception according to which the socialist ideal is a sort of super-slave state in which everyone is well-fed, well-housed and well-clad through the ministrations of a benevolent despotism. Between these two conceptions the crucial choice must be made. I will proceed on the assumption that the former is our notion of what socialism is out to achieve.

2. Under present-day conditions, the alternative is not, as it once perhaps was, between "free" capitalism and socialist collectivism. "Free" enterprise in the traditional sense is already a thing of the past. Our economic life is becoming daily more collectivized, daily more subject to social control and state regulation. In certain countries, in certain industries, in certain areas, this process has gone further than in others but everywhere it is obviously under way. And the process is irreversible. There is no more fatuous utopianism than the belief that either America or the world can return to the capitalism of a century ago.

The alternative is not between a "free" capitalism and socialist collectivism; collectivism in some form is here and is here to stay. The alternative that now confronts mankind is between *totalitarian* collectivism and *democratic* collectivism. Is the Russian road the only road collectivism can take? If it is, then mankind is doomed to decades, perhaps centuries, of slavery, corporeal and spiritual. Such *may* be our fate, but it *need* not be. It is true, and we should face the fact in all its implications, that collectivism *in its very nature* operates powerfully to promote totalitarianism. The odds are thus greatly against us, but there is a chance. Democratic collectivism *is* possible. Lewis Corey has rendered a very great service by his attempt to outline with care the economic and political foundations of a democratic collectivist society.[4] A pluralistic economy, avoiding the concentration of economic control in the hands of the state by distributing it among a variety of public and quasi-public institutions and even, as in agriculture and trade, among private enterprisers, is his basic conception. A new system of checks and balances, based on the effective social power of such voluntary non-state associations as trade unions, is another aspect of his program. I certainly do not insist that Corey's ideas are the only practicable ones, but he has at the very least clearly formulated the problem and given some indications as to the direction in which a solution is to be sought.

It is interesting that Nicolas Berdyaev, the distinguished Russian theologian-philosopher, reaches almost the same conclusion in his recent work, *Slavery and Freedom,*[5] although he and Corey are poles apart in general outlook. Berdyaev urges

> a pluralistic economy, that is to say, a combination of nationalized economics, socialized economics and personal economics, insofar as it does not admit capitalism and exploitation. . . .
> He also calls for decentralization and federalism and a fight against centralized monstrosities. . . . Only decentralization can ward off the danger of the development of bureaucracy.

3. Collectivism is *economic,* an economic device to enhance the possibilities of personal freedom for the great mass of the people. It is not a "higher" form of existence valid at all levels of life. "Only economics can be socialized," Berdyaev well says, "the spiritual life cannot, nor can the consciousness and conscience of man. The socialization of economics ought to be accompanied by the individualization of men and women. . . ." The mystical cult of collectivism is the sworn enemy of democratic socialism; it leads straight to totalitarianism. Socialism more than any other social order must preserve a rigid and inviolable distinction between the things that are Caesar's and the things that are God's—between what society may legitimately interfere with and what is inalienably the domain of the individual conscience—for in no other social order is the boundary so easily transgressed.

4. All this adds up to what might be called personalist socialism, socialism rooted in the ethical philosophy of personalism. In this philosophy, personality is the supreme value in the universe and the self-realization of personality the supreme law.[6]

The entire world (writes Berdyaev) is nothing in comparison with human personality, with the unique person of a man, with his unique fate. . . . Man, human personality, is the supreme value, not the community, not collective realities such as society, nation, state, civilization, church. This is the personalist scale of values.

Society is not an organism, it is not a being or a personality. The reality of society consists in the personalities themselves. . . . The enslaving power of society over human personality is the outcome of the illusion of objectivization. Society is presented as though it were a personality of a higher hierarchical degree than the personality of man. But this makes man a slave. . . . Sociologists who affirm the primacy of society over the individual are in fact reactionaries.

The personalist creed is in essence the Judaeo-Christian doctrine of the transcendent worth of the human soul. It is the Kantian precept that every human being is an end in himself and not merely a means to some external purpose. It is the view championed by the young Marx when he protested against the *Verdinglichung* of man in bourgeois society. It is the core of every ethical philosophy that takes man's moral life seriously.

A socialism genuinely rooted in the philosophy of personalism could hardly become the vehicle of totalitarian power politics. Nor could it easily be betrayed into sacrificing its human values for the sake of security, power or expediency. Whatever else might be its fate, it would not lose its soul.

5. The personalist philosophy is at bottom a religious philosophy. And so personalist socialism would naturally not share the anti-religious bias with which modern socialism is still burdened. On the contrary, personalist socialism would find itself profoundly at

one with the essential spirit of Judaism and Christianity. In the resources of this faith it would find a
deeper understanding of the nature and destiny of
man as well as a vantage point under the aspect of
eternity from which to meet the perplexing problems,
the difficulties and contradictions, that confront an
essentially moral crusade such as socialism when it is
compelled to fight its battles in the world with the
weapons of the world.

I ncreasing numbers of sensitive people, shocked by
the moral disintegration of the contemporary
world, can no longer be content with the glib,
hollow phrases, with the once plausible half-truths
that history has turned into dangerous falsehoods.
They are searching for something deeper and more
fundamental, and their searchings seem to take them
all in the same general direction. Ignazio Silone's long,
painful pilgrimage from communism to primitive
Christianity is both symptomatic and symbolic of the
new drift. If indeed the seed is there beneath the snow,
waiting for the hard winter to pass in order to spring
into life, it is the seed of a new spirituality in which all
that is best in socialist idealism will be absorbed and
transfigured.

Notes

[1] Karl Marx; *The Communist Manifesto.*

[2] Ed. Bernstein: *Die Briefe von Engels an Bernstein,* p. 34.

[3] I have chosen Ramsay MacDonald to cite from because of his unusual
directness of expression, but it should be noted that British socialism has
been less affected by the totalitarian-collectivist perversion than most
other socialist movements, thanks largely to the strong liberal-individu-
alist tradition in British public life and to the religious strain (nonconformist Protestantism) in the British labor movement.

[4] Lewis Corey: *The Unfinished Task* (1942).

[5] Nicolas Berdyaev: *Slavery and Freedom* (1944).

[6] It should hardly be necessary to say that self-realization of personality is utterly different from selfishness. As Berdyaev points out, the highest reach of personal self-realization is sacrificial service to others.

—2—

From Marxism to Judaism

JEWISH BELIEF AS A DYNAMIC OF SOCIAL ACTION

(1947)

U ntil nine or ten years ago, I was a thoroughgoing Marxist. I had spent most of my life in
the radical movement, and Marxism was to me
more than a mere strategy of political action, more
than a program of economic and social reconstruction, more even than a comprehensive theory of history and society. Marxism was to me, and to others
like me, a religion, an ethic, and a theology: a vast, all-
embracing doctrine of man and the universe, a passionate faith endowing life with meaning, vindicating
the aims of the movement, idealizing its activities, and
guaranteeing its ultimate triumph. In the certainty of
this faith, we felt we could stand against the world.

It was a faith committed to freedom, justice, and
brotherhood as ultimate ideals and supreme values.
But it was also a faith that staked everything on the
dogma of Progress, that is, on the unlimited redemptive power of history. Through its own inherent

energies, the materialist Dialectic of history would sooner or later solve every problem, fulfill every possibility, and eliminate every evil of human life, leading mankind through terrific struggles to a final perfection of uncoerced harmony amidst peace, plenty, and untroubled happiness.

The motive power of this redemptive process of history the Marxist metaphysic found in economics. Man's essence was economic, the root of his frustrations and miseries was economic, and his salvation would be economic as well. "Economic development" was the invincible power that in the last analysis determined everything, and in the final outcome would bring the processes of history to consummation and fulfillment: it was the invisible god of the Marxist faith.

But this invisible god operated through visible instrumentalities, through economic classes. The proletariat was the savior of humanity, and the class struggle the engine of salvation. From this conception emerged a system of ethics that I found increasingly untenable. Marxism, it is true, did not admit to possessing an ethical system; it prided itself on its "scientific" character, and scornfully rejected all moral imperatives. But in fact it followed an extreme moral relativism, according to which good and evil were constituted by a shifting class interest.

Whatever served the "interest of the proletariat" was good; whatever ran counter to it was evil. Everything, literally everything, was permitted if only it promoted the "proletarian class struggle." But the proletariat could attain self-consciousness only in its "vanguard party," so that in the end the interest of the proletariat really amounted to the interest of the party. Party interest—power for the party and its leaders—thus became the ultimate, indeed the only criterion of right and wrong.

This ethic of power was very conveniently justified by faith in the redemptive power of history operating through the Dialectic. The Dialectic prescribed the course of world history and to Marx, as to Hegel, *Weltgeschichte* was *Weltgericht*. Only world history could decide who was really right and since world history was bound to decide in our favor, everything we might do to promote the success of our cause—that is, of our party—was justified in advance. Ultimately, the only true moral agent was power, for only power could claim a hearing before the bar of world history.

Such was the faith by which we lived and fought. And so long as this faith remained unchallenged from within, no attacks from without could shake it. Doubts were ignored or else drowned in action.

But reality could not be forever withstood. I do not know what is the secret mechanism by which subconscious processes which have been going on for years are suddenly precipitated into consciousness under the impact of some great event. In my case, it was the course of the Russian Revolution and the development of events in Europe, culminating in the triumph of Hitler, that had this effect. Put to the test, the Marxist faith failed. It proved itself incapable of explaining the facts or sustaining the values that gave meaning to life, the very values it had itself enshrined as its own ultimate goals. It could not meet the challenge of totalitarianism because it was itself infected with the same disease. By the logic of its own development, the ideal of unlimited freedom had become the reality of unlimited despotism. The individual personality, instead of being liberated for self-fulfillment, as Marx and Lenin had promised, was being engulfed in a total collectivism that left no room whatever for personal autonomy. Sacrificial dedication to the welfare of humanity had given way to narrow, ruthless, self-defeating power politics.

It was this latter point perhaps that told most. The disastrous corrosions and corruptions of the Marxist movement in politics seemed to me clearly a reflection of its lack, or rather of its rejection, of an ethic transcending the relativities of power and class interest, and the lack of an adequate ethic to be the result of a radically false religion.

Not that I felt myself any the less firmly committed to the great ideals of freedom and social justice. My discovery was that I could no longer find basis and support for these ideals in the materialistic religion of Marxism. On the contrary, it seemed to me that in its philosophy and ethics Marxism went far toward destroying the very objectives it was presumably out to achieve. I felt intensely the need for a faith that would better square with my ideal, which in tenor, doctrine, and spirit could give impulse and direction to the radical reconstruction of society which I so deeply desired.

For this Marxist religion itself, it now became clear to me, was in part illusion, and in part idolatry; in part a delusive Utopianism promising heaven on earth in our time, and in part a totalitarian worship of collective man; in part a naive faith in the finality of economics, and in part a sinister fetishism of technology and material production; in part a sentimental optimism as to the goodness of human nature, and in part a hard-boiled, amoral cult of power at any price. There could be no question to my mind that as religion, Marxism had proved itself bankrupt.

With Marxism went the entire naturalistic outlook as it affects the nature and destiny of man. I began to see that though man is undeniably part of nature and remains embedded within it, he quite as undeniably transcends it by virtue of his spirit, by virtue of his reason, his imagination, and his moral freedom. I began to see new meaning in the poignant words of Bertrand Russell, himself and uncompromising naturalist, describing man's paradoxical status in nature:

A strange mystery it is that nature, omnipotent but blind, has brought forth at last a child, subject still to her power but gifted with sight, with knowledge of good and evil, with the capacity of judging all the works of his unthinking mother. . . . Man is yet free, during his brief years, to examine, to criticize, to know, and in imagination, to create. To him alone, in the world with which he is acquainted, this freedom belongs, and in this lies his superiority to the resistless forces that control his outer life.

These were the words of a great naturalist philosopher, but naturalism had so far not succeeded in explaining or building on this paradox. And so naturalism seemed to me bound in the end to fail to satisfy any one who demanded something better than the narrow and paltry conception of human life and destiny it offered.

The conclusion I reached as the final outcome of the long and painful process of reorientation was that neither man nor his fate could be understood in terms of an outlook that limited itself to the two-dimensional plane of nature and history, that the ultimate meaning of human life was to be found in a dimension transcending both and yet relevant to both—in a dimension that, in the most genuine sense of the term, was *supernatural*.

To suggest the process by which I and perhaps others found our way out of Marxist materialism and power-worship, I will paraphrase the words used recently in derision by a well-known writer, himself an unreconstructed Marxism, to describe an experience in some ways very like my own. In trying to discover what went wrong with economics—he says—they (that is, people like me) came to politics; but politics revealed that it was tainted and so they strove to cure the taint of politics with ethics; but ethics alone could not withstand the taint either, and so they went on finally to religion.

These are scoffing words, but they are not without their truth. I found in religion what I sought: and that was not an escape from social responsibility, but a more secure spiritual groundwork for a mature and effective social radicalism. The calamitous schism that had so long divided socialism from religion seemed to me to be at last coming to an end: in the profound insights and spiritual resources of religion, socialism would find a philosophy and a dynamic far superior to the shallow materialism that had led it so woefully astray. In short, I came to the conclusion that by abandoning the Marxist metaphysic in favor of a positive religious affirmation, I was becoming a better socialist and, if I may venture the paradox, even a better Marxist, taking Marxism in terms of its best insights and ultimate ideals. For the great contributions of Marxism were, it seemed to me, in the fields of economic understanding, social thought, and political action. And these could best be conserved, I now saw, within the framework, not of a shallow materialism, but of a profound religion that would give full recognition to the transcendent aspects of man's nature and destiny.

In my particular case, finding my way to religion meant finding my way to Judaism. Was this a return or in reality a first encounter? I cannot tell. But I can tell, I think, what it was that I discovered in essential Judaism that came to me as a revelation in my perplexities. If I now describe it in entirely intellectualistic terms, I hope it will not be concluded that I ignore or deny the devotional, mystical, and ritual elements that are so vital to any true religious experience. I limit myself to the intellectual, one might say theological, aspect because that has been foremost in my thinking and has had greater meaning for me in the solution of my own perplexities.

I. God and Man

The very heart of Judaism, it seems to me, is its magnificent conception of the Deity. It is a conception at once profound and paradoxical: a God transcendent, yet working in life and history, infinite yet personal, a God of power, justice, and mercy, but above all a holy God. The worship of a holy God who transcends all relativities of nature and history, as Reinhold Niebuhr has pointed out, saves the soul from taking satisfaction in any partial performance, curbs self-righteousness, and instills a most wholesome humility which gives man no rest in any achievement, no matter how high, while a still higher level of achievement is possible. The worship of a holy and transcendent God who yet manifests himself in history saves us alike from the shallow positivism that leaves nature and history and life all without ultimate meaning, from a pantheism that in the end amounts to an idolatrous worship of the world, and from a sterile other-worldliness that breaks all connection between religion and life. The worship of a holy and transcendent God who is the one God of the universe, besides whom there is no other, saves us, finally, from the many debasing idolatries that are bedeviling mankind today.

The scriptural doctrine of God, as I read it, is also a doctrine of man. For man is created "in the image of God": that is his glory but also his inescapable responsibility. The Biblical doctrine seems to me to hinge upon a dramatic tension both in the nature of man and in his relations with God. On the one hand (Psalms 8:5), man is "but little lower than the angels"; on the other (Genesis 8:21), "the inclination of man's heart is evil from his childhood." In this I see no contradiction, but rather a profound insight into the paradoxical, the ambivalent nature of man. It is an insight that does justice both to his grandeur and to his misery, both to his capacity to transcend self in righteousness, reason, and loving-kindness and to the inescapable limits of self-transcendence because of the irreducible egotism of his nature.

The scriptural conception of man thus refuses to countenance either the fatuous optimism of the Rousseauistic doctrine of the natural goodness of man or the dismal pessimism of the ultra-Calvinist doctrine of his utter depravity. It is at once more realistic and more complex, for it sees both sides in their coexistence and conflict, in their state of eternal struggle out of which is generated that tragic sense of life which is the mark of every high religion. But it is a sense of tragedy that is never final, for with God all things are possible.

The same dialectic tension that converts the human soul into the field of a battle never won, yet always within reach of victory, is to be found in another form in the relations between God and man. "Everything is in the power of Heaven except the fear of Heaven," the Sages tell us. "God in his providence determines beforehand what a man shall be and what shall befall him but not whether he shall be righteous or wicked." We need not take even this partial determinism too literally to see the profound significance of the uncompromising insistence on man's freedom of will. Evil is the result not of the forces of nature or of the promptings of the flesh: that is a Greek-Oriental notion which has had a most unfortunate effect upon our popular moral outlook. Both nature and the flesh are good in themselves, for did not God create both and find them good? Evil is rooted in man's spiritual freedom and consists in the wrong use of that freedom, in sinful disobedience to God.

I find this conception, which as far as I know is unique to Judaism and the religions that derive from it, the only adequate foundation for a significant moral life. It does justice alike to man's creaturely subjection to the moral law as the law of God and to his self-determination as a free moral agent. It combines freedom and responsibility in a synthesis that no philosophy has been able to transcend.

II. Man and Society

If there is one strain that has run through Judaism from the earliest codes to the present day, it is the passion for social justice. No modern attack upon economic exploitation can equal in earnestness and power the denunciations of the Prophets against those who "grind down the faces of the poor." No modern warning against the evils of authoritarianism is so arresting as the words of Samuel rebuking the people of Israel for desiring to subject themselves to the yoke of kingship.

But even more important, it seems to me, is the fact that the scriptural doctrine relating man to God provides the only really adequate groundwork for the ideals of freedom and equality, as well as the only fully realistic justification of democracy in political and economic life.

At the bottom, the affirmation of the freedom of the individual person can be grounded in nothing less ultimate than the belief that he is created in the image of God and is, therefore, a being in comparison with whom all of the nonhuman world is as nothing in worth. It is the belief in the eminent dignity of the human personality—in other words, in the infinite value of the individual human soul. This has received its modern formulation in the Kantian teaching that every man is an end in himself, and is not to be used as a mere means or tool for some external purpose. In the same way, the affirmation of human equality cannot be grounded in empirical fact; it can be grounded in nothing less ultimate than the belief in the Fatherhood of God and the Brotherhood of Man. For men are equal not in power or wisdom or beauty or goodness, but in their spiritual essence, in the infinite worth of their individual souls, in their relation to God. It is this equal relation to God, it seems to me, that alone can serve as the ultimate criterion of human relations. True understanding of this principle—of the value and significance of human personality—came to the world for the first time with the Prophetic insistence on the spiritual autonomy and moral responsibility of the individual person.

The scriptural insight into the ambivalent nature of man makes for a clear and realistic view of power and government. Power of man over man is intrinsically evil, for it involves the subjection of some men to others, the violation of their God-given personal autonomy, *and by that much their enslavement*. Power, moreover, has its own logic of expansion and corruption: it corrupts the wielder as well as those upon whom it is wielded, feeding the pride and arrogance of the one, and instilling a slavish spirit of subserviency in the other. Yet power is necessary, because man's "inclination to evil"—that is, his egotism and self-centeredness—makes coercion at some point necessary in order to protect society from the centrifugal forces of individual and group self-interest. The recognition of power as an inescapable necessity, and yet as a corrupting influence, endows social life with the same sense of tension and pathos that we have noted in the spiritual life of the individual. The moral law, which is embattled in every human soul, is also imperiled, and at least partially thwarted, in every transaction in the world.

It is out of this keen sense of the perils of power, so strikingly absent in traditional Marxism, that democracy grows. For democracy is at bottom an institutional system for the control of power in the interests of freedom and social welfare. It is predicated on the conviction that no man possesses sufficient imagination, wisdom, or virtue to make him a safe repository of the interests of others—that no man is good enough or wise enough to be entrusted with absolute power over his fellow men. This is a principle that applies not only to politics but to economics as well, where it serves as the starting point of democratic socialism, as well as of all other programs of economic reform in the interest of social justice. Democracy is, in effect, a dynamic reconciliation on the social level of man's grandeur and misery, of his eminent dignity as a person and his perennial inclination to sinfulness as manifested in the egoistic self-assertion of power.

Judaism, as I see it, is the sworn foe of the totalitarian state in its claim to absolute control over the individual and all his activities. Unconditional obedience to a universal and transcendent God precludes the possibility of total and absolute subjection to any earthly power. Earthly powers making such claims are usurpers and pretenders to the prerogatives of Deity. They are to be resisted to the bitter end. "For unto Me are the children of Israel slaves," says the Talmud; "they are not slaves unto slaves."

The profound insights of scriptural religion reveal a logic of social action that escapes the pitfalls alike of power-mad cynicism, secular Utopianism, and otherworldly quietism. As against the cynicism that recognizes no rule but power, Judaism vindicates the validity and relevance of the moral law, however impossible it may be to live up to it fully in any given situation. As against other-worldly quietism, it raises the witness of the Prophets and the duty to one's neighbor. As against the secular Utopianism, whether liberal or Marxist, which hopes to achieve perfection within history, it stresses the inescapable relativities of this world and places the grand consummation to come at the *end* of time rather than within it.

It is here that the uncompromising monotheism, the abhorrence of idolatry that distinguish Judaism are, to my thinking, so relevant. The modern world is full of the most obscene idolatries—idolatries of race, of class, of society, of the state, of dictators, of science, even of ideologies. It is most vital to emphasize, as Judaism does, that faith cannot be placed, finally and unreservedly, in any person, institution, or order of this world. To do so would be not only to invite inevitable disillusionment; what is worse, it would be to destroy even the partial good embodied in the person, institution, or order thus idolatrously worshipped. By attempting to exalt a relative into an absolute good, we can but convert it into a total evil. Faith and worship can rest finally and unreservedly only in the transcendent, the ultimate, the absolute, in the one true God; all other faith must be partial, tentative, and provisional at best.

The insights into the nature and destiny of man revealed in scriptural religion supply a dynamic as well as a logic of moral action. For it discloses how the ideal standards of the moral law, though impossible of achievement amidst the intractable forces in man and society, are yet directly pertinent to life in their function as transcendent principles of aspiration, judgment, and action. It is this tension between the immediate relevance, and yet ultimate impossibility of the absolute imperatives of the moral law, that generates the dynamic of moral action in social as well as in individual life.

III. Israel and the World

On this question, I speak with great reluctance and hesitancy, for who can penetrate the mystery of Israel? A sociologist of our time, Carl Mayer, has given it as his verdict that:

> The Jewish problem is ultimately inexplicable. . . . It can be stated, described, and analyzed in so far as its external manifestations are concerned, but it cannot be explained. . . . The Jewish problem in its fundamental aspects appears to be of such a character as to transcend human understanding, and thus essentially belongs to a sphere which is open only to faith. . . .

Judaism is embodied and incarnated in a people which is not a race or a nation or even a religious group in the usual sense of the term. "The Jewish people," says the sociologist I have just quoted, "represent a sociologically *unique* phenomenon and defy all attempts at general definition." The mystery of Israel is one that escapes all categories of nature and society.

This, it is my conviction, is true of Israel, its history, and its scriptures. The history of Israel is not simply the history of an ethnic or cultural or religious group, but in truth a providential history that reveals God's ways with men in a sense in which the history of no other people does. The holy books produced by the Jews are not simply part of the sacred writings of the people of the world: they are the word of God in a way in which the holy books of no other people are. In what way I could not define, but that they are so I cannot but believe.

What I have been saying amounts to an affirmation of the age-old doctrine that Israel is a chosen people. As I read Scripture and history, Israel was chosen both for a mission and for suffering; indeed, the two are probably two sides of the same thing. I believe that Israel was chosen to be a "light unto the nations," to bring the highest reaches of the moral law to the peoples of the world. The Exile and Dispersion came not as punishment of Israel but as an opportunity to spread the word of God to the four corners of the earth. But the mission thus entrusted to Israel creates a tension between Israel and the world: Israel remains *in* the world but is not entirely *of* it. "Like an activating ferment . . . [Judaism] gives the world no peace. It bars slumber. It teaches the world to be discontented and restless as long as the world has not God. It stimulates the movement of history." Thus speaks the Christian philosopher Jacques Maritain. For the sake of this, Israel must undergo persecution, humiliation, agonies of pain and death. Bringing God to the world, Israel must suffer the hatred and resentment of the world against God and his law. Israel as the Chosen People is Israel the Suffering Servant of the Lord, of whom it is written in the words of Isaiah: "He is despised and rejected of men; a man of sorrows and acquainted with grief."

The message of Israel is universal. The Jews, it has been acutely pointed out, are "an ethnic group with a universal religious faith which transcends the values of a single people but which they are forced to use as an instrument of survival in an alien world." This is the irony of Jewish existence: devotion to a universal faith marks off the Jews as a "peculiar" people, a "chosen people," and only too often, an "accursed" people! Where this will end, when this will end, is a mystery within the greater mystery of Israel.

These are the things I must think of when I think of my faith as a Jew. And I must add that I am among those who see fundamental spiritual kinship rather than opposition between Judaism and at least the more Hebraic forms of Christianity. Indeed, I find that many of what I conceive to be crucial Jewish insights are illumined rather than obscured when viewed in the light of the development they have undergone in Christian doctrine. I, therefore, believe that whatever significant differences there may be between Judaism and Christianity considered as total systems, there is real and vital meaning in the idea of a Judeo-Christian religious tradition basically distinct from all other religions of the world.

Thinking about religion, so I have found, is no easy way of arriving at simple solutions. It is not a refuge from reality but a challenge to realistic thinking. It means an endless grappling with problems that are never fully solved. In the course of my reorientation, I have encountered perplexities that I was not even aware of before. What is the ultimate meaning of the ritual observances so central to the Jewish tradition? How are we to distinguish their transient historical from their eternal religious aspect? Or the existing Jewish community, how is it related to, yet distinguished from, the spiritual community of Israel? And what are the implications of the universality of Judaism? At various times in its history, Judaism was an expansive force. Will it ever become such again, or is its expansive role at an end since the rise of Christianity and Islam?

Some of these questions will undoubtedly be answered by time, experience, and increased understanding on my part. But other problems will surely arise in their place. Nor is any answer ever likely to be final or conclusive, for in question of such ultimacy, it seems to me, inquiry must end in an irreducible mystery at the heart of things.

For all my uncertainties, however, there is one remark, or rather plea, I would venture to make. It is an appeal for a renewal of Jewish theology. I have lately been reading Dr. Solomon Zeitlin's book *Disciples of the Wise,* which professes to detail the social and religious opinions of American rabbis, as expressed in answers to a questionnaire. One cannot but be gratified at the advanced views on social and economic questions of the Rabbis. But it would be difficult to feel the same gratification at the general state of their theological views. According to Dr. Zeitlin, the group of nearly 250 rabbis "as a whole, as well as the several wings, is divided between the acceptance of the concept of salvation as (a) achievement of an integrated personality, and (b) participation in efforts for social progress." Thus religion is conceived either as a kind of inexpert psychotherapy or else as an auxiliary social reform agency. In one case as in the other, it seems entirely secondary, and as such, can claim no significant place in modern life. Have we really come to the pass where such profound and tradition-laden words as salvation can mean nothing more; where (to take another example from the study) sin is conceived exclusively in such shallow external terms as "harm to neighbors, friends and business associates; harm to society; support of accepted institutions which are socially harmful"; or where (to take still another example) prayer is interpreted entirely in subjectivistic and sociological terms? I cannot believe it. For this would mean that Judaism has been reduced to nothing more than routine observances and a somewhat emotionalized social ethic. Surely Judaism has not yet come to this pass. What we are witnessing, I think, is the gradual corrosion of faith by the naturalistic and secularist temper of the time. It is a corrosion that can and must be arrested and undone by a vital theology, cast in contemporary terms.

Throughout the world, even in America, there is a widespread hunger for metaphysics, engendered by disillusionment with the shallow formulas and plausible half-truths of positivism. Throughout the world, there is a renewed concern with theology, amounting to a renaissance. Catholicism has its neo-Thomism. Protestantism has its new and vital neo-orthodoxy associated, in various forms, with the names of Karl Barth, Emil Brunner, and Reinhold Neibuhr. What Judaism needs today, in my sincere opinion, is a great theological reconstruction in the spirit of a neo-orthodoxy distant alike from sterile fundamentalism and secularized modernism. I earnestly hope that we will not have much longer to wait for this great and high undertaking to get under way.

—3—

Reinhold Niebuhr: Christian Apologist to the Secular World

(1956)

"I cannot and do not claim to be a theologian," Reinhold Niebuhr states in the "Intellectual Autobiography" that forms the opening chapter of the volume on himself in The Library of Living Theology. "I have taught Christian social ethics . . . and have also dealt in the ancillary field of apologetics." These words of genial self-depreciation have their deeper truth, for the immense influence that Reinhold Niebuhr has wielded upon his contemporaries has come not from any attempt at theological system-building, but from his continuing efforts over three decades to develop a profound and realistic social ethics, and to "defend and justify the Christian faith in a secular age." No case is typical, and yet every case is revealing; it is in terms of the impact that Niebuhr has had upon my own life and thought that I can best communicate what he has meant to the large numbers whom he has reached, not through seminary and church, but in fields of secular life at first sight so remote from religion and its special concerns.

My first encounter with the thought of Reinhold

Niebuhr came in the later 1930's. I was then at a most crucial moment in my life. My Marxist faith had collapsed under the shattering blows of contemporary history—there is no need to retell a story now grown familiar. I was left literally without any ground to stand on, deprived of the commitment and understanding that alone had made life livable. At this point, in a way I cannot now remember, I came upon Niebuhr's *Moral Man and Immoral Society*. It is easy today to see the weaknesses of this early work; it is much more difficult to recapture its impact upon one in my position. It came with the revelation of a new understanding of human existence in terms of which I might reconstruct my life and thought. What impressed me most profoundly was the paradoxical combination of realism and radicalism that Niebuhr's "prophetic" faith made possible. Here was a faith that transferred the center of its absolute commitment to what was really absolute—the transcendent God— and was therefore able to face the real facts of life unafraid, with open eyes. Here was a faith that called into question all human institutions and institutional vested interests, that permitted nothing of this world to parade as final or ultimate, and yet provided an intelligible ground for discriminate judgment. Here was a faith that warned against all premature securities, yet called to responsible action. Here, in short, was a "social idealism" without illusions, in comparison with which even the most "advanced" Marxism appeared confused, inconsistent, and hopelessly illusion-ridden.

How much of this I got from *Moral Man and Immoral Society* and how much from other of Niebuhr's writings then available—for I promptly read all I could get hold of—I cannot now say. What I do know is that this "meeting" with Niebuhr's thought—I did not yet know him personally—quite literally changed my mind and my life. Humanly speaking, it "converted" me, for in some manner I cannot describe, I felt my whole being, and not merely my thinking, shifted to a new center. I could now speak about God and religion without embarrassment, thought as yet without very much understanding of what was involved.

It was not merely a matter of social philosophy, I soon discovered, though that is where it began. Deeper problems of the nature of man and the structure of human existence were to emerge, but the "leap" had been made. Every work of Niebuhr's, almost every article he wrote, enlarged my understanding, deepened my insight, perhaps even confirmed my faith. *The Nature and Destiny of Man* marked the high point at this stage. When some years later I got out my work of theology (*Judaism and Modern Man: An Interpretation of Jewish Religion* [1951]), it was avowedly Niebuhrian in temper and thought.

Perhaps I had better now drop the quasi-autobiographical form of these comments, but not before I point out that I was not alone in experiencing the impact of Niebuhr's thinking at this time. Many of my acquaintances in labor and radical circles testified to the relevance of his "apologetics," some eagerly, others reluctantly, but all with wonder and respect. His prominence in "liberal" causes, his realistic understanding of politics and social issues, above all his early and sophisticated anti-Communism, won him an audience among those in the secular world no other theologian of the time could reach.

The mood of the time was (to quote Malcolm Cowley's words) "a general dismay at the results of five centuries of progress and widening enlightenment." What had gone wrong with man and with history? Niebuhr's answer to these questions came with his rediscovery of the classical doctrine of "original sin," which religious liberalism and secular idealism had combined to deride and obscure. He pointed to the radical ambiguity residing at the heart of every human enterprise, and showed that every achievement of human virtue and rationality bore within itself an element of evil and unreason, which was bound to become demonic precisely to the degree that it was ignored or written off. He uncovered the frightening consequences of human pretensions to establish the Kingdom of God within history by ascribing finality and perfection to historical institutions, structures, and programs. It was modern man's utopian illusions, and his overweening confidence in his own power to "remake the world," that had led to the protracted crisis of the twentieth century. History, as neither bourgeois liberalism, the Social Gospel, or Marxism could understand, was not its own redeemer; it remained ambiguous to the very end, "a tragedy in which all are involved, whose keynote is anxiety and frustration, not progress and fulfillment" (Schlesinger). For redemption, man—even modern science-wielding, history-making man—would have to look beyond.

Man's Nature

This kind of depth understanding of history naturally involves a depth understanding of man. The "nature" of man Niebuhr found in his unique dimension of freedom, in the capacity of the self to transcend all the coherences, whether natural, social, or rational, through which it is provisionally defined and in which it is provisionally enclosed: man is a "being forever surpassing himself infinitely" (Pascal). Yet man is also a creature—relative, finite, incomplete. Out of this tension between man's self-transcending freedom and the inherent limitations of his creatureliness is generated that profound existential anxiety which is at once the mark of the human situation and the precondition of sin. Neither naturalism nor idealism can understand this predicament, for neither sees man in his entirety. Naturalism sees man as simply part of nature; idealism sees him as essentially free spirit or reason; actually he is a self embedded in nature, culture, and society, yet transcending all of these by virtue of the indeterminate possibilities of his freedom. This dimension of human existence which enables the self "to stand as it were above the structures and coherences of the world" Niebuhr recognizes as the "dimension of the eternal," for it is in this dimension of his being that man is driven beyond himself and enters into the dialogue with the divine.

Implicit from the beginning, it seems to me was this "dialogic" strain in Niebuhr's thinking, which has come to mature expression in his latest book, *The Self and the Dramas of History*. With acknowledgment of his indebtedness to Martin Buber, Niebuhr there describes the self as "a creature which is in constant dialogue with itself, with its neighbor, and with God." The very texture of this threefold dialogue of existence is historical. Niebuhr would not go so far as Ortega y Gasset in asserting that "man has no nature, what he has is history"—after all, Niebuhr does stress the natural and social coherences in which human existence is embedded—but he would certainly go along with the Spanish philosopher in insisting that "to comprehend anything human, be it personal or collective, one must understand its history." This direction of Niebuhr's thinking, which seems to me both biblical and existential, has of course brought him into some conflict with the basic ontological outlook championed by Paul Tillich; the cross-controversy between these two friends and opponents, in the new Library of Living Theology volume and in the earlier volume in this series devoted to Tillich, makes fascinating reading. Where Tillich asserts that "all problems drive us to an ontological analysis," Niebuhr insists that "the human person and man's society are by nature historical, and the ultimate truth about life must be mediated historically." It is in this area that the real issue dividing the two great theologians is defined.

Even in the newer framework of his thinking, however, Niebuhr's original interest remains dominant. He is concerned with showing how out of the encounter of faith in the dialogic life, the possibility emerges of a courage and a vision beyond the resources of human wisdom and virtue, a courage and a vision that enable us to accept our limitations and yet make the most of the creative potentialities of our being by seeing both in the larger perspective of the divine purpose. We see the folly of attempting to complete life and history through our own doing, and yet we recognize that our efforts and achievements have their significant place in a "larger plan" in which our fragmentary meanings will be completed in a way beyond our comprehension or control. In this confidence, we may live and work in full responsibility, without lapsing into either self-sufficiency or despair.

Another tendency in Niebuhr's thinking, this time on the political level, is brought to expression in his most recent book. As far back as 1944, in *The Children of Light and the Children of Darkness,* signs of the essentially "conservative" cast of mind of this leading "liberal" could be discerned, for what is *The Children of Light* but a truly "conservative" defense of American democracy? Niebuhr's recent writings combine a more conscious and explicit formulation of this "conservatism" with an embarrassed repudiation of the term. Yet the fact itself cannot be denied. His devastating critique of the French Enlightenment as the cradle of "every error which infects a modern liberal culture in its estimate of the human situation, and [of] most of the errors which reached a tragic culmination in modern totalitarianism"; his bitter characterization of the French Revolution as the source of the illusions which have "produced despotism in the name of liberty, civil war in the name of fraternity, and superstitious politics in the "name of reason," are enough to indicate the basic direction of his political philosophy. Nor should we be surprised to see his earlier "prophetic" radicalism culminate in the "new conservatism"; there is an inner connection between the two, and no real reversal is involved. For the "prophetic" radicalism implied a radical relativization of all political programs, institutions, and movements, and therefore a thoroughgoing rejection of every form of political rationalism. Add to this a renewed emphasis on the historic continuities of social life, and Niebuhr's brand of "conservatism" emerges. It is manifestly not the conservatism of those who are called conservatives in American public life, but it is enough apparently to establish a kinship with Burke and to give Niebuhr a prominent place in all the recent histories and anthologies of the "new conservatism."

Influence in the Secular Disciplines

The sweep of Niebuhr's thinking has led him into many fields, and has driven him to take issue with the dominant tendencies in modern religion and culture. It has also brought his influence to bear upon significant elements outside the conventional scope of the Christian theologian. The impact of his biblical-existential thinking on religiously concerned American Jews is apparent to anyone who is in touch with recent trends, and may be documented by such writings as A. J. Heschel's contribution to the Library of Living Theology volume, "A Hebrew Evaluation of Reinhold Niebuhr," and his book published earlier this year, *God in Search of Man: A Philosophy of Judaism*. Even more striking is the communication Niebuhr has been able to establish with many of the younger men in history and political science, of whom Arthur M. Schlesinger Jr. and Kenneth Thompson—both have valuable essays in this volume—may be taken as typical. Niebuhr, on his part, gratefully acknowledges that of late he has had a particularly appreciative understanding from men in these secular disciplines, and I too can add my testimony from my own experience on the campuses of this country. This influence he attributes to the fact that "these disciplines are most critical of the illusions of our culture." Perhaps it is also due to the fact that kind of theology he teaches seems to the men in these disciplines particularly near to their concerns and particularly germane to their problems. It is a theology that—as Arthur M. Schlesinger Jr. long ago pointed out—restates the basic insights of biblical faith "with such irresistible relevance to contemporary experience that even those who have no decisive faith in the supernatural find their reading of experience and history given new and significant dimensions." Perhaps, too, it may, with God's help, lead them to see "faith in the supernatural" in a new light.

Niebuhr's thinking in the past three decades has ranged far and wide over the areas of Western culture, yet he is no doubt right in saying that throughout he has "not strayed very far from [his] original ethical and apologetic interests." He has merely been able to make these interests take in all the major concerns of our time.

Part II

JEWISH RELIGIOUS THOUGHT: ISSUES AND PERSPECTIVES

—4—

Has Judaism Still Power to Speak?

A RELIGION FOR AN AGE OF CRISIS

(1949)

The revival of creative theological thinking is generally recognized as one of the significant events in recent intellectual history. Theology, as we are beginning to learn, is not just a scholastic wordgame of abstract system-making, remote from life. It has something to say, something directly relevant to the fearful predicament in which modern man finds himself. "The Christian account of human motivation," Arthur M. Schlesinger Jr. points out in commenting on a work of Reinhold Niebuhr, "is massive, subtle and intricate, and it throws light on certain present dilemmas which baffle liberalism or Marxism. Whatever you may say about Augustine, he would not have been much surprised by the outcome of the Russian Revolution."

In the past generation, Christian theology has made an impressive effort to rise to its proper task—which is to interpret life and history, man and the universe, in ultimate terms. Without rejecting the insights gained on other levels of analysis, it has striven to include and

transcend them, to fuse them into a single
Weltanschauung that can serve at once as the ultimate
logic and dynamic of life.
   But what about Jewish theology? We have long
prided ourselves on being universally recognized as
the People of the Book. What have we done to make
the Book relevant to the perplexities of our age? What
has been our response in terms of creative religious
thinking, theological interpretation, or prophetic witness? What word has Judaism had for mankind in
agony?

The revival of Christian theology followed upon
World War I, which put an end to the smug
self-satisfaction of Western civilization and
therewith to Western man's high illusions of approaching omnipotence and perfectibility. It may be said to
date from that day in 1919 when Karl Barth stood in
his little parish church in Safenwil, Switzerland, called
upon to say something meaningful to a congregation
still shattered by the impact of the war. He took up his
Bible and preached. As he himself describes it, he was
like a man who, uncertainly climbing the dark and
winding staircase of a church tower, reaches for the
bannister to steady himself, and gets hold of the bell-
rope instead.
   The echoes of that bell, which reached the world in
the *Römerbrief* that same year, have not yet died
down. The steady stream of writings that have come
from Barth's pen in Switzerland, in Germany, and then
in Switzerland again, have had an immense effect in
reshaping religious thinking on the Continent, in Britain, and in America. From Switzerland too has come
the voice of Emil Brunner, the Zürich theologian,
whose systematic works have had an even greater direct influence in the English-speaking world. Barth
and Brunner are neo-Reformation theologians—that
is, their work is primarily a reinterpretation of the

Reformation tradition of Luther, Calvin, and Zwingli. Originally closely identified, they have now developed important and perhaps crucial differences. Both have found partisans and followers throughout Protestant Europe and America. Concurrently, significant new trends have also appeared in the Roman Catholic and Eastern Orthodox communions. The Catholic revival in France predates somewhat the First World War but its major contributions fall in the postwar period, and the reworking of Thomism in contemporary terms, in particular the development of the idea of Christian Personalism, is linked with the name of Jacques Maritain. The intellectual renaissance in Eastern Orthodoxy is limited to a handful of Russian thinkers living in exile (the late Nicholas Berdyaev was perhaps best known), but is none the less brilliant for that.

In the United States, neo-Reformation theology has found its exponents among men like Reinhold Niebuhr, H. Richard Niebuhr, Paul Tillich (in this country since 1933), Robert L. Calhoun, and John C. Bennett. What they have had to say has perhaps had more meaning for Americans, so obviously is it cast in terms of our own experience.

Most characteristic of all these theologians, Catholic, Protestant, and Orthodox, is the immediate bearing of their teaching upon the fundamental problems of life. These men are very far from being the cloistered recluses theologians are popularly supposed to be; they are actively and deeply concerned with the world and the affairs of men. Their work is permeated with a profound sense of contemporaneity.

The one unifying motive in neo-Reformation theology has been the effort to find a "third way," a way free from the inadequacies of old-line fundamentalism and latter-day modernism. This third way, it has been felt, is to be gained not by eclectic compromise but by achieving a fresh synthesis of Reformation thought which would turn the insights of scriptural religion to bear upon life, human nature, and history.

Protestant neo-orthodoxy, as it has come to be known, thus begins with a double rejection from which it proceeds to a strong affirmation. Neither rationalism nor mysticism: dialectic theology—this is the first of its affirmations. The pretensions of reason to answer the ultimate questions of life are challenged. At the very most, Brunner says, reason is able to point to the transcendent reality, but it can never, unaided, apprehend or establish relations with it. (Barth is unwilling even to make that concession to human reason in the field of religion.) But if reason is challenged, so is mysticism, which claims immediate apprehension of the absolute and ultimate union with it. As against both rationalism and mysticism, these theologians take what has been called an "existentialist" position: *faith is decision.* Dialectic theology sees the thinker first of all as a man who has to make practical decisions in life, and among these decisions the most crucial is the one by which he stakes his life on his affirmation of God—it is a portentous "wager." "The truth concerns me infinitely now," said the early Barth, recalling Kierkegaard, and although Barth later abandoned the term itself, existentialist thinking remains basic to the best in neo-Reformation Protestantism. Out of the existential decision—out of the divine-human encounter in which man confronts God across the abyss which separates the human from the divine—is generated the tension of spiritual life. Neither reason nor mystic union can resolve it, in spite of their sweeping claims. Such tension is ultimately expressible only in paradox, which Reinhold Niebuhr defines as "a rational understanding of the limits of rationality, . . . an expression of faith that a rationally irresolvable contradiction may point to a truth which logic cannot contain."

The new Protestantism recognizes the service liberal theology has rendered in breaking the grip of a sterile fundamentalism, but it maintains that liberalism has been unable to meet the test. Theological liberalism—so runs the indictment—has systematically striven to break the tension that is the spring of spiritual energy by affirming the continuity of God with man instead of the "otherness" of God; by preaching an unwarranted confidence in the powers of human reason despite its clear limitations and corruptions; by insisting on the "innate" goodness of man and the essential unreality of sin and evil; by looking for the gradual realization of the Kingdom of Heaven in the course of social progress. Liberal theology is accused of having merely sanctified the relative standards of secular bourgeois society and having served as a sounding board for its prejudices, even to the point of virtually discarding the Bible except as "inspirational reading" or "great literature." In short, liberalism in theology has been a near-secular cult of "adjustment" and "peace of mind" at a time when these are counsels of spiritual death.

Against all this, the new theology takes Scripture seriously, though—and here it breaks with fundamentalism—not always literally. (How the Bible can be understood as revelation without danger of falling into bibliolatry is given profound theoretical treatment in Brunner's *Revelation and Reason* and H. Richard Niebuhr's *The Meaning of Revelation.*) It reaffirms Kierkegaard's insistence on the "eternal qualitative difference between God and man." The favorite preposition of liberal theology is *within*," H. Richard Niebuhr comments acutely, "that of post-liberal theology, *over against.*"

This radical distinction makes possible a fresh appreciation of the meaning of sin and evil in human life, which has become, perhaps, the most familiar aspect of the new theology. The inordinate pretensions of the human spirit, man's efforts to deny and overpass his creatureliness—his pride, his egocentricity, deep-rooted tendency of each person to make himself instead of God the center of his universe—reflects the radical sinfulness of human nature ("original sin"). It is the other side to man's undoubted capacity for self-transcendence in reason, imagination, and moral freedom, and constitutes both a limitation and source of corruption of that capacity. In Reinhold Niebuhr's work we see excitingly described the insidious ways in which all motives, even the basest, are idealized, and all ideals, even the purest, are in fact compounded with the self-interest of those who promote them. It is a perspective capable of assimilating the best of Marx and Freud.

The new theology is preeminently a crisis theology. It was born in a time of crisis; it reflects the contemporary crisis of society; it expresses the permanent crisis in which man finds himself in this world.

Crisis here means the perennial plight of man, who, like Kafka's K., sees the goal, is driven to motion, yet cannot find the way—who desperately needs the truth, strains to attain it, yet can never be sure that he has reached it. But crisis also means judgment (Greek: *krisis*)—the divine judgment under which man and all his enterprises stand. "The worst sin is man," says Kierkegaard, "is self-assurance, the source of which lies in man's lack of realism in facing himself."

The Kingdom of God, as the neo-Reformation theologians conceive it, can never be simply identified with historical "progress." It always transcends and stands "over against" history, yet is always relevant to it as judgment and fulfillment. More, the power of the Kingdom breaks through into human existence. Every one of our achievements, it is true, is ambiguous; but each achievement nevertheless contains a genuine "hint" of the Kingdom. This is the source of the moral dynamic which makes possible working *within time* to speed the "grand consummation at the end of time." The final elimination of evil, it is recognized, is not possible in the life of man—"Perfection is an eschatological conception, an 'impossible possibility,' " says Paul Tillich—but, under judgment of God, man must never rest so long as there is evil in the world, while at the same time he must never permit himself to be deceived as to the quality of his achievement. Here we have a "utopianism" that can resist corruption, a theologically grounded social activism that can actually face and deal with reality.

Neo-Reformation theology is neither absolutist nor relativist in the usual sense; it holds to what may be called a God-centered relativism. Only God is absolute; everything else—literally everything, every idea, institution, or movement—is infected with relativity, for there can be no human situation that does not stand under the judgment of God. Once we confess and acknowledge God, Barth says, everything which is not God is "criticized, limited, made relative," and absolutizing the relative is idolatry. Such radical depreciation of everything short of God once drove Karl Barth to the utter devaluation of the world of nature and culture. It was this that led to his separation from Emil Brunner in the early 1930's. With the mounting European crisis and the war, Barth's attitude underwent a change, signified by his militant anti-Nazism. Apparently, however, the change was not a permanent one, for the same almost nihilistic tendency is to be detected again in his present-day attitude of unconcern for the fate of Western civilization as against Soviet Communism. Tillich was quite right, it would seem, when as far back as 1935, he criticized Barth's special type of dialectic theology in the following terms:

"When I am asked, what is wrong with the 'dialectic' theology, I reply that it is not 'dialectic.' A dialectic

theology is one in which 'yes' and 'no' belong inseparably together. In the so-called 'dialectic' theology,
they are irreconcilably separated. . . ."

Brunner, the Niebuhrs, and Tillich himself—each in
his own way—has been able to maintain the dialectic
tension so that the relativization of everything under
God has not meant a turning aside from life and
history, but rather the achievement of a standpoint
from which both may be apprehended and dealt with.
A relativism rooted in the absolute is the hallmark of
neo-Reformation theology. It makes evident the tragic
dimension of life for it does not hide the degree to
which man's best aspirations are corrupted in his own
soul and imperiled in the world. But it points beyond
tragedy and despair—to the coming of the Kingdom,
to the realization of the "impossible possibility."

T
he work of William Temple, the late Arch-
bishop of Canterbury and easily the most distinguished Anglican theologian of recent times,
may be conceived as an effective absorption of central
neo-Reformation insights into the main body of Anglican tradition. His chief importance lies, perhaps, in
his effort to work out a Christian social ethic that will
be relevant to the times and yet refrain from identifying the church with any particular social program.
His work in connection with the Malvern Conference
(1941), in which he was the leading spirit, and his
popular Penguin brochure, *Christianity and Social
Order*, have made his point of view well known among
large numbers in Britain and America.

The Catholic Humanism (or Personalism) of
Jacques Maritain stresses the eminent dignity of the
human person as a spiritual being and his transcendence over the total claims of society. It is rooted in the
doctrine of "theocentric humanism," which Maritain
finds in St. Thomas and which he opposes to the
"anthropocentric humanism" that he asserts has

brought contemporary civilization to the brink of disaster. He has had to contend with powerful resistance in Catholic ranks, for neither humanism nor personalism has ever been much stressed by the Church. Indeed, one gets the impression that what Maritain is attempting to do is to recapture a side of St. Thomas' teaching which has been rather consistently ignored since the 13th century. Closely linked with Maritain's thought is the Catholic existentialism of Gabriel Marcel and other French writers. Maritain himself has lately contended that St. Thomas' "philosophy of being" is existentialist in the true sense of the term.

The two leading Eastern Orthodox thinkers—Berdyaev and Father Bulgakov—were both Marxists to start with and have retained their social radicalism as part of their theology. Reflecting the diverse influences of Kant, Dostoevsky, Marx and the mystic Jacob Boehme, Berdyaev has developed, in a series of works—the best known of which is, perhaps, *Slavery and Freedom*—a personal theology widely different from Western patterns and rooted in the Russian Orthodox tradition. He is par excellence the philosopher of freedom, of free creativity. He condemns all types of *objectification*—that is, depersonalization—of man through institutions, organizations, laws, rites, or dogmas. In place of such "enslavement," Berdyaev calls for the free communion of love. His social philosophy is indeed one of Christian anarchism or personalist socialism, which recognizes the necessity of a certain degree of economic collectivism but categorically rejects the collectivization of any other aspect of life.

Bulgakov has sketched his own development "From Marxism to Sophiology" in an article under that title in the *Review of Religion* for May 1937. His criticism of Marxism is acute and realistic. His own "Christian humanism" or "social Christianity" is rooted in the Orthodox concept of *sobornost,* or free union, which brings him close to Berdyaev's sphere of thought. Both opposed the Bolshevik Revolution and were driven from Russia, but both regard the revolution as the perversion of a profoundly true idea and as punishment for the fearful sins of pre-revolutionary church and society. Berdyaev particularly is a firm believer in the Orthodox idea of the universalist-messianic mission of Russia: it is in Russia that "the way is being prepared . . . for the new Jerusalem of community and the brotherhood of man."

Virtually all the important figures in the renewal of Christian theology—Karl Barth, Emil Brunner, Reinhold and Richard Niebuhr, Paul Tillich, Jacques Maritain, William Temple, Nicolas Berdyaev, and Father Bulgakov—are to be classified as social radicals in the sense of being anti-capitalist and anti-totalitarian in their understanding of the Christian social imperative.

Indeed many of the leaders in the new theological movement took active part in the European resistance. As Horton (*Contemporary Continental Theology*) pointed out in 1938, "for a liberal Protestant, prepared to admit the reality of contemporary natural knowledge of God, it is a delicate question where to draw the line between the true and the false in this contemporary German [Nazi] sense of God. Not so for Karl Barth. He stands over against this in complete prophetic opposition, like Amos at Bethel or Elijah at Mount Carmel. . . . He calls upon all faithful Christians to take to the catacombs rather than bow the knee to the new Baal." To Barth and those who, after much hesitation, followed him in the German Confessional Church, to the church in Holland and Norway, the crisis of Hitlerism was no mere political, economic or cultural crisis. It was a religious crisis: it was man deifying himself, man establishing the God-state. That is why men who had never shown any interest in politics suddenly became rebels, why quiet, respectable citizens did not shrink from martyrdom. At that moment of crisis, the new theology became a force in history.

I n a very profound sense, what goes by the name of the "crisis of our time" is a Jewish crisis. Not only has it brought frightful disaster to millions of Jews on the European continent; what is perhaps more significant, the fate of the Jew has become essentially typical of the fate of contemporary man. The demonic evil and unreason which mankind loosed upon itself in the course of the past generation found in the Jew its first and chosen victim: anti-Semitism has established itself as the projection of the deepest impulses of human sinfulness. In the Jew, the archetype of the outsider standing forever at the brink of nothingness, the alienation of contemporary man, his malaise and homelessness in the world, find their most intense expression.

Immediately after the First World War, a brilliant renaissance of Jewish thinking, ripened in the previous decade, came to fruition in Germany. Jewish religious existentialism, linked with the names of Martin Buber and Franz Rosenzweig, and in a sense too with that of Hermann Cohen, the great neo-Kantian philosopher, was born. In his *Religion of Reason from the Sources of Judaism,* published immediately after his death in 1918, Cohen had already, as Franz Rosenzweig was quick to see, transcended the abstract rationality of the academic tradition and achieved an essentially existentialist position.

It was Martin Buber, however, who developed the "new thinking" in a way that made it an immediate power in Western culture. Buber is probably the greatest religious existentialist thinker since Sören Kierkegaard; his philosophico-theological achievement is immense—his *I and Thou* is already an acknowledged classic—and his effect on contemporary thought deep and far-reaching. His affinities with neo-Reformation thought on the one hand and with Berdyaev's personalist approach on the other—so complex and manysided is his thinking—have made him a powerful germinal force in contemporary theology, much more perhaps outside than within the limits of the Jewish community.

The central idea of Buber's thought is given in his celebrated distinction between the two primary attitudes, the two orders of living, the two fundamental types of relation, of which man is capable: I-Thou (person-to-person) and I-It (person-to-thing). Through the I-Thou encounter emerges the primary reality of the spiritual life: neither the I nor the Thou, says Buber, is ultimately real but the I-Thou meeting, the "between-man-and-man." The person—the "single-one"—is born of the I-Thou encounter: without a Thou there can be no I.

Yet man's attitude cannot possibly be cast permanently in the I-Thou relation. To survive, he must know and *use* things—and it is the intrinsic tragedy of life that he is only too often driven to treat persons as things. "Without It man cannot live. But he who lives with It alone is not a man."

To Buber, in his thoroughgoing existentialism, man's freedom is decision. "The man who thinks existentially," he says, "is the man who stakes his life on his thinking." It is through the decision of faith, upon which man does indeed stake his whole life, that in the last analysis he gains his freedom and becomes a person, a "single-one."

Though in his view, personality is generated out of the I-Thou relation and is therefore not ultimate in the sense of many radical individualists, Buber is insistent in his personalist emphasis. "Man can have dealings with God only as a single-one," he repeats. "The individual human person is unique and irreplaceable." Because of his personalist emphasis, Buber feels compelled to set limits to mysticism, which he has valued highly and to which he was personally attracted; it is communion, not union, with God that is the proper goal. He rejects too the rationalism that thinks it can "comprehend" God in an intellectual formula. "God may be addressed, not expressed," is Buber's profound insight. God as the transcendent Thou in the ultimate I-Thou encounter is, of course, "wholly other," as the Barthians have stressed; but he is also "wholly present." Buber, in the authentic Jewish tradition, refuses to suppress either the transcendence or the "hereness" of God.

B uber's ethic is rooted in his I-Thou philosophy. Evil in human relations is the conversion of the "other" from a Thou into an It—objectification or depersonalization, in Berdyaev's terminology—the utilization of a person as a means to an external end, in Kant's. Thus, Buber, like the neo-Reformation thinkers, finds the root source of human sin in the making absolute of the self. As against this, there is the self-giving love of a genuine I-Thou relation. Such love does not mean the suppression of self: "It is not the I that is given up, but the false self-asserting instinct. . . . There is no self-love that is not self-deceit . . . but without being and remaining one's self, there is no love."

In his social philosophy, Buber, like Berdyaev, sharply counterposes the free community "resting on self and self-responsibility" to the collectivity in which every person is institutionalized and turned into an It. In true community, he teaches, just as in true love for the "other," God enters as a "third": "The true community does not arise through people having feelings for one another (though indeed not without it), but through first, their taking their stand in living mutual relation with a living Center, and second, their being in living mutual relation with one another." He defines an important aspect of his social philosophy in a very telling polemic against Carl Schmitt and Friedrich Gogarten, who try to exploit a one-sided doctrine of the utter depravity of man to justify the authoritarian state. Buber eloquently vindicates individual man against the total claims of state and society. Man he sees as "essentially" neither good nor evil nor simply the indeterminate possibility of either, but in the most precise sense of the words, both-good-and-evil, "good and evil together." Only as against God can radical evil be ascribed to man, he insists, "because God is God and man is man and the distance between them is absolute."

This feeling for tension in the human situation appears strikingly in Buber's interpretation of the Messianic vision. "Redemption," he says, "occurs forever and none has ever occurred": the Kingdom of God is here among us as a power and a summons and yet always remains as the promise of fulfilment at the "end of days." Out of this polarity of the "already" and the "not-yet" is generated the dynamic of spiritual life. Buber, too, grounds his theology of social action—he is, of course, a convinced socialist—in his eschatology. "What he seeks," Ernst Simon points out, "is the 'demarcation-line' between the unconditional demand and the always only conditional realization."

Buber does see the possibility of a really "organic" community in which a We is formed through a complex of person-to-person associations. Such an organic community, he believes, was exemplified in the Hasidic movement, at least in its best days. Hasidism he regards as one of the great spiritual achievements of Israel, along with Prophetism and early Christianity— and Zionism too, the Zionism of the *halutzim,* who strove for the realization of the spiritual potentialities of Judaism. Buber's Zionism is linked with his conception of Israel. Israel is not just one of the "nations of the world": it is "something unique, unclassifiable, a community that cannot be grasped in the categories of ethnology and sociology." Israel is the people of spiritual creativity: "Salvation comes from the Jews; the fundamental tendencies of Judaism are the elements from which a new gospel for the world is always elaborated."

With Buber stands Franz Rosenzweig. Rosenzweig's tragic yet triumphant life—he died in 1929 at the age of 43 after eight years of an encroaching paralysis that finally deprived him even of the power of speech—constitutes a moving experience. His writings—*The Star of Redemption,* his one complete work; his shorter pieces and his letters—reflect a profound and penetrating intellect, in its very texture existentialist; it is humiliating to note that almost none of his writings has yet appeared in English.[1]

Having reached his existentialist position after a hard struggle with an idealist heritage, Rosenzweig traced, in life as well as in thought, the road that leads "from unimportant truths of the type 'twice two equals four,' to which men lightly assent, . . . through the truths for which a man is willing to pay something, on to those which he cannot prove true except with the sacrifice of his life and finally to those the truth of which can be proved only by the staking of the lives of all the generations." I say in life as well as in thought, for Rosenzweig's life—his existential decision for Judaism at the very moment when he was ready for conversion to Christianity—was precisely such a "wager" with destiny.

Rosenzweig too saw the ultimate reality in the I-Thou encounter, in "speaking and answering." The metaphysic of speech became a salient part of his philosophy: in a significant sense, his and Buber's translation of Scripture into German—or rather "re-translation of Holy Script into Holy Word"—was a work of theology, of an inwardly working theology of the world. His whole system, as elaborated in that strange work, *The Star of Redemption,* is based on a series of "correlations" between the primary elements of ultimate reality—God, man, and world—to which the divine-human encounter is crucial.

The "mystery of Israel" obsessed Rosenzweig, the passionate "life-thinker." For him, as for Buber, "salvation comes from the Jews." Judaism is the "eternal fire," Christianity, the "eternal rays"; Judaism, the "eternal life," Christianity, the "eternal way." While Israel stays with God, the Christian is sent out to conquer the unredeemed world. But he is always in danger of relapsing into paganism and when he does, when the pagan within him rises in revolt against the yoke of the Cross, he vents his fury on the Jew; that is the "secret" of anti-Semitism. "The fact of anti-Semitism, age-old and ever-present though totally groundless," Rosenzweig wrote to his mother, "can be understood only by the different functions which God has assigned to the two communities—Israel to represent in time the eternal Kingdom of God, Christianity to bring itself and the world toward that goal." Only when that goal is reached—at the "end of time"—will the final reconciliation and fusion take place; then all will indeed be one in the recognition of the unity of the Divine Name.

The time of Buber and Rosenzweig boasted of other names as well. There is Gershom Scholem, in whose scholarly studies of Jewish mysticism, suggestions of rich theological ideas may be perceived. In his writings on the "essence of Judaism," Leo Baeck has given the "liberal" viewpoint a new depth and power. And then there was Franz Kafka.

Perhaps in the current deluge of Kafka exegesis it is necessary to insist that Kafka was after all a creative artist, not a theologian. Yet it is not to be denied that, on the level of interpretation at least, *The Castle* is a powerful theological myth of man's search for salvation in a world marked, in Buber's words, by a "special human homelessness and solitude," while *The Trial* is an imaginatively projected study of human guilt and divine judgment. Nor will the perceptive reader fail to note the relevance of many of Kafka's episodes and symbols to the "mystery of Israel," to the position of the Jew in the world. However one may differ on interpretation—and no interpretation of a great creative artist can ever be final or exhaustive—I do not think it can any longer be denied that Franz Kafka was a religious thinker of a stature we are only now beginning to appreciate.

The ardent intellectual life of German Jewry did not cease with the triumph of Hitler. If anything, it grew more intense, for now it began to search for the meaning of the awful catastrophe that was overwhelming it. But the end came all too soon and the voice of German Jewry was silenced. The center now shifted to Jewish Palestine. There an immense cultural work was going forward. Hebrew was being reborn as a living language; a rich literature was springing up, scholarly work of all sorts was being energetically prosecuted. But aside from the recent German immigration, only two figures seem to have made themselves felt as creative religious forces in the course of the past generation, Chief Rabbi Abraham Isaac Kuk and Dr. Judah L. Magnes.

Dr. Magnes was no theologian in the narrower sense of the term, but his pronouncements through the passing years had a genuine prophetic ring. In a cowardly age, he spoke out and no opposition or abuse was ever able to silence him. But what is perhaps most important, he spoke and thought in thoroughly religious terms. It is a great pity that so many have allowed factional heat or differences on what are, after all, secondary questions to obscure their appreciation of this great man. Rabbi Kuk infused the age-old Orthodox tradition with new energy. His writings are the reflection of a life of genuine sanctity and gain much of their power therefrom. His personal influence was perhaps even more potent than his writings; he has left a deep and lasting impression on important sections of the new Palestine.

Aside from these men, what Palestine has to show is hardly impressive. But how much less impressive is the picture presented by the United States, this land where lives the bulk of modern Jewry! It is true that the heritage of Solomon Schechter has been developed in new directions by such independent thinkers as Louis Finkelstein and Max Kadushin. It is true that Samuel S. Cohon has for more than a quarter of a century pursued serious theological work in the Reform-liberal tradition. It is true, too, that Reconstructionism, the creation of Mordecai M. Kaplan, has a notable achievement to its credit: it has evolved the only relevant "philosophy" of our Jewish existence in America. Its theology, however, still retains far too much of naturalism and pragmatic humanism so that it is always in peril of passing over into sociology on the one side or collapsing into mere ethical sentiment on the other.

Beyond this, what American Jews have to show in the way of theology and religious thinking is hardly more than routine reiteration of inherited formulas, Orthodox or modernist, the ostentatious parading of platitudes, the anxious effort to identify Judaism with the latest version of the "American way of life"—plus one or two less useful popularizations. The whole story is told when we note that the largest Jewish community in the world—numerous, active, and prosperous, involved in so many Jewish enterprises—does not possess one single significant journal of Jewish theology.

The fact is that neither the world catastrophe nor the Jewish disaster, with which it is so inseparably linked, has evoked any creative response on the part of present-day Judaism. The age of Buber and Rosenzweig, with all its achievement and promise, must be recognized as hardly more than an isolated episode in the almost unrelieved mediocrity of Jewish religious thinking in recent decades.

Is it primarily the desperate insecurity of Jewish existence during the past thirty years that is responsible, as so many have suggested? Has preoccupation with mere survival absorbed so much of Jewish energy as to leave little or none for reflective thought transcending the moment? Insecurity and disaster are nothing new in the history of Israel, but never in the past did they paralyze the sources of spiritual creativity. On the contrary, every great achievement in Jewish religious thought came into being in response to crisis.

Nor can the inadequacy of the Jewish theological response be attributed to the alleged anti-theological bias in Jewish religious tradition. This alleged aversion to theology is, to a large extent, nothing but a latter-day fiction. If theology is understood in terms more comprehensive than scholastic system-making, Jewish thought has almost always—at least until recently—been theological. From the scriptural writers and Prophets to Rosenzweig and Buber, Jewish thinking has been a continuing effort to interpret problems and events in terms of the divine-human encounter and the working-out of God's providence.

The renunciation of theology in modern times is not so much a continuation of Jewish tradition as a more or less definite break with it, although it must be said that there are aspects of the tradition itself that have made this break possible.

This abrupt break with tradition reflects the belated entrance of the Jews into the modern world. For the great mass of Jews in Eastern Europe, there was no Renaissance; within one or two generations, they passed directly from the Middle Ages into modern secularism. For all its great cultural achievements, Emancipation brought confusion and disorientation from which Jewry has not yet recovered. In the rout of traditional Judaism, the very notion of religious thinking was all but lost. More, in the self-hatred that this period of demoralization bred, theology was rejected not only because it was theology but also, and perhaps primarily, because it was *Jewish,* because it bore the ghetto-stigma of Jewishness.

The metaphysical climate of opinion has changed drastically since those days but the after-effects are still strong.

The religious tradition itself has not been entirely unambiguous. The polarity of Jewish religion has been noted more than once in the past. Over fifty years ago (1893), Ahad Ha-Am wrote his penetrating essay, "Priest and Prophet," in which he pointed out the reciprocal relation between the two contrasting types of Jewish spirituality. At one pole is the prophet, standing outside the sinning community—"over against" it, in fact—to denounce its evil ways. He is "a man of strife and of contention to the whole earth." But he is also—and for that very reason—the inspired agent of crisis-creativity, the spiritual pioneer who conquers new frontiers of religious understanding. Very different is the priest. The priest, in Ahad Ha-Am's words, "appears on the scene at a time when prophecy has already succeeded in hewing out a path for its idea." His task is not spiritual pioneering but everyday normalization, cultivating the ground gained by the prophet and reducing it to order. He is the respectable man standing at the head of—"within"—the respectable community to guide and rule it. "The idea of the prophet produces the teaching of the priest." but it is a teaching that no longer has the urgency and utter immediacy of the prophetic message.

Essential Jewish tradition takes as normative *both* prophet and priest, or rather the tension between them. It is a tension that manifests itself, not so much in the succession of historical epochs with varying emphasis, as in an ambivalence within each historical period and even within each genuine spiritual leader.

But there is ever the besetting temptation to reduce the polarity to the one-sided routine of priestly "normalcy," thus draining Jewish spirituality of its originating force. Rabbinism was born out of the Pharisaic movement, which was clearly a prophetic protest against priestly superficiality and laxness, and many of the finest examples of post-scriptural prophetism are to be found in rabbinical ranks. Yet Rabbinism too, as Ahad Ha-Am indicates, only too often tended to lose its prophetic spirit and sink to the level of priestly routine.

For many generations now, priestly "normalcy" has been taken as the true spirit of Jewish religion and every suggestion of prophetic urgency impatiently brushed aside. A hidden "liberalism" permeates and enfeebles conventional Jewish religion, even the most orthodox. Judaism, we are assured, is not a crisis-religion but an affair of "everyday normal life." Yet if there is one religion in the world that owes everything to crisis, it is Judaism. Judaism was born out of crisis; Israel is the crisis-people par excellence. In tradition, it is the great crisis of the Exodus that is the central point of reference for everything Jewish. The crisis culminating in the fall of the two kingdoms and the captivity served as the background for the prophetic movement. The crisis under the Hasmoneans gave birth to Pharisaism. The crisis following the destruction of the Temple witnessed the far-reaching reconstruction of Judaism by Johanan ben Zakkai. Where is there another record of crisis so unrelieved and so continuous as that contained in the historical books of Scripture or indeed in the entire body of Jewish history?

Jewish existence itself is caught up in an inescapable ambiguity: is it ethnic or is it religious? Ideally, it is both, reflecting the universal and particularist components in the pattern of Jewish destiny. But this polarity too has been broken and reduced to a one-sided falsification, in the form either of old-line Reform Judaism or of secular nationalism. The non-Jew striving to achieve a more profound, more significant spiritual orientation can do so only in religious, and usually only in specifically Christian, terms; the "scientific," aesthetic, and sociological cults of yesterday no longer have much appeal. The Jew too strives to affirm himself, but unlike the Gentile, he can affirm himself as Jew, at least up to a certain point, entirely in non-religious terms. To be a "good Jew"—how ambiguous is the phrase!—he need not affirm the religious tradition of Israel; he can be a fervent Zionist, an ardent Hebraist or Yiddishist, or a valiant fighter against anti-Semitism. Corresponding to the Christian affirmation of the non-Jew, there is, for the Jew, not merely Judaism or Jewish religion; there are also the *ersatz*-Jewish faiths—Jewish nationalism, culture, social service, "anti-defamation"—all moving on the secular level, all unable or unwilling to break through to the religious.

N ow all of these things—nationalism, culture, social service, "anti-defamation"—are fine things, worthy things, *in their place*. It is only when they make pretensions to absoluteness as *total* affirmations—it is only when, as I have said, they present themselves as *ersatz*-Jewish faiths in place of Jewish religion, rather than subordinate to it—that they become mischievous. To mistake the part for the whole, the relative for the absolute, is surely the most dangerous pitfall in spiritual life.

This atmosphere is so pervasive that it affects even those who sincerely believe themselves free from it. They too—rabbis, scholars, and theologians—make their interpretations and judgments, do their thinking, in wholly non-religious terms. It simply never occurs to them to make what they preach really and deeply relevant to the crucial problems of modern life; aside from a few platitudes, they have nothing to say that is not better said by the psychologist, sociologist, or political leader. By the logic of compensation, it is precisely this failure that has given the *ersatz*-Jewish faiths, especially Zionist nationalism, the opportunity to claim with a great deal of cogency that it is they who are exercising the prophetic function, they who are saying the new and meaningful word. And in some sense they are—particularly in contrast to the sluggish mediocrity of conventional Jewish religion. But in the final analysis, it is merely a pseudo-prophetism.

It cannot remain so. It cannot be that Judaism has spent its force, that the ancient People of the Book possesses no religious, no theological, no prophetic word for our time. Perhaps events under way today may bring about a drastic change and release the creative forces of Jewish spirituality. But until then the matter must remain in the problematic form given to it by Dr. Magnes: "Has Judaism still the power to speak in these days of mankind's crisis?"

Notes

[1] A volume including a biography of Franz Rosenzweig and an anthology of his writings, prepared by N. N. Glatzer, is published by Schocken Books.

—5—

Rosenzweig's "Judaism of Personal Existence"

A THIRD WAY BETWEEN ORTHODOXY AND MODERNISM

(1950)

There is hardly an aspect of Jewish life and thought that Franz Rosenzweig did not touch with his creativity. But there is one achievement of his that seems to me to be of imperishable significance: he was among the first to point the way to that return to faith which is a mark of our time. He it was who—along with his slightly older contemporary, Martin Buber—showed that the ancient faith of prophet and rabbi was not merely compatible with the externals of modern culture—that was easy—but was in fact the answer to the deepest problems of the Jew's existence in the contemporary world. Because Franz Rosenzweig did not simply inherit his faith as a matter of course, but had to win it for himself, his word possessed, and still possesses, an extra-ordinary power. In his own person and thought, Rosenzweig showed that the depth, the vitality, the closeness to real existence for which the new generation was longing, could be found in the resources of Jewish religion when that religion was properly understood. Wherever there are Jews who are earnestly striving to understand the meaning and relevance of their faith, there Franz Rosenzweig will have his word to say. Rosenzweig blazed the trail of a new way in Jewish religious thinking—a "third way" equally distinct from, and opposed to, the traditionalism of conventional Orthodoxy and the rationalistic modernism of "liberal" religion. He laid the basis for a kind of Jewish religious thinking that is traditional yet vital, true to the deepest insights of Biblical and rabbinic teaching yet fully relevant to the demands of contemporary existence. He showed that Jewish religion can be something very different from either a scholastic fundamentalism out of touch with modern life or a rationalistic modernism out of touch with Biblical truth. In his very conception of religion and religious thinking, in his understanding of the eternal problems of Jewish and human existence, he was a pioneer. He re-thought the problems of Jewish religion—or rather, we should say, he re-lived them in his own life—and out of his own life he was able to forge a new way of Jewish religious thinking, a new conception of the ancient faith, that never fails to strike fire in the heart of those who seek God out of the necessities of their existence.

Franz Rosenzweig was born on December 25, 1886, at Kassel, Germany, into a substantial, in many ways typical, German-Jewish bourgeois family. His great-grandfather in the Rosenzweig line had come from Eastern Europe with a rabbinical ordination but had settled down at Kassel as a manufacturer. His paternal grandfather was a chemist, his maternal grandfather the principal of a Jewish school. His father was a successful industrialist and respected civic leader. The Rosenzweig family was formally affiliated with the Jewish community but its Jewishness was empty of all content. The last link with the past was a great-uncle, Adam Rosenzweig, with whom the boy sometimes went to synagogue.

The young Franz at first studied medicine, but after 1908 he transferred to Freiburg to work in modern history under Meinecke, and somewhat later he went to Berlin. He was a brilliant student and made a deep impression on Meinecke and other scholars under whom he studied. His doctoral dissertation was on Hegel; almost simultaneously he wrote a work on Schelling. In other words, his career followed the course laid out for a gifted young scholar. Nor was it really extra-ordinary, at least in Rosenzweig's circle, that he should manifest an interest in theology; he and his friends heatedly debated the great issues of religion and philosophy. But in these discussions Judaism never seriously figured. Rosenzweig seems to have felt that it was quite possible for the religiously concerned young Jew to become a Christian but that it was no longer possible to become a Jew: from the Judaism with which he was familiar, he simply could not see how he could establish his religious existence in Jewish terms. He was thoroughly disgusted with the "religionless" Judaism of the bourgeois world in which he lived. Indeed, in 1909, Rosenzweig even encouraged his cousin Hans Ehrenberg to convert to Christianity.

In 1913 came his own great crisis. His religious concern had been growing intense, and he was in almost continuous discussion, particularly with his Christian friend Eugen Rosenstock (now in this country teaching at Dartmouth). The entire night of July 7, 1913 was devoted to one such interchange. "In that night's conversation," Rosenzweig himself relates, "Rosenstock pushed me step by step out of the last relativist positions which I still occupied and forced me to take an unrelativist standpoint. . . . Any form of philosophical relativism [became] impossible for me." He had now made the standpoint of religious faith his own, but that very fact called his Jewishness into question. There was no role whatever that the Judaism he knew could play in religious existence. And so, in July 1913, he decided to become a Christian.

Before his conversion could be consummated, however, Rosenzweig went to the Yom Kippur services held in a little Orthodox synagogue in Berlin. There something happened—exactly what has never become known. But when it was over, Rosenzweig was convinced that he could live his religious existence as a Jew and that his place was in the People Israel. It was for him now, as he put it, to "return to where I have been elected from birth."

Rosenzweig now set himself to studying Jewish sources and to following the thinking of Hermann Cohen—the great neo-Kantian philosopher who became, in his later years, a Jewish thinker of importance. But before very long, the First World War broke out, and Rosenzweig joined the army. He spent most of the time on the Balkan front, where the fighting was not severe and where he had considerable opportunity to think, study, and write. He published some articles, the most important being *Zeit ist's* ("It Is Time") on the subject of Jewish education. In November 1917, he wrote a long letter to his cousin Rudolf Ehrenberg, in the course of which he dealt with revelation and a whole series of other theological problems; this letter, he afterward said, became the "germ" of his "system."

But before he was to develop that system he had still another significant experience to undergo. In May 1918, the army transferred him to Warsaw, where for the first time he really came into touch with East European Jewry. He was profoundly and lastingly impressed by what he saw. The image of the "integral"

Jewish existence of the Polish Jew remained with him throughout his life as a kind of yardstick against which to measure the "fragmentary" existence of the Jew in the Western world. When he returned to the Balkans in August 1918, he began to write his great philosophico-theological work, *Der Stern der Erlösung* ("The Star of Redemption"). He wrote feverishly on army post cards and scraps of paper, which he sent to his mother for transcription. Of course, there was later revision, but it still seems almost unbelievable that a work so complex and intricate in its internal organization could have been composed in this manner.

Returning home after the war, Franz married Edith Hahn (June 1920) and settled in Frankfort on the Main, where he took over the direction of the Freie Jüdische Lehrhaus. This was a remarkable institution, which became the source and center of a veritable renaissance in German Jewish religious thought. Drawing to itself some of the most creative intellectual forces of German Jewry, it tried to reestablish the integrity of Jewish "learning" in a vital, non-academic, non-scholastic sense, and, despite its brief career, it left an indelible mark on Jewish thought. In 1922, Rosenzweig also accepted the recently established chair of Jewish theology at the University of Frankfort, after he had declined a very flattering offer of an important university post in history.

That very year, when he was thirty-four, Rosenzweig was stricken by a creeping paralysis from which he was never to recover. Little by little, it affected his whole body, even his organs of speech. And yet, such was the spirit of the man that the next few years were the most productive of his life! "In this period," writes Nahum N. Glatzer, "he completed his *Jehuda Halevi;* he wrote the long essays on Jewish law, on Hermann Cohen and on the 'New Thinking.' [In this period] Rosenzweig and Buber began to translate the Bible into German. This translation induced the two men to write a number of fundamental articles on Biblical problems. . . . In a number of extensive book reviews. Rosenzweig dealt with current trends from a broad point of view. . . . In his 'leisure hours.' Rosenzweig, who had a thorough musical training, reviewed recordings of classical music and wrote a few interesting chapters of musical history."[1] And this, when all he could move was but one finger!

"With the help of nurses"—again I quote Glatzer—"he was placed in an armchair; his chin was supported by a small cushion that kept his head from dropping; his right thumb miraculously retained some power of movement, though slow and indistinct. This thumb he moved—his arm supported by a sling—over a plate containing the letters of the alphabet. . . . His wife, sitting beside him, combined the letters into a word, the words into a sentence, and the sentences into elaborate articles, epistles, books."

Aside from *Der Stern der Erlösung,* virtually everything of major importance that Rosenzweig produced was written under such conditions. And throughout this race with death, Rosenzweig retained his intimate contacts with his friends and his lively interest in the outside world and the various enterprises with which he was connected. He died on December 10, 1929, just as he was approaching his forty-third birthday.

Most of Rosenzweig's published writings, aside from his early philosophical work, are to be found in three books: *Der Stern der Erlösung* (three volumes); *Kleinere Schriften,* a large collection of articles; and *Briefe,* which contains much of his voluminous correspondence. Next to nothing has been translated into English.

For Franz Rosenzweig, religious thinking is not legalistic argumentation or arbitrary speculation, as it has only too often been in Orthodox circles; nor is it sentimentalizing on the beauties of "ethical monotheism," with the modernists. It is "life thinking," existential thinking, which seeks not to discover external facts or to establish universal truths but to "make sense" of existence, of one's own existence. It is therefore not the kind of thinking that one can engage in "objectively," as in science or philosophy.

"Objective thinking" is objective in two senses: it treats what it thinks about as an object, and it thinks about it as a spectator, in detachment, with the elimination of the so-called personal equation. But this is not the kind of thinking that one can do about human existence. For the self—one's own or another's—is not object but subject; to "objectify" the self is simply to destroy it. Nor can existence ever be genuinely thought about from the spectator's detached point of view. The thinking that is adequate to existence is a thinking of involvement and concern in what is thought about; it is thinking in which a man makes his decision, affirms his commitment, and ventures everything on it. This is what Rosenzweig calls the "new thinking" and he gives it the following formulation:

"The idea of 'making' truth true (Bewährung) is the basic idea of the new theory of knowledge . . . and the static concept of objectivity is replaced by one that is dynamic. . . . From those unimportant truths, truths of the type 'twice two equals four,' to which men lightly assent with the expenditure of no more than a trifle of mind-energy—a little less for the ordinary multiplication table, a little more for the theory of relativity—the way leads to those truths for which man is willing to pay something, on to those which he cannot prove true (bewähren) except with the sacrifice of his life, and finally to those the truth of which can be established only by the staking of the lives of all the generations."

This conception of "making true" (Bewähren) by commitment, decision, and venture is at the heart of the "new thinking." It is what Emil Brunner means when he speaks of the "knowledge of faith" as being "not theoretical knowledge but 'existential' knowledge—that is, knowledge of such a kind that is it only fully realized as practical decision and wholly excludes the attitude of a mere spectator." The teachings of religion, Rosenzweig constantly repeats, cannot be appropriated merely by the intellect; they must be made part of one's existence to be truly understood. Is this "new thinking," then, simply "subjective" in the bad sense, without discipline or control? Rosenzweig denies it. "A philosophy, if it is to be true," he explains, "must be philosophized from the actual viewpoint of the philosophizing person. . . . There is no other way of being objective than by honestly starting from one's own subjectivity. The duty of being objective requires that one retain sight of the entire horizon, not that one look out from a standpoint different from that on which one is standing, or even from 'no standpoint at all.' One's own eyes are certainly no more than one's own eyes; but it would be foolish to think one had to pluck them out in order to see rightly."

Religious thinking, in this sense, is really inseparable from religious existence out of which it emerges and which it reflects. To Rosenzweig, religion is not philosophy or sentiment or conduct; it is a kind or quality of existence.[2] Faith is a divine-human encounter, a meeting, in which man makes his total commitment to God and God offers his grace to man. The life of faith—religious existence—is lived on a plane where God and man are linked by the characteristic bond of personal communion: the word—the word of revelation and prayer. The "new thinking" is thinking that somehow partakes more of the nature of speech, dialogue, than of abstract thought.

"The difference between the old and the new thinking lies in the need of 'the other,' and, what is really the same thing, in taking time seriously. To think means to think *for no one* and to speak *to no one*, but to speak means to speak *to some one* and to think *for some one;* and that some one is always an entirely definite some one, who has not only ears . . . but also a mouth." The life of faith is thus lived between God and man; it is life "in the second person," *dialogic life,* to use Buber's pregnant phrase. The God of Jewish religion is not a remote lawgiver; nor is he an idea or a synonym for ideals and sentiments. The God of Jewish religion is a God who "speaks and hears," a God who enters into life at every point and without whom no moment of life can have meaning.

Indeed, man's very being is "respons-ible," and dependent upon God's word for its origin and maintenance. As Karl Löwith has said: "It is only through God's calling Adam, 'Where art thou?' that the latter's 'Here I am' reveals to man, in the answer, his being as related to God. The ego is at the outset wrapped up in itself and dumb; it waits for its being called—directly by God and indirectly by the neighbor." Man, in other words, possesses his being as a Thou which arises in response to the I which is God. Human existence is thus intrinsically religious existence.

The God of our faith reveals himself through his words and his deeds. "He has made known his ways to Moses, his acts to the children of Israel" (Ps. 103:7).

The problem of revelation—and of the Bible as revelation—is one of the crucial problems of Jewish and Christian faith. To oldline Orthodoxy—what we in this country call fundamentalism—every word of the Bible, especially of the so-called "Five Books of Moses," is literally the word of God, dictated by him and therefore incapable of error. Many Orthodox Jews would even extend this doctrine of inspiration and infallibility to the rabbinic writings, particularly to those dealing with halachah (Law). To the modernist, on the other hand, revelation is usually nothing but a figure of speech. The scriptural writers, he concedes, were "inspired." but this means little more than saying that a Shakespeare or a Plato or a Buddha was inspired; the "inspiration" of the prophet is identified with the imagination of the poet and the illumination of the mystic or philosopher. As to the Biblical writings themselves, they are, to the modernist, interesting compilations of myth, legend, and folklore, in which are embedded a number of high ethical teachings. After all, has not criticism shown that even the Pentateuch is a patchwork of documents from different times, sources, and historical settings—in other words, a compilation made by man rather than a single whole dictated by God?

Rosenzweig agrees that Scripture is a compilation made by men, but he nevertheless insists that it contains the revelation of God. God reveals himself through his encounter with man, and the Bible is preeminently the record of the divine encounter with Israel, in which God makes known his will and displays his judgments and mercies. Of course, the books of the Bible were put together and edited by men in the course of centuries and therefore contain God's word only as it has passed through the medium of the human heart and mind: does not the Talmud itself say that "the Torah speaks in the language of men"? But it contains God's word nevertheless. It contains it, yet is not identical with it. The whole tradition of scriptural interpretation reflects the effort to discover the message of revelation in the record of scripture. This is a work that is never complete and that each of us, in his own religious existence, though taking cognizance of the tradition that has come down to us, must in the end do for himself.

The celebrated translation of the Bible into German made by Buber and Rosenzweig was based on Rosenzweig's profound conception of Scripture as revelation. Granting that the various books of the Bible are compilations from various times and sources, Rosenzweig points out that the *meaning* of Scripture is to be discovered in how these parts are put together, just as in a mosaic the meaning of the picture emerges from the way the separate tiles are arranged and not merely from what the tiles in themselves "say." It is the whole that counts—and Scripture is a whole, a *Gestalt*, a unique and organic entity. Rosenzweig regards the Redakteur—the name for the compilers and editors of the Biblical books—as the key figure in the development of the Bible:

> "Our difference with Orthodoxy [he writes to Dr. Jacob Rosenheim, the Orthodox leader] consists in this, that from our belief in the holiness and uniqueness of the Torah and its character as revelation, we cannot draw any conclusions as to its literary origins or the philological value of the received text. Should Wellhausen prove right in all his theories . . . our faith would not be affected in the least. . . . We too translate the Torah as a single book. For us too it is the work of one spirit. . . . We call him by the symbol which critical science . . . uses to designate its assumed redactor: R. But this symbol R, we expand . . . into *Rabbenu*. For he is our teacher; his theology is our teaching."

In the same spirit, Rosenzweig understands the relation between Scripture (written Torah) and tradition (oral Torah). To the Orthodox, he writes, "the oral Torah is a stream parallel to the written Torah and sprung from the same source. For us, it is the completion of the unity of the Book-as-written through the unity of the Book-as-read. Both unities are equally wonderful. The historical view discovers multiplicity in the Book-as-written as well as in the Book-as-read; multiplicity of centuries, multiplicity of writers and readers. The eye that sees the book not from the outside but in its inner coherence sees it not merely as written but as read. In the former, it sees the unity of teaching; in the latter, it finds the unity of learning, one's own learning together with the learning of centuries." Clearly, this approach to Scripture presupposes the election of Israel. The compilation of the Bible is part of the literary history of the Jews, just as the compilation of the Homeric poems is part of the literary history of the Greeks. It is only because of Israel's unique position that its literary history is more than a mere record of human creativity and becomes the working out of the divine intent in communication with men. Scripture is indeed a human document, and therefore by no means infallible in its parts; but God fulfills his purposes through the doings of men, and so this human document can become the vehicle of divine revelation.

It is in terms of the basic affirmation of the election of Israel that Rosenzweig understands the Torah as Law (halachah). Again, he finds inadequate both the Orthodox and the modernist conceptions. To the conventional Orthodox Jew, the Law is something external, a list of 613 particular commandments, every one of them given by God on Sinai and thereafter carefully arranged, interpreted, and codified: these he is to perform. To the modernist, they are simply remnants of ancient folkways, of little religious significance today, at best merely of sociological, aesthetic, or sentimental value. Rosenzweig, in a brilliant essay, *Die Bauleute,* and a letter, *Göttlich und Menschlich* (end of November 1924), outlines his own position.

Halachic observance is the "acting-out" of the Jew's affirmation of the chosenness of Israel and its "separation" as a "priest-people." You shall be holy unto me, for I have separated you from among the nations that you should be mine" (Lev. 20:26): in this proclamation lies the meaning of Israel's existence and the ultimate grounding of the halachic code of ritual observance. The Jew who, himself and in his own religious existence, receives the Torah, receives it not only as a teaching about the election of Israel but also as a code—a "holiness-code"—in terms of which he is to enact this teaching into the pattern of his life. Rosenzweig commends "the Pharisees of the Talmud and the saints of the Church" for knowing that "man's understanding extends only as far as his doing." Religious observance is, in effect, the *doing* of one's religious convictions; the two cannot be separated.

Jewish observance is halachah, for the Jew lives "under the Law," and the special discipline to which the halachah subjects him is the commandment of God involved in the election of Israel. But to say this is a far cry from asserting, as the fundamentalists do, that the particular, detailed observances that confront the Jew at any time are the eternal prescription of God, communicated to Moses on Mount Sinai. The commandments *(mitzvot)* are not fixed and eternal; they have arisen, have changed, and many of them have lost their effectiveness with the passage of time. As with Scripture, so with halachah, it is fruitless, even meaningless, to attempt a single and definitive differentiation between the "human" and the "divine." Yet one cannot accept the "general principle" of election as important and divine but relegate the particular commandments to the rank of the merely peripheral, the "merely human." The "general principle" cannot be *understood*—means nothing existentially—unless particular commandments are *observed.* "The general theological connection [between chosenness and Law] comes to life for us only when and where we actually fulfill it as individual commandment."

Die Bauleute was addressed as a letter to Martin Buber, who took a rather negative attitude to halachah as Law, and who objected to its "ritualistic" emphasis. But the halachah in Rosenzweig's presentation is very far indeed from legalistic ritualism. Buber himself, moreover, speaks somewhere of the "mysteries whose meaning no one learns who does not himself join in the dance." The halachic pattern in Rosenzweig's view may be said to be the "dance" in which the Jew learns the mystery of the election of Israel. It is a "dance," moreover, in which the individual Jew finds himself as a Jew. Religious observance must be personally appropriated; it must be not just halachah, but halachah-*for-me*. The entire body of halachic tradition, ever changing yet ever the same, confronts the individual Jew as *Gesetz* ("law" in the external sense). To be operative, it must be turned into *Gebot* (commandment" in the inner sense). "*Gesetz* must become *Gebot*, which, the very moment it is heard, turns into deed. It must recover its contemporaneity *[Heutigkeit]*." This, however, is not to be achieved through "obedience to the paragraphs of a code." "In the end, it is not a matter of will but of ability-to-do *[Können]*. Here the decisive thing is the selection which our ability-to-do makes from among what is to be done *[das Tubare]*. This selection, because it does not depend upon the will but upon the ability-to-do, must necessarily remain an individual matter." Only personal ability to fulfill the precept can decide. "The doing comes forth only . . . at the point where at the voice of the *Gebot*, the spark leaps instantaneously across from 'I must' to 'I can.'" No man can decide for another what he can or cannot appropriate; each must decide for himself—in responsible recognition of the claim that the tradition of the Law has upon him, but for himself nevertheless. "What anyone is able to do, he alone knows; the voice of his own being, to which he is to listen, can be heard only with his own ears. . . . Nor does anyone know that the other's not-being-able may not in the end mean more for the building up of the teaching and the Law than our own being able. . . ." Rosenzweig, who started with nothing, became more and more traditional in his observance as time went on, but his philosophy of halachah never changed. Personal appropriation in religious existence remained his touchstone.

One of Rosenzweig's most profound and significant insights is his conception of the nature of Christianity and its relation to Judaism. In thinking through the problem, he finds himself once more in conflict with both Orthodoxy and modernism. Conventional Orthodoxy is without any real sense of the organic relation between the two faiths. By and large, it sees no religious or theological problem at all; its attitude to Christianity (to the *goyim*) is largely determined by the bitter experience of Jews in so-called Christian lands. On the other hand, most modernists take the position that all religions are essentially the same, being different cultural expressions of one and the same "religious spirit." All possess the same basic truth, and all are in part, though not perhaps to the same degree, corrupted by ignorance and superstition. For the modernists, too, there is no special problem.

But for Franz Rosenzweig, who takes seriously the claim of Judaism to supernatural truth and yet cannot ignore Christianity's kinship to it, there is a problem. And this problem he treats with a depth and originality that will make all future thinking on the subject dependent on his work.

In dealing with the problem of Christianity, Rosenzweig explicitly associates himself with the insights suggested in the teachings of the great Jewish philosphers of what he calls "the classical period of the construction of dogma systems in Judaism." What he finds in the older Jewish thinkers, he deepens and develops in his own characteristic manner. Judaism and Christianity are to him essentially of one piece, one religious reality: Judaism facing *inward* to the Jews, Christianity *outward* to the Gentiles. The two faiths are organically linked as complementary aspects of God's revealed truth. Yet they are not the same; they are distinct and different in their being and in their function. Judaism is the "eternal fire," Christianity the "eternal rays"; Judaism is the "eternal life," Christianity is the "eternal way." While Israel stays with God, Christianity goes out to conquer the unredeemed world for Him. And Christianity would not endure as a force for redemption did not Israel remain in its midst, in its very being serving as a witness to the Eternal.

Borrowing the imagery of Judah Halevi, Rosenzweig speaks of the historical revelation of Israel as a seed, which, falling on the ground of paganism, produces a tree—Christianity—in the fruit of which it reappears in another form. Christianity is, in fact, "Judaism for the Gentiles," through which the peoples of the world are brought to the God of Israel. Yet as close as are the two, so are they different, and the difference is not to be overcome by "liberalism" or good will, since it is rooted in the different functions and vocations set for them by divine providence. Only when the goal is reached and the world redeemed, only at the "end," will the final reconciliation and fusion take place; then all will indeed be one in the recognition of the unity of the Divine Name. Until then, "only with God . . . is the truth one. Earthly truth remains split into two." It is for each—the Jew and the Christian—to remain loyal to his vocation and his vision of the truth, which is the truth-for-him and as such valid before God. For "truth is a noun only to God; to men, it is really best known as an adverb, 'truly [wahrlich], as the measure of inner faithfulness" (Agus).

It follows from this general conception that Christian existence contains within itself the tension between paganism and revelation. The Christian is always in danger of lapsing into paganism, in rebellion against his fate and vocation as Christian. It is in this phenomenon, in the Christian's own incompleteness, in his own "not-yet," that Rosenzweig finds the hidden source of anti-Semitism. "The fact of anti-Semitism, age-old and ever-present though totally groundless," he concludes in a letter to his mother, "can be understood only by the different functions which God has assigned to the two communities—Israel to represent in time the eternal kingdom of God, Christianity to bring itself and the world toward that goal." Whenever the pagan in the Christian rises in revolt against the yoke of the Cross, he vents his fury on the Jew whom he hates not as Christ-killer but as Christ-bringer. The notorious proto-Nazi anti-Semite, Houston Stewart Chamberlain, saw this very well. "The Jew," he was wont to wail, "has spoiled everything with his Law and his Cross."

Rosenzweig's teaching on Christianity is the first, and remains the only serious, attempt to develop a Jewish theological framework in which the two religions will be seen in their relation to God's providential plan for the salvation of mankind. Rosenzweig does not deny that in some sense God is to be discerned in all religions, but he insists that only Judaism and its counterpart Christianity are in full truth *revealed* religions. Only they are divinely ordained as God's appointed way for the realization of his kingdom among men. Together, they constitute the "*Überwelt*," in which eternity enters into time and God into the world.

Everything in Rosenzweig's thinking about Jewish existence stems from and returns to the election of Israel. For the very cornerstone of Rosenzweig's Jewish faith is a passionate belief in the uniqueness of Israel and of its divine vocation in the world.

Rosenzweig never tires of reiterating that Israel is not "like unto the nations," neither in its origin nor in its nature and destiny. "The saga of the eternal people, different from those of the other peoples of the world, does not begin with autochthony. . . . Israel's ancestor is a wanderer, with the divine command to leave his native land and go to a country that God will show him. Thus begins the story as told in the sacred books. Only by exile does this people become a people." Nor does it possess a fatherland in the usual sense. Rosenzweig was no Zionist, at least not in the familiar nationalistic acceptation of the term—though he had a strong love for Zion. "A fatherland of which a people becomes part by ploughing itself, as it were, into it . . . such a fatherland the eternal people does not possess. The land [Zion] belongs to it only as the land of its yearning—as the Holy Land." Until the "end," when the "yearning" and the "promise" will be fulfilled, Israel's destiny remains inescapably dual, centered alike upon Zion and the Exile.

To Rosenzweig, Israel is a people defined by the covenant of election, a people eternal and "forever inexplicable, a disturbance to state and to world history. The power of world history breaks down before [it]."

The "peoples of the world" are always straining, through their historical enterprises and institutions, to bring time to a stop and secure for themselves a measure of eternity. But for God's people eternity is ever present. Israel lives in eternity because it "represents in time the eternal kingdom of God." It lives as a "holy people" and by its very being bears witness to the Holy One. It lives and waits—for the great "day of the Lord" when redemption will come, for Israel, for mankind, and for all being. Israel, the elect people, finds its vocation as the Suffering Servant of the Lord. Rosenzweig's vision is essentially the Prophetic conception which Salo Baron describes as "the idea of a Jewish people beyond state and territory, a divine instrument in man's overcoming of 'nature' through a supernatural process in the course of 'history.' "

I n this brief sketch, it has been possible to touch upon only certain aspects of Rosenzweig's thought. Not even an allusion has been made to the imposing quasi-metaphysical structure that constitutes the architectural framework of his *Stern der Erlösung*. But I think I have included those aspects that are especially important for an understanding of the quality of his Judaism. What is so amazing in Rosenzweig's thinking is his ability to transform ancient doctrines and theological formulas into a living power. He has at his command all the knowledge and learning of his time, but he must go beyond. No real understanding of the deepest problems of life is possible, he is convinced, except in terms of man's relation to God. To Rosenzweig, such words as God, revelation, divine providence, election, vocation, the Kingdom of heaven, stand for immediate and vital realities without which it is impossible to think seriously about existence. That is why he is always saying that "theological problems require to be translated into human and human problems pushed on into theological."

For the Jews of today, Rosenzweig has a word of special relevance. For he shows us how we can affirm the authentic religion of Israel without falling into obscurantism, how we can lead a life true to Torah without falling into legalism and superstition, how we can dedicate ourselves to the vocation of Israel without falling into racial or nationalistic chauvinism. What Rosenzweig fought against with every fiber of his being was the routinization, the secularization, the sentimentalization of Judaism. On this ground he opposed fundamentalism; on this ground he opposed modernism; on this ground he opposed nationalistic Zionism. And he was able to develop a Judaism free from these distortions. This is his legacy to us of this generation and to the Jews of the generations to come.

Notes

[1] Nahum N. Glatzer, "Franz Rosenzweig," *Yivo Annual: I* (1945). Glatzer was a friend and coworker of Rosenzweig's and followed Martin Buber in Rosenzweig's chair at Frankfort. The only important studies of Rosenzweig in English with which I am acquainted are Glatzer's memoir, Jacob Agus's chapter on Rosenzweig in his *Modern Philosophies of Judaism*, and Karl Löwith's "M. Heidegger and F. Rosenzweig," *Philosophy and Phenomenological Research*, September 1942.

[2] Rosenzweig even disliked using the term "religion" for Judaism and Christianity, for he felt that it implied the separation of a particular field called "religion" from total reality. "The special position of Judaism and Christianity consists precisely in the fact that even though they become religion, they still retain within them the power to free themselves from their religiousness and to find their way back to the free field of reality. . . . They were originally something quite 'unreligious'—the one a fact [the fact of the People Israel], the other an event [the 'Christ-event']."

—6—

The "Chosenness" of Israel and the Jew of Today

(1955)

I n all the vast and complex heritage of Jewish belief, that element, which, according to Solomon Schechter, was so pervasive that it hardly needed to be explicitly formulated, has for many Jews of today become the most difficult to accept, perhaps even to understand. The overwhelming majority of American Jews, like the overwhelming majority of other Americans, "believe in God," and take this belief to be the essence of their religion. But that God has in some sense singled them out for His service and made of them a "chosen people," this they find strange and incomprehensible. The "chosenness" of Israel, once the Jew's fundamental conviction about himself and his place in the world, has to all appearance become meaningless, if not actually unintelligible, to the great mass of American Jews of our time.

And yet, despite appearances, it is my feeling that this belief is very far from being as obsolete and meaningless as so many present day Jews think it is. On the contrary, recent events, as well as a good deal of current Jewish self-analysis, would seem to have given it a reality and relevance it did not appear to possess in the days before Hitler and Stalin. It is my conviction, in other words, that if the modern Jew will only bring himself to face the fact of his Jewishness in the context of contemporary life, he will rediscover the meaning and power of the ancient doctrine of "chosenness."

I

Recent history (1955) teaches a strange lesson, which we modern Jews had lost sight of in the bright age of liberal cosmopolitanism. Roger Shinn, in a notable study, makes this lesson explicit in an illuminating comment: "Hitler found in the Jews *(by their very existence)*, and in faithful Christians *(by their religious protests)*, a reminder of the universalism . . . he could not tolerate" (emphasis added). What Dr. Shinn is saying here is something which we all must acknowledge once we really face the facts, that somehow the Jew, *simply by being a Jew,* constituted an offense and a challenge to Nazi totalitarianism in its time, as he does to Communist totalitarianism today. The Christian, so recent history teaches us, can make his peace with the totalitarian powers by apostasy, by ceasing to be a Christian; only the Christian who remains "faithful" and makes a "religious protest," as Dr. Shinn puts it, is a real threat to the totalitarian despot. And very much the same is true of the secular humanist; he too can abandon his humanistic creed and make his peace with the regime. But the Jew? Strangely enough, it is not what the Jew happens to believe or affirm that makes him so intolerable to the totalitarian; it is his *Jewishness,* his *being a Jew.* And of his Jewishness, of his being a Jew, he cannot rid himself, do what he may.

If we look a little closer, we discern some logic in this insensate totalitarian hatred of the Jew. Totalitarianism is essentially the absorption of all human life by the state. The meaning of human existence is felt by totalitarianism to be completely comprehended in the national community, of which the state is the embodiment. That is why totalitarianism is inherently chauvinistic, and why chauvinism always harbors a totalitarian potential. The very idea of a dimension of human existence that transcends the social and political, and passes beyond the limits of society and state, is something that cannot be tolerated in a system whose maxim is "everything in and through the state, nothing outside the state," and whose claim is to the totality of life. In such a society, it is possible, as I have suggested, for the Christian or the secular humanist to save himself and make his peace with the regime by abandoning his Christian witness or his humanistic ideals, by surrendering whatever may challenge the self-enclosed ultimacy of the totalitarian state. But the Jew somehow has this challenge built into his being, because built into his being is a trans-national, trans-cultural, trans-political dimension that makes him irrevocably and irreducibly "different." He may resent his being "different," he may desire to get rid of it; he may even make a strenuous effort to come to terms with his world and conform to its totalistic pattern—but so long as he remains a Jew, so long as he remains known as a Jew, he cannot possibly succeed. The Christian and the secular democrat have it within their power to cease to be Christians or democrats; but can the Jew ever "un-Jew" himself? Can he, by anything he may do, rid himself of that in him which makes him so intolerable to a Hitler or a Stalin? History gives its own answer, and that answer is unequivocally in the negative.

It would seem, then, as though the Jew were "chosen," through his very Jewishness, to be a witness against totalitarianism. If we define the conviction that nothing of this world, no idea, institution, or individual, no man, or nation, or "ism," may be divinized and worshipped as something ultimate, if we define this conviction as the "principle of anti-idolatry," then we can state it as the inescapable lesson of history that the Jew is the living embodiment of this principle. He is that not only because the principle stems directly from his religious tradition, but also and more fundamentally because any violation of it—any tendency to absolutize a man, a nation, a culture, a system, or an "ism"—sooner or later brings with it a threat to his very existence as a Jew, no matter how otherwise well established in society he may be. The Jew, it has been said with considerable insight, is a kind of living litmus paper by which the spiritual health of a society or culture may be judged.

This fact, so clearly evidenced in recent history, is not peculiar to our time. The tendency of ideas, institutions, and systems to absolutize themselves is perennial in human affairs; man is always prone to make absolute, idolatrous claims for himself and his works, and to strive to comprehend all life in their terms. Whenever that happens, and to the degree that it happens, the Jew falls into trouble: his merely *being a Jew* is felt to be an intolerable challenge and affront. Whether it is the Hellenistic effort to establish a divinized world culture, or the medieval attempt to exalt Christendom as indeed the very City of God, or the Nazi and Communist efforts to erect a divinized total state: it is always the Jew who is the enemy to be singled out and destroyed.

In the face of such facts, it would seem hard to avoid the conclusion that somehow, in some way, the Jew has, through the centuries, been made to serve a certain very distinctive function in history—the function of calling into question, *by his very Jewishness,* the self-idolizing, self-absolutizing tendencies in men and society. The fact may be variously interpreted and explained, but it remains a fact, a hard, undeniable fact, a fact that would seem, on the face of it, to give real contemporaneous content to the traditional Jewish conviction of "chosenness." For after all, as Buber has pointed out, the important thing "is not whether we feel or do not feel that we are chosen . . . [The important thing is rather] that our role in history actually has been unique." It is history in the first place that speaks to the modern Jew about the meaning of his "chosenness."

II

But history is not something that comes upon the individual from the outside; it is really the interior life of man externalized. Does not the testimony that history gives of the "chosenness" of Israel reflect, and is it not reflected by, the sense of "chosenness" that permeates the life and behavior of the individual Jew, however much he may repudiate the doctrine?

It is a mere commonplace, yet an important truth nevertheless, that the Jew, whatever his position in society or his field of activity, is aware not only that he is "different," but that something different is expected of him—in the first place, by himself. The Jewish businessman will acknowledge a special ethical obligation ("There are certain things a Jew doesn't do!"), even as he violates it and tries to make up for his shortcomings by philanthropy. The Zionist may vehemently asseverate, and perhaps even believe, that he is just another "nationalist" striving to regain his "national homeland," but he betrays himself in his every word and thought which breathes the passion of the age-old messianic idea. The Jewish socialist too reveals the messianic origins of the impulse that animates him, and indeed often relates his "idealism" to "Jewish ethics," just as the Jewish scholar or scientist will find his intellectual concern quite natural in view of the "Jewish tradition of learning" and the "Jewish zeal for truth." I have myself heard Jewish labor leaders, men remote indeed from the faith and practice of

Judaism, explain confidentially that their "progressivism" was somehow the consequence of their being Jewish. These things are matters of common experience, and I have yet to find a Jew who does not in some manner or form exhibit this profound sense of "difference" and special vocation. It is simply a fact that "consciously or not, the Jew moves in the context of a long and special history and religio-ethical tradition that lays upon him, whether as a burden or as a badge of pride, the sense of being 'chosen' . . ." (Elliot E. Cohen, ed., *Commentary on the American Scene*). Let the Jew who rejects the doctrine of "chosenness" examine his conscience and see whether these words do not ring true to the inmost reality of his being.

A phenomenology of Jewish character as affected by the hidden conviction of "chosenness" still remains to be written. It would have to include cases like Disraeli, about whom a recent critic remarks acutely that his "awareness of being 'different' gave him self-confidence and an abiding detachment," and it would have to include others with whom the consciousness of difference has made for anxiety and self-rejection. It would have to show how the Jew's recalcitrance to becoming totally absorbed in his environment and in the claims of success and power has given him a keener social vision and a greater sensitivity to social evil, but also how at the same time it has made him more susceptible to utopian schemes and to entrapment in false messianic movements like Communism. It would have to indicate how the consciousness of being a Jew often operates to create a high sense of *noblesse oblige,* but also how it can degenerate into the senseless arrogance that makes the word "Jewish" stand for everything right and proper and its antonym *"goy"* for everything gross and brutish. It would have to show how the Jew, in his Jewishness, acquires his "intellectual preeminence," but often at the price of becoming, for good or bad, a "disturber of the intellectual peace," "an alien of uneasy feet," "an intellectual wayfaring man, a wanderer in the intellectual No Man's Land, . . . seeking another place to rest, further along the road, somewhere over the horizon . . ." (Thorstein Veblen). Everywhere the hidden effects of the sense of "chosenness" would reveal themselves, and testify that through this sense of being "chosen," an extra dimension has indeed been added to Jewish life and personality.

The reference to Thorstein Veblen may serve to remind us that in recent years it has been the sociologists, psychologists, and historians, rather than the theologians, who have, in however indirect a manner, called attention to the Jew's hidden sense of "chosenness" and to its wide ramifications in individual and social life. A considerable documentation could be compiled from the writings of these specialists, but such documentation would, after all, be not nearly so impressive as the everyday testimony that the Jew himself gives in his thinking, feeling, and behavior, in his very life as a Jew in a non-Jewish world. The events of the past two decades have strikingly reversed the earlier trend toward "assimilation" on the part of American Jews; a new urge to self-identification as Jews is to be noted among all sections of American Jewry, particularly perhaps among the younger people. But this has raised in a new form an old problem of profound significance: *What does it mean to be a Jew?* It cannot be simply by virtue of belonging to a particular race, or to a particular nation, or to a particular culture, or even to a particular religious denomination, that one is a Jew. Many and diverse racial strains are to be found among Jews; Jews have, and have long had, the most varied national origins, allegiances, and cultures; and even those Jews who renounce the Jewish religion, or religion in general, somehow remain Jews. The answer to the question, "What does it mean to be a Jew?", is not an easy one; perhaps no final or complete answer can be given. But is it not true that when the Jew of today, whether he is "religious" or "non-religious"—perhaps even sooner in the latter case than in the former—comes to examine himself in order to make sense of his Jewishness, some inkling of "difference," of "chosenness," necessarily enters into his own understanding of himself as a Jew?

III

Sociologists, psychologists, and historians not blinded by doctrinaire formulas have, as I have suggested, long noted and documented these facts of Jewish existence as they manifest themselves in individual life and society. They have their interpretations and explanations, of course. There is no occasion whatever for quarreling with them, for there is a great deal of truth in what they say as far as it goes. The anomalous position of the Jew in the non-Jewish world, his marginality, his apparently ineradicable minority status, do indeed make him an "outsider," somehow *in,* but never entirely *of,* the world in which he finds himself. Thus he can hardly avoid putting a note of interrogation to every established dogma or institution; his very being a Jew does that, whether he desires it or not. His very Jewish "particularism," because it transcends every national and cultural boundary, becomes strangely enough a vehicle and witness to universalism. The distinctivenes of the Jew, his sense of "difference" and "chosenness," as well as his special role in history are thus understood as functions of his anomalous position in society.

This may be granted, but the question always arises: *Why* this unique and anomalous position in which the Jew is forever barred from losing himself in the mass and becoming "like everyone else"? Other groups there are which have been marginal and "unadjusted" in this or that society, under such and such circumstances—but the Jew is marginal and "unadjusted" everywhere, at all times, under all circumstances. However genuinely at home he may feel in his society, he remains the "eternal outsider," and neither he nor his society can ever really lose awareness of this fact. Explaining it all in terms of anti-Semitism merely begs the question. What is this anti-Semitism that has accompanied the Jew from the beginning of his historical career till this very day, despite all changes in social, economic, political, and cultural conditions? Is it not, after all, really the obverse of the problem of Jewishness? The sociologists, psychologists, and historians can teach us a great deal, but when they have had their say, the fundamental fact still remains a fact, neither "explained" nor explained away: Jewish existence, individual and collective, bears witness to a sense of "difference" that is immediately recognizable as the substance of the traditional belief in "chosenness."

I t is at this point that the modern Jew, who shies away from the explicit doctrine of "chosenness," ought to begin to question himself. Is it not true that his own sense of being "different" and standing under a special responsibility points beyond itself? Does not the sense of "chosenness" raise the question of *"chosen" by whom?* The question may be phrased in various ways, employing or avoiding the traditional vocabulary, but posed in some manner it must be by the Jew who is not afraid to pursue the logic of his Jewishness. Most modern-minded Jews, if they can get themselves to face the question at all, tend to answer it in terms of "history" or "destiny"; not so long ago, quasi-racialist theories of "innate gifts" and a special *Volksgeist* of Hegelian provenance were quite popular. But do not all such answers, welcome as they are in testifying to the ineradicable conviction of "chosenness," tend to turn history, or destiny, or the alleged

Volksgeist into a kind of god before which we must bow as the ultimate law of life? And somehow this kind of god we cannot swallow. There is something in us that responds to the warning, "There is no god but God," and drives us beyond all premature and arbitrary absolutes to the transcendent.

Dostoievsky, who cannot be accused of too great a fondness for Jews, once affirmed his conviction that no Jew, whatever he might say, could really be an atheist. We can now see what he meant. The Jewish "atheist," if he is a Jew at all, in effect proclaims: "There is no God, but we are His people!" He may vehemently, and quite sincerely, assert that he does not "believe in God," but does not his very being as a Jew testify to the *existential* belief still alive within him that "there is no god but God" and that the Jews are His people?

What I am contending, in short, is that the Jew's sense of his "chosenness"—and this sense would seem to be operative in all Jews who hold themselves to be Jews, and perhaps even in those who reject their Jewishness—is an implicit *religious* affirmation which inevitably points beyond itself to the God who acts to "choose." Jewish existence, as Dostoievsky saw, is intrinsically religious and God-oriented. Jews may be led to deny, repudiate, and reject their "chosenness" and its responsibilities, but then their own Jewishness rises to confront them as refutation and condemnation. "God, Torah, and Israel" do indeed form the indivisible unity of tradition, each member of the triad implying, and being implied by, the others.

IV

This approach to the question may seem rather devious to those accustomed to think of religion as a system of abstract metaphysical propositions about God and morality. From such a point of view, "belief in God" comes first as the foundation of "ethical monotheism," and only afterward, if at all, comes the corollary of the "chosenness" of Israel. But such is not the way of Jewish religious tradition, Biblical and rabbinic. In Jewish religious tradition, it is the conviction of "chosenness," of Israel's being the covenanted people of God, that is the central fact. The God of Jewish faith is not an abstract "Supreme Being," but the God of Abraham, Isaac, and Jacob, the God of Israel, the God of the Covenant, who redeemed His people from the darkness of Egypt and "chose" them to be His witnesses forever. This is the primordial confession of Jewish faith: the conviction of "chosenness" lies at its very heart.

In Jewish tradition, the People Israel is conceived of as neither a nation nor a religious group in the ordinary sense; in Jewish tradition, Israel is understood as a people "called" into being by God to serve His purposes in the world. It is understood as a community created by God's special act of covenant, first with Abraham, whom He "called" out of the heathen world, and then, supremely, with Israel collectively at Sinai. The "choosing" is also a *calling*, a vocation, "a summons and a sending"; what Israel is called to is best expressed in the rabbinic formula, *kiddush ha-Shem*, the "sanctification of the Name." Stripped of its mystical and metaphysical overtones, this rabbinic formula means to bear witness to the God of Israel amidst the idolatries of the world, to proclaim in word and deed, in life and thought, that "there is no god but God," and to "give the world no rest so long as it has no God" (Jacques Maritain). The late Judah Magnes was speaking true to the Biblical-rabbinic teaching when he declared: "It is the Jew's historical function to question, to challenge, to deny every idolatry which the world in its self-delusion comes to worship, whether this idolatry be of nature, of science, or of state and society—and beyond these, to point to God. This is his real reason for existence."

The vocation of Israel as witness against idolatry emerges with particular force in the relations between

Jew and Christian, Israel and the Church. "It is important that there always be Judaism," Paul Tillich, the distinguished Protestant theologian, has testified. "It is the corrective against the paganism that goes along with Christianity . . ." No one who recalls the experience of the churches in Germany during the days of Nazism will fail to see the relevance of Tillich's words; their truth is a truth evidenced by the whole history of Christendom. The Christian who is tempted to bow the knee to the idolatrous gods of his society and culture, will always find in the Jew an accusing witness against him, for in the Jew he will see the victim of the idols he is prone to worship.

Anti-Semitism is the "natural" consequence of this witness to God in a world beset with idolatry; however it may express itself, at bottom anti-Semitism reflects the revolt of man and society against the God of Israel and His absolute demand. This was obvious in pre-Christian anti-Semitism, but it is also true of anti-Semitism in the Christian world, where "hatred of Judaism is at bottom hatred of Christianity" (Maritain). For, as Franz Rosenzweig so clearly saw, "whenever the pagan within the Christian soul rises in revolt against the yoke of the Cross, he vents his fury on the Jew." Very much the same view has been set forth by a number of recent psychologists and sociologists, who see the Jew as representing the "bad conscience of Christian civilization" and anti-Semitism as a kind of revolt against the "spiritual collective super-ego" (Ernst Simmel). We recall what the rabbis say of the Mountain of the Covenant: "It is called Sinai because *sinah,* hatred [toward Israel] came down to the nations because of it" (b. Shab. 89b).

Although it converts Jewry into an "exposed signal station flashing a warning of the wandering of Satan upon the earth" (Magnes), the "chosenness" of Israel has always been the bulwark of its existence. It was the conviction of "chosenness" that enabled the Jew to defy the powers of destruction and to reverse the normal patterns of history. Military defeat and the annihilation of nation and state did not mean the end of Jewry or the extinction of its hopes; on the contrary, it inspired the emergence of Israel in a new form and with a more profound consciousness of its destiny. Precisely because his Jewishness has never been completely tied to state or territory, to culture or nation, but has always been defined in terms of the suprahistorical reality of his "chosenness," the Jew has been able to survive all the disasters of history. The Jew has always found a home in the Covenant whenever he has been at odds with the world, for it is the Covenant that is his true "fatherland," and the world that confronts him with the need for redemption.

Within the corporate vocation of Israel, the individual Jew, according to Biblical-rabbinic teaching, finds his own "calling," and therewith also the meaning and power of his life. He sees himself a "son of the Covenant," upon whom has been laid a great and special responsibility of "sanctifying the Name." He understands that the fateful question for him is not, as religious "liberalism" would have it, "Shall I or shall I not be a Jew? Have I or have I not been 'chosen'?" The real question he finds on an altogether different level; it is: "Shall I recognize my 'chosenness', my special 'calling', and live an *authentic* life; or shall I deny it, and as a consequence, live an *inauthentic* one?" Judaism, in sum, means living out the affirmative decision.

It will thus be seen that in the tradition of Jewish faith, Judaism, Jewishness, being-a-Jew, is not primarily or essentially a doctrine, a moral code, or a system of observances, although it does in some way include all of these. Judaism, Jewishness, being-a-Jew, in the tradition of faith, is primarily and essentially a *vocation*, a "calling" under God, which defines the Jew's position and responsibilities in the world. The Jewish religious tradition, on its human side, may best be understood as the Jew's attempt through the ages to discern, define, and implement his vocation under God.

V

To the believing Jew of tradition, the "chosenness" of Israel was a central fact, a basic reality, illumining every aspect of his existence as a Jew. Yet for most Jews today, even for those who hold themselves to be religious, the doctrine of "chosenness" is a scandal and an offense. We have a vague distaste for it; it somehow runs counter to our modernity and to too many of our intellectual and moral presuppositions. Even though, as I have been insisting, the Jew cannot help but exemplify the hidden conviction of "chosenness" in his life and thought, the modern Jew, at least, feels very uncomfortable with the doctrine and is moved to reject it whenever he comes face to face with it.

Why is this doctrine of "chosenness" so hard for the modern Jew to accept, even when he still lives in its light? The reasons, I think, are of various orders. There are, first, the intellectual, or philosophical, objections, frequently held by people who profess a religious view of life. A truly rational and universal God, it is maintained, could not do anything so arbitrary as to "choose" one particular group out of mankind as a whole. It is indeed "odd of God to choose the Jews" because it is odd of God to "choose" anybody. God is the God of all alike, and therefore cannot make distinctions between nations and peoples. To this is added the moral argument that the doctrine of "chosenness" is little better than crude ethnocentrism, in which a particular group regards itself as the center of the universe and develops doctrines that will flatter its pride and minister to its glory. Such notions are held to be primitive and unworthy of being embodied in a "mature" religion.

These arguments are, in fact, far from modern. They were all advanced, almost two thousand years ago, by pagan philosophers like Celsus, who made them the basis of a powerful polemic against Judaism and Christianity. What can we say to these arguments, whether ancient or modern? Well, in the first place, it may be pointed out that to be scandalized by the universal God acting in and through the particularities of time, place, and history, is to conceive the divine in essentially impersonal, intellectual terms. Universal ideas are impersonal and timeless, and if religion is simply the apprehension of universal ideas, then of course the particularistic claims of Jewish faith are absurd on the face of it. But if religion is a matter of personal relation and action, as both Judaism and Christianity affirm, the matter takes on an altogether different aspect. Truly personal relations are never universal; they are always concrete and particular. And while an idea or a doctrine may be made available to all men universally and timelessly, action must necessarily be particular in the sense that it is action here and now, in reference to this particular group or person rather than to another. The insistence on historical particularity contained in the notion of "chosenness" is thus seen to be part of the Biblical-rabbinic affirmation of a *"living"* God, who meets man in personal encounter in the context of life and history. Within the framework of Jewish faith, therefore, the doctrine of "chosenness" constitutes no incongruity; it is only to abstract and self-sufficient human reason that it constitutes a scandal and offense. But then to abstract and self-sufficient human reason, all history, in its inexpugnable particularity, must constitute the same kind of scandal and offense.

Nor does the moral argument hold up any better. The most superficial reading of Scripture is enough to indicate that the teaching

about the "chosenness" of Israel is as far as possible
from being an ethnocentric device of self-flattery and
self-glorification. The covenant by which Israel is
"chosen" is never held to mean that Israel is better, or
wiser, or more deserving than the "nations of the
world"; on the contrary, the fickleness, obduracy, and
disobedience of the people is constantly emphasized to
highlight the miracle of God's love and steadfastness.
Nor is the "chosenness" interpreted as implying special privilege for Israel; just the reverse, the "choosing"
is a demand and a summons upon Israel; involving
greater obligation, heavier responsibility, a harder destiny, and a sterner judgment: "You only have I known
among all the families of the earth; *therefore* will I
visit upon you all your iniquities" (Amos 3:2). Finally,
though the "choosing" of Israel is the "choosing" of a
particular group to act in the particularities of time
and history, its purpose is universal, to promote the
supreme welfare of all mankind: "In you [Abraham]
shall all the families of the earth be blessed" (Gen.
12:3), "I the Lord have called you in righteousness . . .
and have made you a light for the nations" (Is. 42:6).
Whatever may be the corruptions which the doctrine
of "chosenness" has suffered at various times in the
long history of the Jews, the doctrine itself, as it appears in normative Jewish faith, is anything but the
crude ethnocentrism its critics accuse it of being.

But, of course, neither the philosophical nor the
moral argument really gets to the heart of the difficulty. The fundamental objection of the Jew, today as
ever, is not that the doctrine of "chosenness" offends
rational or ethical principles, but rather that it places
an altogether unbearable burden upon him and condemns him to be "different," the "eternal stranger,"
the "marginal man," the "suffering servant."
Throughout the centuries, the Jew, being human, all
too human, has rebelled against the "yoke of the Covenant," and has demanded the right to be "like unto
the nations." The Bible is full of the protests of the

"natural" man in the Israelite against the demand of God and the destiny of Israel, and current discussions about the "normalization" of Jewish life reecho these protests in a hundred different ways. "Chosenness" is a *calling,* "a summons and a sending," a "summons" to obedience and a "sending" to service, sometimes even to suffering and death, and those who do not find it in their hearts to be able to obey and serve and suffer—and how many of us can truly say that we do?—are only too prone to deny the calling and reject the doctrine in which it is embodied.

It is, however, part of the force of divine providence (or of historical factuality) that the protests of the recalcitrant Jew against the unwanted distinction have rarely been more than a vain cry of outrage and embitterment. Life and history—the man of faith would say God—have somehow refused to free him of the burden of his uniqueness, and he has gone through the ages an often unwilling witness to the God he is tempted to deny.

VI

To the traditional Jew, the "chosenness" of Israel was a central fact, ever present in his consciousness. The *kiddush* he repeated on Sabbaths and festivals was a constant proclamation of it; in the *Alenu,* the climax of the daily liturgy, he thanked God for it; in every prayer, he was reminded of it. Indeed, no phase of his life was without some acknowledgment of the "chosenness" of Israel. It was the cornerstone of his personal existence as a Jew, as it was of the corporate existence of Jewry.

For the Jew of today, everything has become problematic. Yet ultimately, the Jew of today too must come face to face with the fact of his Jewishness, and every attempt to do so almost at once raises the question of "chosenness" and demands an answer. The "chosenness" of Israel, whether believed in or not, is an inescapable fact for the Jew. He cannot think or live as a Jew without in some way implying it. For better or for worse, it confronts him as a destiny which he cannot escape because he cannot escape himself and his history.

—7—

Socialism, Zionism, and the Messianic Passion

(1956)

The true Israelite is torn with discontent and possessed with an unquenchable thirst for the future." In these words, Ernst Renan, who had his moments of insight, expressed the inner meaning of the messianic passion that has informed Jewish life through the ages. For the "thirst for the future," the orientation of the whole being to that which is to come, is the very essence of messianism, and messianism is the very essence of the historical existence of the Jew. Like the sense of "chosenness," with which it is so closely linked, the messianic passion has characterized Jewish spirituality through all mutations of belief, culture, and social circumstance. It has permeated the thinking and feeling of believer and unbeliever alike, even of those who have felt compelled to reject it as a doctrine along with the faith in which it is grounded. Quite literally, it is the Jew incarnate.

Through the millennia of Jewish history, messianism has assumed many and diverse forms and has come to expression under the strangest guises. Prophetic promise, apocalyptic vision, sacrificial suffering, mystic thaumaturgy, military and political adven-

---

ture, have each, at one time or another, been the manifestation or instrument of the messianic dynamism that has given Jewry and the world no rest through the ages. No aspect of Jewish life, no period of Jewish history, has been left untouched by the messianic urge to "realize" the future. Even our own secularist age has felt the impact. Indeed, the two most significant movements in Jewish life in the past century—socialism and Zionism—reveal with particular force the messianic sources of Jewish creativity. They also raise the question of what happens to the messianic impulse when it is robbed of its transcendence and diverted to secular goals. The experience of these two movements, in this country particularly, is striking evidence of both the power and the ambiguity of the Jewish messianic fervor in the secularized world of today.

I

What is messianism? What are its authentic and essential elements, the beliefs that go to make up the messianic "idea"? Through all its metamorphoses and historic transformations, messianism has always borne witness to certain fundamental convictions about life and reality, and among such convictions the following may well be regarded as central.

Messianism, in the first place, has meant taking history seriously as something real and important. This is by no means self-evident. In the philosophies and spiritualities of the world, history—the doings of men in time—has almost without exception been brushed aside as something unreal and unimportant, "a tale told by an idiot, full of sound and fury, signifying nothing," in comparison with the timeless and immutable. To the Hindu, it is the *maya*-world of illusion; to the Greek, the dreary realm of "eternal recurrence." To the Hebrew alone, history has from

the beginning been that which is real, the texture of
human existence, the medium of man's encounter with
God, the stuff of creation, revelation, and redemption.
Our Western feeling for history is almost entirely of
biblical-Hebraic provenance, with little meaning outside that context. The Hebrew sense of history is indeed so great that nature itself is "historicized" and
given an historical destiny. All that is real and important is, to the Hebrew mind, historical, engrossed in
the fateful drama of history. Man's life is real insofar as
it enters creatively into this historical drama. This is
the first element making up the messianic idea.

The second element is the thirst for fulfillment.
Messianism means seeing history—that is, the human
enterprise in time—as real and important, and for that
reason seeing it as destined for fulfillment and completion. A history in its nature unconsummated and incapable of consummation is a history essentially without
meaning. The passionate hope and expectation of
fulfillment emerges with power despite, or rather because of, the endless frustrations, ambiguities, and
contradictions of actual existence. In the messianic
conviction, the "wrongness" of the present is neither
the first nor the last word of reality. The "wrongness"
of the present is seen as a "falling away" from an
original "rightness" and as destined to be overcome
and rectified in the final fulfillment. The messianic
vision is thus a vision of a grandiose three-phase
drama, consisting of a *protological* first phase, of an
historical middle phase, and of an *eschatological* end
phase. The "discontent" with the present, which Renan finds so characteristic of the messianic passion, is
rooted in both the bitter sense of loss of the original
"rightness" and the deep yearning, the "unquenchable
thirst" for the restoration that the future, the "absolute future" of fulfillment, will bring. The passion for
the future is thus a passion for the "true life" for which
man was meant ("chosen"), which he has lost, and to
which he will, in the "fullness of time" once more be

restored. N. N. Glatzer has well described this essential outlook in summarizing the historical teaching of the Tannaim:

> Election, defection, and return [he says] are the three periods in which history is seen running its course . . . Election without defection would be an assumption of paradisal historylessness; the fall gives impulse to history. Fall without return, however, would mean history surrendered and planless. Between fall and return, history completes its course.[1]

Messianism means not only taking history seriously and seeing it destined for rectification and fulfillment; it means, in the third place, staking the human hope for the messianic future on the ultimate, on the Power in whose hand all outcomes lie. Man enters into the messianic process; his deed is in a very real way essential, and yet it is not to himself that he looks for the final outcome, but to that which is beyond and on which he depends. In the traditional biblical-rabbinic eschatology, it is God who sends his Messiah to usher in the new age; yet men somehow participate in what is done. In the humanistic versions, it is History, conceived as an immanent creative force pervading and energizing the actual course of events, that brings the fulfillment, though again not without more obviously human participation. The strange dialectic of human action, taken up and made use of by that which is beyond, is well expressed in the rabbinic saying, when the saying is taken to refer to the entire human enterprise: "It is not for you to complete the work, but neither are you free to desist from it" (Abot 2:16). "It is not for you to complete the work"—but completion there is; "neither are you free to desist from it"—yet, in the end, it is not you who fulfills and completes.

These are the three essential elements of the messianic idea: history is real and significant—it is destined for fulfillment and rectification—in the course of a great historical drama which man indeed participates in with the fullness of his power, but which looks for its completion to the ultimate beyond.

It is hardly necessary to point out that, so understood, the messianic idea has informed Jewish spirituality and Jewish existence from whatever beginnings we may find in history or tradition. Throughout the Bible, from first page to last, from the earliest "documents" to the latest redactions, the divine-human encounter, which is the substance of the biblical account, takes place in the full context of history, as an historical encounter, and a future is looked to that in one form or another is a future of restored "rightness." In the prophetic promise, the messianic hope becomes explicit, and rises to grandiose heights in the vision of Israel the messianic people, from whom will come the Messiah of God to restore Israel and the world to their proper destiny and to usher in the "end of all things," in the kingdom without end. Later apocalyptic takes up the same theme, though it introduces a determinist and dualist note little known to authentic prophecy. In the earliest rabbinic tradition, the messianic conviction is already central, the corporate hope of Israel being linked with the hope of personal destiny through the teaching about the "resurrection of the dead."

In all these forms, prophetic, apocalyptic, and rabbinic, it enters into primitive Christianity, where the futuristic note remains strong despite the conviction that, in a real sense, the "end" has already come in Christ. Later Christianity, however, mutes this note, and almost extinguishes the messianic passion, by its success in "spiritualizing" the biblical eschatology and in virtually identifying the Kingdom of

God with the Church. Radical messianism goes underground, to burst out from time to time in heretical
and sectarian movements, above all in the teaching of
Joachim of Floris, that strange twelfth-century monk
who projected the vision of an imminent "third age"
of the "Spirit," in which the world, having passed
through the two earlier ages of the "Father" and the
"Son," would be caught up, renovated, and trans-
formed in final perfection. Joachim was condemned,
and his immediate followers suppressed, but a kind of
subterranean Joachimism persisted through the centuries, breaking out again in the turmoil of the Reformation and even in more modern times.

But it was among the Jews, and in Judaism, that the
messianic passion burned with fervor in the Middle
Ages. All talk of the redemption already come and of
the embodiment of the Kingdom of God in the Church
could have little meaning for the Jew who felt the
"burden of the unredeemed world" as something more
palpable than the most palpable facts of life, and who
somehow could not discern the lineaments of the prophetic vision of the Kingdom in the actual Church that
confronted him. Because the Jews had never "been
stilled by anything which [had] happened," they remained "wholly directed toward the coming of that
which [was] to come."[2]

The messianic passion and the messianic idea permeated Jewish history through the Middle Ages into
modern times. In Cabbalism, it often assumed
thaumaturgical forms directed toward "forcing the
end"; for long stretches of time, it remained apparently latent in a quietist "waiting for God," in the
profound conviction that redemption comes through
suffering; on occasion, it burst forth in such demonic
expressions as those associated with the names of Sab-
batai Zevi and Joseph Frank. Throughout, it was sus-
tained and nourished by the liturgy of the synagogue,
which breathes the messianic passion in its every
prayer and its every blessing. The hope and expecta-

tion of the Messiah became, indeed, as Franz Rosenzweig has said, that "by which and because of which
Judaism lives . . ."3 And whatever form it assumed,
however strange and untraditional, however heretical
or repellent, it preserved in some way the authentic
marks of the messianic idea: "discontent" with things
as they are and an "unquenchable thirst for the future" of fulfillment and perfection.

II

With Enlightenment and Emancipation, toward the end of the eighteenth and through
the nineteenth century, the whole traditional structure of Jewish faith and practice began to
crumble. First to go, for increasing numbers who came
under the influence of the secularizing trend in modern Western culture, was belief in the Sinaitic revelation and observance of the halachic way of life; frequently enough, the belief in God was abandoned as
well, along with much of the rest of the religious
heritage. But messianism remained, messianism and
the hidden sense of "chosenness" with which it is so
organically bound up. The messianic idea underwent
drastic transformation, the messianic passion was directed into new and strange channels, but neither the
idea nor the passion disappeared with the disintegration of traditional Judaism. In a way, perhaps, messianism became even more central in the secularized
Jewish consciousness, for it was pretty much all that
was left for these "modern" Jews of the Jewish spirituality that had come down through the centuries.
The two great Jewish movements that arose at this
time bear the mark of this "de-religionized" messianism.

From earliest times, Jewish messianism had revealed
a twofold theme, a theme of double alienation and
double restoration. There was first the alienation of
the world from God, its defection from the divine

source of its being; and there was next, the alienation of Israel from the Land, coming as a consequence of its faithlessness to the God by whose promise the Land had been made its possession. Both of these alienations—or better, both of these phases of the one primal alienation—were understood under the figure of "exile": the "exile" of mankind (Adam and Eve) from the presence of God, the "exile" of Israel from the Promised Land. Both of these were interpreted also as aspects of the suffering of the compassionate God— the "God of the sufferers," to use Buber's celebrated phrase—the God who takes man's suffering upon himself; and so the double "exile" became the "exile of the Shechinah," the "exile" of God from his creation and his people.

But if the alienation was double, so was the restoration to come. The restoration of Israel to the Land, and of the world to God, were the two facets—"particularist" and "universalist," to use the familiar terms— of the integral messianic vision. It is important to recognize that these two restorations were not separable, but were conceived of as two aspects, or phases, of the one great act of fulfillment. And, indeed, in the authentic biblical-rabbinic view, it could not be otherwise, for in this view, Israel as the "people of God" was the instrument of God for the redemption of the world, so that the destiny of the world and the destiny of Israel were in the end one and the same. "Particularism" was a means toward a "universalism" of redemption of which not even the allegedly universalist Greeks could dream. "In the [messianic] future, the Jew was concerned with building a house for all mankind, the house of true life."[4]

With the disintegration of the unity of Jewish life and thought under the impact of modern culture, these two phases, or aspects, of the messianic idea became disjoined, and each assumed a separate and autonomous existence in a radically secularized form. The "particularist" phase of Jewish messianism found expression in Zionism; the "universalist" phase, in socialism. Despite all efforts to reunite them on a secular basis—in socialist Zionism or in Zionist socialism—no real synthesis could be achieved. In the Jewish tradition of faith, they had been held together by God, whose creation the world was, and as whose instrument Israel acquired its place in the total scheme. But with God dropping out of the picture, nothing could prevent the decomposition of integral messianism into these two distinct, and often opposed, movements.

Actually, however, the matter was somewhat more complex. A large segment of "emancipated" Jews in nineteenth century Europe and America simply lapsed into the liberal humanism that pervaded Western culture until the first world war. This liberalism meant a utopian idealism, on the one side, and a local nationalism, on the other. It was an American Reform rabbi—and not a "German" either!—who in the 1840's proclaimed: "America is our Zion and Washington our Jerusalem." It was Abraham Geiger who, in his manifesto at the second *Rabbinerversammlung* at Frankfurt am Main in 1846 declared: "We perceive the kingdom of heaven on earth constantly approaching through the endeavor of humanity . . . We are already entered into redemption: liberty and virtue have increased; everything becomes better . . . the Jewish teaching concerning the Messiah is approaching its realization with vigorous steps . . ."[5] It is surely obvious that despite Geiger's invocation of the "Jewish teaching concerning the Messiah" and the American rabbi's reference to "Zion" and "Jerusalem," despite, too, the gospel of "ethical monotheism" which they so fervently preached, the authentic content of the Jewish faith had been voided and the power and meaning of the messianic idea made to nothing. For a messianism in which the Jew, as man and as Israelite, is at home in the world, a messianism indeed in which everything is seen as progressing nicely toward the ideal, is no messianism at all; it is simply a complacent, self-satisfied delusion that at last all is going well in this best of all possible worlds.

Socialism and Zionism were made of sterner stuff and possessed of a different temper. Both felt a strong sense of the "wrongness" of actual existence and were driven by a deep urge toward restoration and rectification. The origins of both movements are many and complex. Into Zionism went the sharp resentment of the "almost assimilated" Jew at the recrudescence of anti-Semitism in the "enlightened" nineteenth century, in the very home of Enlightenment, France and Germany; into it went also a revived ethnic nationalism, and a longing to "normalize" Jewish existence; into it went finally the ancient and traditional "love of Zion" that had drawn the Jews of all ages to the Holy Land. But what gave the Zionist movement of a half century ago its peculiar vitality was the channeling of the messianic passion in its particularist aspect into a political movement of redemption—the "redemption" of Jewry by its restoration to the Land. Socialism, too, was the product of many converging forces: the French Revolution and the unleashing of the modern class struggle; the rise of large-scale industry and the dreams of "technocracy" it engendered; the *élan* of bourgeois radicalism overpassing itself. But again what gave it its special appeal and dynamic was the messianic passion for universal redemption it embodied and exploited. An underground, much modified "Joachimism," combined with a strain of Jewish messianism torn from its proper moorings, provided the structure and pattern, as well as the driving power, of the new secular religion. Marxism obviously arose as a secularized version of Jewish-Christian messianism, with History replacing God and the Proletariat taking the place of the "chosen people" as the instrument of a redemption that was seen as proceeding in the familiar three-phase movement from "primitive communism" through "class society" to the "new socialist order" of the future. Thus from its very birth modern socialism bore within itself the essential sign of its messianic origin.

Zionism and Socialism represented not only the splitting of integral messianism into two autonomous movements; they represented also the radical secularization of the messianic idea in the modern world. Secularization means the denial of the transcendent and the reduction of reality to the two dimensions of nature and society. In regard to messianism, it means the rejection of the suprahistorical and the conversion of the pattern of redemption into an immanent historical process, taking place entirely within the confines of history itself. History becomes the ultimate power, and history-making collective man—not individual man, who shrinks into nothingness—his own savior. The "beginning" and "end" of history, the original and restored "rightness"—in Jewish-Christian tradition, suprahistorical realities "before" and "after" history—become points *within* history. Eschatology thus turns into utopia; instead of the realistic understanding that history is bound to remain precarious, contradictory, and ambiguous to the very end, looking for its rectification and fulfillment to God, we are presented with a vision of a redemption and perfection to be achieved by man, collective man, within current time and history. Socialism looked to the establishment of the "house of true life" not in the "absolute future" signifying the "fullness of time" and the "end of days," but in the course of history, at some particular time— if not today, then tomorrow, or the day after tomorrow. Zionism dissociated the ending of the *Galut* and the Ingathering of Israel from the total eschatological picture of the "end of days," and made it a particular and isolated historical task. The whole transcendent context of the messianic hope was thus eliminated with the secularization of its elements.

The "finitization" of eschatology involved in its secularization means also its idolatrization, for it is plainly idolatrous to convert a particular time or event in history into the "absolute time," with absolute and final significance, since this means the absolutization—that is, the divinization—of the goals or values in the utopian fulfillment. In pseudo-messianic socialism, the Movement, the Party, the New Social Order becomes absolutes, beyond all judgment and criticism. In pseudo-messianic Zionism, the absolutization of the Jewish people and of the Zionist task leads to an ethnolatry that has given many thoughtful Zionists pause. The consequences of pseudo-messianic utopianism in any form are too obvious in recent history to require any elaboration here.

The point I want to make is rather different. It is not merely that there are types of socialism and Zionism which are not pseudo-messianic and so do not fall under the strictures here advanced; it is rather that even pseudo-messianism has its function in the movement of history toward its fulfillment. "The expectation of the coming of the Messiah . . . ," Franz Rosenzweig pointed out long ago, "would be a meaningless theologoumenon, a mere 'idea' in the philosophical sense, . . . if the appearance again and again of a 'false Messiah' did not render it reality and unreality, illusion and disillusion . . ."[6] At a time of spiritual decadence, when all sense of Jewishness was being dissolved in a smug and complacent adjustment to the modern world, Zionism, with all its illusions and extravagances, sounded a warning and a call—a warning that all was not well even in the modern liberal-constitutional state in which the Jew was emancipated and enfranchised, and a call to authentic Jewish existence. Even many opponents of Zionism recognized the role that Zionism was playing in bringing a sense of Jewishness to the "dejudaized" Jews in Western Europe in the early part of the century. On the other side, socialism, with all its utopianism and moral ambiguities, was bringing a sense of destiny and a hope for the future to the "displaced" masses of proletarians and intellectuals in modern industrial society. "[Marx] spoke of a promised time . . . Millions of people were through Marx put in the Jewish attitude to history, and looked forward with messianic expectation to the coming of the time . . . To this extent, he was a prophet . . . But Marx also was a false prophet . . . He proclaimed the false Messiah . . . He linked his promised era to a . . . final program that would round off and complete history . . . He proclaimed the coming rise to power of the proletariat as the fulfillment of time, as the final justice. That was false prophecy . . . But he was a prophet."[7]

It is not necessary to overlook the sinister consequences of the idolatrous pseudo-messianic element in Marxism, particularly as that has entered into the perverted structure of Soviet communism, to recognize, as does Maybaum in the words just quoted, that Marx did indeed put millions of people in the "Jewish attitude to history," and to that extent was indeed a "prophet."

Again it was Franz Rosenzweig, the non-socialist and non-Zionist, who out of his deep messianic understanding saw the strange role that socialism and Zionism were playing in the history of his time. "Just as the Social Democrats, even if they are 'atheists'," he wrote to his friend Hans Ehrenberg in April 1927, "are more important for the establishment of the kingdom of God through the church than the church-minded, . . . certainly than the vast mass of the semi- or wholly indifferent, so are the Zionists for the synagogue."[8] Both, he felt, were doing a work in furtherance of the

divine purpose, however insistently they might deny
the very notion of such purpose.

Yet we must never forget that significant as was the
role they played in a cause beyond their ken, socialism
and Zionism, in their pseudo-messianic form, were
affected with a deep inner vice.
They were utopian and idolatrous, and increasingly
fell under the sway of the evils generated by utopianism and idolatry. In them, the unity of the messianic idea in its "universalist" and "particularist"
aspects was hopelessly split, and messianism itself
sundered from its transcendent source and origin.
That they achieved so much is indeed testimony to the
strange ways in which divine providence works in
history, using 'unbeliever" as well as "believer" for the
fulfillment of its purposes.

III

Zionism, on any appreciable scale, came late to
America, but Jewish socialism came fairly
early, with the great immigration at the end of
the last century. The mass of Jewish immigrants from
eastern Europe were of traditional religious background, and attempted, usually with indifferent success, to maintain the old ways in the new world. They
quickly adjusted themselves to the conditions of ethnic
group existence in America, and fell in with the general patterns of American life. A strong minority, however, were social radicals of one sort or another,
largely Socialists or Anarchists. In the early days of the
immigration, many of these radicals hardly considered
themselves Jewish; their cultural life and associations
were rather with the radicals and intellectuals of the
countries from which they came: they were Russians,
Rumanians, and the like. A few persisted in their non-
Jewish identification, but the vast majority, fortified by
later accessions of Yiddishists, located themselves in
the Jewish community, of which they became the real

"creative minority." The Jewish community in New York and other large cities was dominated culturally by its radical elements in a way and to a degree without parallel in any other ethnic-immigrant group in this country.

The radicalism of this immigrant generation was, by and large, part of their Jewishness. It entered into the complex of *Yiddishkeit* in as intimate and organic a fashion as did the old religion in the case of their Orthodox fellow Jews. It was, in fact, the "religious" or ideological aspect of their Yiddish culture, which embraced the totality of their lives, at least that part of their lives which was lived in the ethnic group. Of Zionism, in its modern form, there was relatively little in those early days.

The second generation—the American born or bred children of the immigrants—presented a very different picture. The young people of the second generation were marginal to a really painful degree. They were at home in neither of the two communities in which they lived, neither in the Jewish ethnic group of their parents nor in the larger American community toward which they looked. The second generation reacted to its double alienation—"too American in the home, too foreign in the school"[9]—in various ways, but the two extreme reactions are perhaps most important for us. Some reacted by an attempt to overcome their alienation through an intensified assertion of their ethnic group loyalties with a passion and vehemence unknown to their parents, for whom ethnic belonging was more or less a matter of course. Others, at the other end of the second generation spectrum, attempted to overcome their alienation by transcending group affiliations in a radical internationalism or cosmopolitanism. The former turned to Zionism; the latter, to socialism or Communism. "Zionism was the outlet, particularly for the second generation," Handlin writes of the segment at the one extreme. "This group was especially perplexed, as all second generations were, by the question of their place in American culture, confused by specific problems of social and economic adjustment, and anxious over the meaning of anti-Semitism."[10] "Torn away from the old moorings and not yet anchored in the new realities," Sherman writes of those at the other extreme, "large sections of the second generation presented fertile ground for the most radical social ideas and the most revolutionary views . . ."[11] Zionism and social radicalism became the expressions of characteristic second generation reactions of American Jewry.

Yet they were characteristic with a difference. Zionism was ethnic nationalism, to be sure, but how different from the ethnic nationalism of the second generation Germans, Poles, or Hungarians. Jewish socialism was second generation radicalism, of course, but whereas in the second generations of other immigrant groups such radicalism was relatively insignificant in the life of the community, among the Jews socialism and Communism swept over large parts of the second generation and left a deep mark on American Jewish life. The difference was precisely the result of the breadth and intensity coming from the messianic passion that went into the two movements. Jewish messianism thus entered into the life of the second generation to define its most characteristic responses to the American environment.

The third generation of American Jewry, now rapidly emerging, is unlike both the second and the first. It is thoroughly American, at home in America, no longer marginal in the second generation sense. But it has the problem of identification in a way that the first and second generations did not have, for while it is definitely American, it is faced with the task of distinguishing itself from other Americans, Americans of other "heritages." It is meeting this problem in a characteristic American fashion, by attempting to establish its own heritage through religious identification and affiliation. The third generation typically thinks of its Jewishness as adherence to a religious community, to a Jewish religious community, existing side by side with equivalent Protestant and Catholic communities in the tripartite scheme of American religion. The "return" of the third generation to religious self-identification and synagogue membership needs no documentation.

Significantly, this "return" to religion, or rather the relatively secure adjustment to American reality of which the return is, in large measure, a reflection, has led to the rapid dissolution of the ideologies and movements which, in the second generation, were an expression alike of its messianic impulse and its cultural alienation. Zionism and Jewish social radicalism, in their earlier and more authentic meanings, have faded away almost before our very eyes. Very little is left of either the immigrant generation "Yiddish" socialism or of the second generation cosmopolitan variety, and very little is left of the ideological Zionism of a decade or two ago. Almost everybody today is a social liberal, and everybody is a friend of the State of Israel, but what remains of Zionism or social radicalism in the old sense? Of course, the dissolution of these ideologies and the decline of these movements have taken place in the larger context of a world situation very different from that in which the second generation lived and moved. But the effect of the kind of adjustment the third generation of American Jewry has made to American reality, and made it with a singular appropriateness to American conditions, cannot be denied or ignored. Zionism and Jewish socialism in America were essentially second generation phenomena, and they are disappearing with the emergence of the third.

And what of the messianic passion? That too seems to be disappearing. Third generation American Jews are increasingly becoming like other Americans of the like generation; their distinctiveness, at least on the surface, is rapidly diminishing. The "intellectual preeminence" which Veblen once noted is no longer so marked; nor is the restlessness, the "unadjustedness," of these "aliens of uneasy feet" (again Veblen). The decline of the messianic passion among American Jews is part of this picture; it is also part of the new-world situation, in which the sense of *kairos*, of "the time is at hand," has given way to a sense of the void. The messianic Jew is as if born to be the prophet of the *kairos;* he is hardly cut out to be the guardian of the void in an age of no promise.

Has the messianic passion then vanished from the Jewish soul? It cannot be. Jewishness is messianic or it is nothing. "True messianist or false messianist," Arthur Cohen has rightly said, "the Jewish intellectual"—and the Jew is always in some sense an "intellectual"—"is a messianist."[12] The messianic passion cannot be drained from his being without draining away his Jewishness; so long as a trace of the latter remains, so will the former. The messianic passion is not dead; it is dormant.

Third generation adjustment is a fact, but it is not the final or ultimate fact in American Jewish life. The world situation of the void is also a fact, but it is not the final or ultimate fact in human history. In its proper time, a new *kairos* will appear; a new restlessness, a new "discontent," will arouse the Jew, the American Jew as well, to his messianic vocation. Whatever is of enduring value in Zionism and Jewish social radicalism is not lost; it will, in its time, be taken up, reassessed, and made part of the new manifestation of the messianic idea, of which we today have no conception, but which we know is to come. Let us prepare ourselves and those who come after us to be the servants of the new *kairos* with a messianic passion that is integral and restored to the transcendent source and origin from which it has drawn its power through the ages.

Notes

[1] N. N. Glatzer, *Untersuchungen zur Geschichtslehre der Tannaiten*, pp. 35–36.

[2] Martin Buber, "The Two Foci of the Jewish Soul," *Israel and the World*, pp. 35, 39.

[3] Franz Rosenzweig, *Jehuda Halevi*, p. 239; N. N. Glatzer, ed., *Franz Rosenzweig: His Life and Thought*, p. 350.

[4] Martin Buber, *Drei Reden uber das Judentum*, p. 91.

[5] There is a strong echo of this liberal utopianism in the Pittsburgh Platform (1885) of American Reform Judaism: "We recognize in the modern age of universal culture of heart and intellect the approaching of the realization of Israel's great messianic hope for the establishment of the Kingdom of Truth, Justice, and Peace among men."

[6] Franz Rosenzweig, *Jehuda Halevi*, p. 239; N. N. Glatzer, ed., *op. cit.*, p. 350.

[7] Ignaz Maybaum, *Synagogue and Society*, pp. 57–58.

[8] Franz Rosenzweig, *Briefe*, p. 580; N. N. Glatzer, ed., *op. cit.*, p. 157.

[9] Marcus L. Hansen, *The Problem of the Third Generation Immigrant*, pp. 6–7.

[10] Oscar Handlin, *Adventure in Freedom*, p. 217.

[11] C. Bezalel Sherman, "Three Generations," *Jewish Frontier*, July 1954.

[12] Arthur A. Cohen, "Messianism and the Jew," *The Commonweal*, July 15, 1955.

—8—

Judaism as Personal Decision

(1968)

Religion, as I see it, is not merely a metaphysic of the universe, although a philosophical element enters into it; nor is religion simply an experience of the holy, although a mystical element enters into every valid religious experience. Religion is essentially a quality of existence. It is "man's life insofar as it is defined by his supreme loyalty and devotion." This definition by Robert Calhoun indicates that religion is existence, and that the basic problem of religion is the basic problem of existence—the problem of ultimate allegiance and commitment.

The decision of faith, which everyone is obliged to make because he is a living human being, defines the nature and character of his existence. In non-human animals, life is the unfolding of the pattern of their nature. But man's nature is open, not closed. This fact constitutes his freedom. Every vital decision of life contributes to the formation of his being, and the most crucial and vital decision of life is a decision of faith. Radical self-understanding is ultimately possible only in terms of faith, for it is only in terms of faith that our existence is defined and that we can really understand ourselves.

Objective vs. existential thinking

Religion is thus, in the first place, commitment. We can clarify what commitment means by distinguishing between two types of thinking that are characteristic of the human enterprise. One I call "objective" thinking, the other "existential" thinking. There is a basic difference between the two, although they are naturally combined and fused in actual life. Objective thinking is the kind of thinking that has standing in philosophy and in the sciences. It is detached, disinterested thinking. It tries to eliminate the "personal equation," to use a term familiar in the methodology of science. It is contemplative, speculative thinking; thinking about something from the outside, as an object. It is the thinking of a spectator, the thinking about the game that is going on in the playing-field from the point of view of the spectator in the grandstand. In this kind of objective thinking, truth is ready-made and external. It exists outside and independent of man; he has to conform to it as he thinks.

But there is another kind of thinking—the thinking not of the spectator in the grandstand watching the game, but of the player in the playing-field who thinks about the game as he plays it. This kind of thinking is not detached; it is involved, caught up in, "engaged." Something of the thinker himself is at stake in what he is thinking about. It is thinking in confrontation, in meeting, in encounter. Instead of being spectatorial, speculative, contemplative, it is active, the thinking of a participant. It is "the thinking of the existing subject about his existence as he exists his existence" (Kierkegaard). In this kind of thinking, truth is not external or ready-made; it is personal, and it is "made true," at least in part, by commitment and action.

The objective type of thinking is relevant to science and speculative philosophy. But where human existence is concerned, only existential thinking would seem to be appropriate. Existential thinking is the thinking relevant to the problems of life, especially and preeminently to personal relations, ethics, and religion. Religious faith is at bottom an act of commitment. It is staking one's life on truth to be "made true." The truth of faith is not a ready-made, external truth; it is a personal truth that has to be "verified" by commitment and action. It is a truth that demands the staking of one's life on the venture because the decision of faith is indeed the total determination of life. As Milton Steinberg once put it, "As a man thinks about ultimates, so he deals with immediates," including his own existence. Faith is essentially neither a state of mind, as the rationalists claim, nor a compendium of propositions about a divine metaphysics, nor a state of feeling, as the mystics would contend. Faith is a structure of being-in-action because human being is itself essentially and inescapably being-in-action. Faith is thus a restructuring of existence, similar to a mass of iron filings that is restructured when a magnet is brought near: nothing new is added, the filings were there before, but everything is different.

Who am I?

The great question of human existence, whether it is asked or not, is: "Who am I?" Human life, in one form or another, is an attempt to define and answer this question. The answer for the Jew is, however, double: "I am a human being, and I am a Jew." The problem of faith, from this point of view, is the problem of making sense of both parts of this answer. What do I mean when I say I am a *human being*? What are the implications of this assertion for my existence? And what do I mean when I say I am a *Jew*? Two levels of self-understanding and commitment are involved here. One is the ultimate determination of personal existence which is defined in terms of God. The other is the ultimate determination of Jewish existence which is defined in terms of Israel, the people Israel, the people of God.

The ultimate determination of personal existence requires a definition of what it means to be a person. What does it mean to be a self? H. Richard Niebuhr answers this question in a profound and classic manner: "To be a self is to have a god"—a god with a small "g." Human existence, in contra-distinction to non-human being, is ultimately god-related. It is intrinsically existence in terms of an ultimate concern—of that by which, and for which, one lives—which is the god of one's existence. Human existence is self-transcending because the human condition is a condition of tension, of crisis, of anxiety. We live in two worlds. We are immersed in the context of nature, yet somehow we transcend the dimensions of nature. Man is finite; but, alone of all finite beings, he *knows* he is finite. Therefore he can never rest easy in his finitude; he is ever striving to reach beyond it. Man is mortal; but, alone of all mortal beings, he *knows* he is mortal. Therefore he can never rest easy in his mortality; he is ever straining to overcome it. Man is a creature; but, alone of all creatures, he *knows* he is a creature. Therefore, he can never rest easy in his creatureliness; he is forever striving to raise himself above it. Man is the kind of being who cannot stay put: he cannot rest within his creaturely limitations. Human existence, when we attempt to live and understand it in merely human terms, is self-contradictory and self-destructive.

Limit situations

Certain situations in life serve to bring man's efforts in achieving autonomy to an abrupt and tragic halt. They are what Karl Jaspers calls fundamental "limit situations," situations which bring a man to a sudden awareness of his dependent and transient nature and make him conscious of the inadequacy of the empirical mode of existence and therefore of his ordination to transcendence. Freedom is such a "limit situation." Human existence is specifically existence in freedom; yet freedom meets its limit and crisis in the determinism of nature and thought. The moral sense is another "limit situation." Human existence is specifically existence in the moral dimension; but the moral sense meets its limit and crisis in the scientific picture of a universe drained of value. Still another "limit situation" is human effort. Human existence is existence in action; yet the ongoing activity of human life meets its limit and crisis in the ambiguity and transitoriness of all human achievement. Man strives and works and builds yet he knows, or should know, that everything is here today and gone tomorrow. The things we build are not the solid, everlasting structures we imagine them to be; they are sand castles on the beach, which the next wave of history may wipe out. The ultimate "limit situation" is life itself. Life meets its limit and crisis in death. Death, it has been said, is the ultimate crisis in life.

Human existence conceived simply in its own terms comes up against these "limit situations" and necessarily reveals its own self-destructive logic. As a result, we experience that "lostness," that anxiety and insecurity that characterize human life. Man feels himself alone and homeless in the universe. He is forever teetering at the brink of an abyss of meaninglessness and nothingness—in Housman's phrase, "a stranger and afraid in a world I never made." Moreover, there is a restlessness in human existence that reflects the insatiability of the human spirit. Once you've got everything you want, you find that you don't want anything you've got. This restlessness and insatiability are a consequence of the freedom of the human spirit. Man is never content to rest in the limitations of his being. He is always striving to transcend himself, to ground his existence in a larger whole beyond himself so as to give it meaning and security. This is what Richard Niebuhr means when he says that "to be a self is to have a god." To live a human life is to live in terms of something that is the object of one's supreme loyalty and devotion, that which gives content, meaning and direction to life. Faith is a person's relation to his god. In this sense, every man has his god and his faith, whether he knows it or not, whether he wants to or not. The meaning of being human is to have a god, to live in faith.

The basic choice

The real problem, therefore, is not *whether* to have faith or not, *whether* to affirm a god or not. A man can no more escape having a god and living in faith than he can escape the necessity of eating or breathing. As Feodor Dostoievski said, "Man must worship something; if he does not worship God, he will worship an idol made of wood, or of gold, or of ideas." Thus, the real question is not *whether* faith, but what *kind* of faith, faith in *what*. Some faith for living there must be, and the kind of faith we live by defines the kind of life we lead.

The basic choice is startlingly simple. It is: *God or an idol!* The choice is inescapable and all-important. It is a choice between some god with a small "g" and God with a capital "G." We must have something ultimate, some object of supreme loyalty and devotion, to give content, meaning, direction and value to life. This object of our supreme loyalty and devotion may be something of this world, something partial, relative, conditioned—some value, idea, person, power, movement, institution or program—taken and exalted to ultimacy and absoluteness, made into the god of our existence. Or it may be the God who transcends and is beyond all things of the world. There is no other choice. To take something of this world and worship it as God is what the Bible and our religious tradition know as idolatry. The choice is between idolatry and God-centered faith.

These are the two roads. Where does each of them lead? What are the consequences of the choice?

The evil of idolatry is not due to the badness of the thing idolized. The things of the world are good things in their place. The evil of idolatry resides in the fact that a partial and limited good (and all goods of the world are merely partial and limited) is taken and exalted to absoluteness. It is the process of idolatrization that does the mischief; it turns a partial good into a total evil. A story in the Mishnah illumines this insight. The Jewish elders in Rome were asked: "If your God has no pleasure in the worship of idols, why does He not destroy them?" To which they replied: "If a man worshipped things of which the world had no need, God would make an end of them, but lo, they worship the sun and the moon and the stars and the planets. Shall God destroy the world because of fools?" The things which are worshipped are good things; all things that God has created are good. The folly—which is not merely ignorance but a kind of perverseness—consists in elevating partial and relative goods to absoluteness, that is, in worshipping them as if they were God.

Consequences of idolatry

The first consequence of idolatry is, therefore, *delusion*. This is what the Bible means when it says that idolatry is "vanity," foolishness. The man who makes something of this world his god, is driven to distort the rest of reality to suit the demands of his idol. The structure of his existence is distorted because a partial view or value is made absolute.

Something that is only part of reality is exalted into the be-all and end-all of life and made the measure of all things.

A second consequence of idolatry is *enslavement*. Our religious tradition speaks of idolatry as "demonism." The implication is clear and compelling. The man who makes anything of this world his god makes it his master. This is true whether he worships his business, family, or nation, or some ideal, movement or social program. The moment he makes it his god—that for which, or by which, he lives—he exalts it beyond criticism or control. It becomes his master and he becomes its slave. The truth of the biblical teaching about idolatry is abundantly verified in the experience of mankind.

A third consequence of idolatry is an ethic of *dehumanization*. If we take something of this world and make it our god, that something, precisely because it is something *in* and *of* the world, divides the human race into two parts—one part within the magic circle defined by the idol; the other, much larger part, without. A man who makes his family or his nation his god, divides mankind into two parts—those within his particular family or nation, who are fully human and entitled to be treated as human beings, and those outside the family or nation, who are not really human in the same sense and who are quite expendable where the interests of family or nation are concerned. Every idolatry involves a "segregationist" ethic of this kind, for it exalts something of this world and defines an "in-group" that, by its very nature, is held to be superior to the rest of the human race. Idolatry and dehumanizing ethics go hand in hand.

Faith is liberating

The consequences of a God-centered faith are radically different. Insofar as a man grounds his existence in God, he is protected against the delusion and distortion that come with idolatry. He will not permit himself to regard anything of this world with such utter devotion that he will make its standpoint absolute and twist all of reality to conform thereto. Nothing of this world can make absolute claims on him. God-centered faith thus makes for *realism*. But it is also a *liberating* faith. Our subjection to the God beyond is our charter of freedom in this world for, insofar as we are and remain loyal to Him, we will reject the claims of anything in this world to absolute loyalty, absolute devotion, absolute allegiance—whether that claim be made on an economic, social, political, intellectual or even spiritual level.

Being the servant of God, man is free from subjection to mere man. A rabbinic saying illustrates this point to perfection. "Unto me are the children of Israel slaves," God is represented as saying in the Bible; to which the rabbis add: " . . . therefore not slaves unto slaves." Thomas Jefferson applied this maxim to the realm of politics when he said that "Resistance to tyrants is obedience to God." The tyrant is one who claims for himself the absolute allegiance that is due to God alone. The "tyrant" may be a man or an institution, an organization, a system or an idea. In every case, the man of God-centered faith will answer the demand for absolute, total devotion with a resolute *no*. He will not permit himself to be enslaved by anybody or anything of this world, because the only master he acknowledges is God. He will deal with everything critically; he will see everything in its proper perspective; he will keep everything under control and not permit himself to be overwhelmed by the things of the world—which are all good things, but good things *in their place*. He will know how to keep them in their place.

Ultimate equality

God-centered faith is a liberating faith. It frees one for controlling and dealing with the things of the world. It is also a faith that makes for an ethic of human worth; indeed, only on the basis of such a faith can an ethic of human worth really be established. In every empirical respect—physical, biological, social, psychological, even moral and spiritual—men are manifestly unequal. An ethic that sees men merely as natural beings is bound to declare that, while all men are human, some are more human than others. But the man of God-centered faith sees men not merely as natural organisms but as persons in their God-relationship. He therefore sees beyond all empirical inequalities, and perceives something supremely significant in which all men are indeed alike—their God-relationship. The empirical inequalities among men do not disappear. They remain important, but they are overshadowed by the ultimate equality of all men in the face of a God who is transcendent and sovereign. Here, and here alone, we have the ground for a radical ethic of human worth and dignity.

Idolatry makes for delusion, enslavement, a dehumanizing ethic. God-centered faith makes for realism, freedom, and an ethic of human worth and dignity. But there is still a deeper level of comparison and contrast. Idolatry does not lead to any real self-transcendence. In idolatry, the self merely finds and worships itself writ large. It never gets beyond itself. Hence there is no ultimate security at all. In God-centered faith, there is the possibility of genuine self-transcendence. In God-centered faith, we are offered a security beyond—and shattering—all earthly securities. It is the security of the "peace that passeth understanding," which is never the work of psychological techniques, but always the gift of God received in faith. As Augustine puts it: "For Thou hast made us for Thyself alone and our hearts are restless till they rest in Thee."

A human decision

The decision for or against God is the primary decision of life. We have to make it by virtue of the fact that we are human beings. If we do not decide for God, it is not as if we "withheld judgment" and made no decision at all; if we do not decide for God, quite inevitably we decide for some idol, with all the consequences of idolatry.

The decision confronts us as a demand. The demand is given in the biblical injunction: "Choose you this day whom you will serve." Note the nature of this demand. It is not philosophical or mystical; it is a straight "political" demand or, rather, a straight "theo-political" demand. What is asked for is absolute loyalty and service to God, who is to be acknowledged as sovereign Lord and Master. And the authentic Jewish answer is the one Joshua gives: "As for me and my house, we will serve the Lord." To live an authentic human life means that we will serve the Lord. To live an authentic human life means that we ground our existence in the living God and thus stand protected by our faith from the demonic idolatries that beset us on all sides. That is what the decision of faith is—the choice of a God, the supreme venture of life.

The decision of faith, if it is genuine, is not merely or even primarily an intellectual decision. It is a decision that defines our life. Above all, it is a commitment of the whole person. It is a decision of faith in which one stakes one's life on a truth which one has to "make true" through commitment and action.

To be a jew

We define our humanness in terms of the god we worship and the truth we live by. What then does it mean to be a Jew? Again, I am not raising a question of objective academic research but of existence. When I ask the question, "What does it mean to be a Jew?" I am really asking the question, "What does it mean *for me* to be a Jew?"

It is easier to define what being a Jew is *not*. To be a Jew is not to be a member of a distinct and separate race. According to anthropologists, Jews are racially and ethnically one of the most mixed groups in the world. No definition in racial terms can serve to define them. Nor does being a Jew mean being a member of a distinct and separate nation, if we employ the word "nation" in the sense in which we speak of the English, French or American nations. Nor is it possible to define Jewish existence in cultural terms. Aside from religion, there is no cultural character or trait that is unique and common to all Jews. Neither can Jewish existence be defined simply in terms of membership in a religious denomination. A man is a Baptist if he adheres to a Baptist church, affirms the basic Baptist beliefs, or does both. Many Jews in America adhere to no synagogue, hold no religious belief, and indeed call themselves atheists. Yet it would be a gross violation of the usage of the term to deny them the appellation "Jew." In short, being a Jew is not like being a member of a race, nation, cultural group, or even of a religious denomination.

Any attempt to define Jewishness in secular-empirical terms, on a level that makes no reference to one's relations to God, is futile. The well-known anthropologist, Melville J. Herskovits, after a prolonged attempt to define the Jews exclusively in secular and empirical terms, finally comes to this conclusion:

> It is . . . apparent that it is neither race, nor such an aspect of physical type as nasality, nor a "Jewish look" that affords terms in which the question, "Who are the Jews" is to be answered. In like manner, language, culture, belief, all exhibit so great a range of variation that no definition cast in terms of these concepts can be more than partial. Yet the Jews do represent a historical continuum. . . . Is there any least common denominator other than the designation "Jew" that can be used to mark the historical fait accompli which the Jew, however he may be defined, seems to be? It is seriously to be questioned.

The fact is that there is no way in which Jewishness can be adequately defined or given positive content on a secular, empirical level. Therefore, Jews trying to understand their Jewishness in secular terms have regularly been driven to a negative conception of Jewishness. They view their Jewishness primarily as the result of an historical irrationality, anti-Semitism, which forced the label "Jew" on them. Being herded together, they will develop some common traits; basically however, they have nothing in common except the label "Jew." Jews are Jews simply because they are treated—that is, mistreated—as Jews by the world. The world will not let them *not* be Jews, whatever that term may mean.

Negative jewishness

This view is inadequate though it contains some truth. If it were true that Jewishness is nothing positive, but simply a label signifying the way a Jew may be treated by the world, why should anyone want to remain a Jew or retain for himself and his children a meaningless and onerous burden? Being a Jew in the world, at best, brings with it annoyances and handicaps; at worst, it can involve great perils. It may be difficult to throw off one's Jewishness; but to yield to difficulties without an effort to overcome them is an unworthy defeatism. If being a Jew means nothing but being branded as "Jew," it clearly is something to be discarded as quickly as possible. Such is the logic of secular Judaism, and many secular Jews have recognized it, much to their own perplexity. The secular Jew frequently wants to remain a Jew, yet is unable to understand or explain what it is he wants to remain, or why.

The meaning of Jewish existence can be affirmed and understood only in faith. Jewish existence is something unique; on this, the theologian and sociologist, the Jew and the Christian, agree. Martin Buber, the Jewish philosopher, says that "the existence of Israel is something unique, unclassifiable; this name marks the community as one that cannot be grasped in the categories of sociology and ethnology." Carl Mayer, the Christian sociologist, reiterates that "the Jewish people represents a sociologically unique phenomenon and defies all attempts at definition." This uniqueness makes no sense in secular-empirical terms; it is intelligible only in terms of faith. To quote Buber again: "We have but one way to apprehend this positive meaning of this negative phenomenon, the way of faith. From any viewpoint other than faith, our inability to fit into a category would be intolerable, something contrary to history, contrary to nature; but from the viewpoint of faith, our inability to fit into a category is the foundation and meaning of our existence."

A convenant folk

I can answer the question, "What does it mean to be a Jew?" only in faith. Jewry—Israel collectively—can understand itself only in faith. The tradition of Israel, the ongoing tradition of self-understanding of Israel in relation to its God, has always defined Israel as a covenant folk—not as a race, nation, or culture group, but as a covenant folk. Israel is not a nation like other nations; it is not a nation at all. As Jewish teaching has always understood it, Israel is a people brought into being by God to serve Him as a kind of task-force in the fulfillment of His purposes in history. Israel's special relation to God is defined and established in the covenant which binds it to God. Apart from the covenant and the vocation it implies, Israel is as nothing, and Jewish existence a mere delusion. But in terms of the covenant and the vocation it implies, Jewish existence becomes supremely significant and meaningful to the Jew.

The vocation to which Israel is appointed by divine covenant is traditionally defined in the term *kiddush hashem,* "sanctification of the Name"—standing witness to the living God amidst the idolatries of the world.

The world is idolatry-ridden and in rebellion against God; men are forever striving to throw off their allegiance to their rightful Lord, the living God. The vocation, the function of Jewry, is to remain loyal and to stand witness to its Lord and the Lord of all being amidst this universal rebellion and disobedience; to say no to every idolatrous pretension; to reject every claim of an earthly power—whether person, institution, or idea—to finality and absolute devotion; to call men to knowledge and service of the living God, to whom alone absolute devotion is due. In word and deed, individually and corporately, in inner life and in outward action, "to give the world no rest so long as the world has not God" (Maritain)—such is the vocation of Israel. This conviction concerning Israel's nature and destiny is neither an empirical finding nor a sociological conclusion; it is a commitment of faith.

When I say that Israel is a covenant folk, appointed for this vocation, I am not describing a scientific notion. No sociologist or anthropologist can confirm— or refute—the statement. What I am saying is that, from the standpoint of faith, I interpret my Jewish existence as covenant existence. I am engaging in existential, not objective, thinking. This conviction concerning Israel's nature and destiny, held in faith, illumines one's self-understanding as a Jew as nothing else can, because every attempt to understand Jewishness apart from the standpoint of faith, apart from the covenant, ends in negativism and nihilism. It is impossible to understand Jewish existence positively on any other level.

The inescapable choice

This conviction held in faith affords an unshakable ground for Jewish existence and survival. Again, a basic choice is involved—a choice between covenant existence and some form of secular idolatry. The choice again is inescapable. It defines my existence as a Jew. The terms of the decision are either self-affirmation in faith as a Jew, or self-surrender to some secular idolatry. No other alternative is possible. Even "conversion" to Christianity, if it is sincerely based on faith, implies prior self-affirmation as a Jew, as Franz Rosenzweig has pointed out.

The crux of decision is given in terms of demand and response. The demand is: "You shall be unto me a kingdom of priests and a holy nation." The response determines whether my existence as a Jew shall be authentic or inauthentic. I can affirm my existence as a Jew in terms of covenant existence and thus make my Jewishness a source of meaning and power for life. Or I can attempt to deny and reject my covenant existence. In this case, my Jewishness becomes a curse and burden, and a source of self-hatred with its psychological and sociological consequences. We are, in a measure, free to choose, but we are not free *not* to choose. It is for each of us to decide; it is our fate that is at stake. And when we make the decision, it must be a genuine decision—a commitment of the whole person to a truth, which we are now ready to "make true" with our life.

Affirmation on two levels

On both levels of faith, Judaism is decision and commitment. It is just as much decision and commitment on the corporate level of Israel as on the personal level of the affirmation of God. On both levels, it involves an ultimate affirmation, which is at once an ultimate allegiance and the staking of one's life on a truth that is nevertheless to be "made true" by commitment and action. On both levels, this personal commitment is both the ground or security, and the illumination of existence.

But the two levels are essentially one. For the God of personal existence—"*My* God"—is the God of the covenant—the "God of our fathers." For the Jew, the decision for God is a decision for the covenant, and the decision for the covenant is a decision for God. The Jew finds the living God of faith in and through Israel, in and through the covenanted people of God, that has stood witness to God through the ages and that sees the meaning of its hard and perilous existence only in its world-challenging and world-transforming vocation.

Part III

ANTI-SEMITISM AND JEWISH SURVIVAL

—9—

The Theology of Antisemitism

(1948)

I n the historical crisis of our time many ideas and movements once confidently accounted for in economic or sociological terms are revealing themselves as at bottom theological. Of no contemporary problem is this truer than of the problem of antisemitism, the "metaphysical" face of which not even the most naturalistic age could obscure. Antisemitism is not just one of the social questions of our time. From a certain point of view it may be considered the root question; for it points straight to the heart of the spiritual malady of the contemporary world.

The great merit of Dr. Eckardt's book *Christianity and the Children of Israel*[1] is that he views antisemitism from this broad perspective. He sees it as a phase of the idolatrous self-alienation of man, of the outworking of human sin in history. And because his approach is so fundamental, it enables him to deal perceptively with many related issues and to climax his inquiry with a profoundly interesting discussion of the relation between Judaism and Christianity. "A Theology for the Jewish Question"—that is at once the title of the last chapter and the real subject of his work.

Dr. Eckardt is a young theologian trained at Union

Theological Seminary, now teaching philosophy and religion at Lawrence College, Wisconsin. His frame of reference and fundamental categories are derived from the thinking of contemporary neo-Reformation theologians: Karl Barth and Emil Brunner in Europe, and Reinhold Niebuhr, H. Richard Niebuhr and Paul Tillich in this country. Not the least valuable feature of his book is its heavy documentation from these writers, including extensive excerpts from letters and unpublished manuscripts. By the subtlety and incisiveness with which he pursues his inquiry, he convincingly demonstrates the power of the theological approach.

The book begins with a brief sketch of the plight of the Jews, followed by an analysis of the more important types of explanations and interpretations of antisemitism. Economic, ethnologic, racial, religious, psychological: one after the other the author examines them, assesses their measure of validity and points out their shortcomings. Individually or all together, they fall short of encompassing the full enormity of the phenomenon. Something much more fundamental is indicated, something that goes beyond the relatively superficial levels of economics and politics and probes to the heart of the "human condition," that dares to ask the basic question: "What is man?" Such an approach cannot be anything less than theological.

This approach, of course, does not deny the insights gained on other levels of analysis; it strives to include and transcend them. Particularly akin to theology is the psychological viewpoint. Both alike concern themselves directly with the human self, although from radically different points of view. As we shall see, the analysis of the inner motivation of antisemitism given by the positivist Freud bears a startling likeness to the insights of the theologians.

"The Jews embody a transcendent mystery": the mystery of Israel confronts us at the very outset of any consideration of the "Jewish question." The Christian sociologist Carl Mayer and the Jewish philosopher Martin Buber agree: "The existence of Israel is something unique, unclassifiable. This name marks the community as one that cannot be grasped in the concepts of ethnology or sociology" (Buber). The mystery of Israel is one that escapes all the conventional categories of nature and society.

The mystery of Israel, as the historian Salo W. Baron has put it, is the mystery of "a people beyond state or territory, a divine instrument in man's overcoming of 'nature' through a supernatural process in the course of 'history.' " In his own account of the divine vocation of Israel, Dr. Eckardt employs Paul Tillich's counter-position of the gods of space and time. Israel has been chosen to bear witness to the universal God of history (time) against the pagan gods of space; to contend for the one transcendent God against the idolatries of the world; to proclaim the Messiah and the coming of the Kingdom against the inordinate pretensions to finality of secular life.

If this is indeed the vocation of Israel, is it any wonder that Israel has felt the heavy hand of oppression throughout the ages? Men are in rebellion against God—that is the meaning of "original sin" as an inescapable part of their nature—and they vent their fury upon the silent witnesses of the God of justice. "The people of time," Tillich explains, "cannot avoid being persecuted because, by their very existence, they break the infinite claim of the gods of space, which expresses itself in will-to-power, imperialism, injustice, demonic enthusiasm and tragic self-destruction." A pastoral letter of the Dutch Reformed Church in 1943 proclaimed: "The enormous and unrestrained hatred of the Jews comes from natural aversion for the 'Jewish God' and the 'Jewish Bible,' for they [the Nazis], like nothing else, reveal the true nature of paganism."

But antisemitism is not merely revolt against God and His law. Among Christians it is particularly and especially a manifestation of a hidden hostility to Jesus as the Christ. Christian ambivalence towards Christ is explicitly noted by Dr. Eckardt. Calling it the "attitude of acceptance-rejection," he traces all its involutions. His conclusion is: "We reject the Jews in order to reject Jesus as the Christ. Hatred of the Jews is the result of our hatred of Christ." Antisemitism, in short, is anti-Christianity: "Christianity is a Jewish religion, Christ was a Jew." These are almost the very words of Freud, whom Dr. Eckardt quotes:

> One might say that they all [the antisemitic peoples of the Christian world] are "badly christened"; under the thin veneer of Christianity, they have remained what their ancestors were, barbarically polytheistic. They have not yet overcome their grudge against the new religion which was forced on them, and they have projected it on to the source from which Christianity came to them . . . The hatred of Judaism is at bottom hatred of Christianity. . . .[2]

The pogrom is the reenactment of the Crucifixion. We think of the iconography of Chagall's moving canvases and recall Berdyaev's passionate indictment: "Throughout all their long history, Christians have by their deeds crucified their Lord, crucified him by their anti-Semitism. . . ." What Berdyaev suggests, Dr. Eckardt makes explicit:

> Christianity has placed itself in the forefront of the forces persecuting the Jewish people . . . The whole Christian world carries the accessory guilt, if not the full guilt, for Adolf Hitler's slaughter of the Jewish people . . . The

Christian world failed to act . . . Is it not possible that our indifference to Nazi persecution
of the Jews and our own complicity in anti-
Semitism can only be explained in terms of our
hatred of Christ?

Dr. Eckardt distinguishes his interpretation from
the similar one of Maurice Samuel in *The Great
Hatred* on the ground that his own implies the confession of Jesus as the Christ. Yet, as he himself points
out, "even if this confession is false, the fact that men
believe Christ to be the one who calls them to a
unique decision is sufficient to provoke the kind of
reaction to Christ we have noted." His real difficulty is
to get his specifically Christian explanation to cover
the well-known cases of pre-Christian and non-Chris-
tian antisemitism. Without in the least wishing to
detract from the cogency of his analysis, I would venture to suggest that the conception which I have formulated and which Dr. Eckardt quotes twice in his
book seems to meet the problem more adequately:
"Bringing God to the world, Israel must suffer the
hatred and resentment of the world against God and
his Law. Israel as the Chosen People is Israel the Suffering Servant of the Lord . . ."

The theologies of the various schools within
Christianity have important implications for
the "Jewish question." The touchstone is the
kind of claim the Church makes for itself and its
creed. Religious absolutism, Dr. Eckardt rightly believes, is a most dubious position. Absolute devotion
to anything short of the Absolute is idolatry; and the
fruits of idolatry are bound to be evil even when the
relative value that is "absolutized" is something so
exalted as Church or creed.

By attributing absolute value to the Church, and by
equating the creed of the Church with absolute truth,

Roman Catholicism falls under the category of religious absolutism. So does Protestant fundamentalism for its absolutizing of the Bible and its claim to possess the true faith "once for all delivered unto the saints." It is in the inordinate pretensions of each, and in their more or less explicit "religious anti-Judaism," that Dr. Eckardt finds the peril of antisemitism. His criticism, though severe, perhaps too severe, is not undiscriminating; for he notes carefully the elements in the thought and action of each Church that tend to mitigate its theoretical intransigence and to make for a more humane attitude towards the Jews.

Nor is Dr. Eckardt less sparing in his analysis of absolutist strains in neo-Reformation theology, which "finds its one Absolute in the conviction . . . that Jesus is 'Christ' or 'Lord.' " (Dr. Eckardt himself shares this conviction, but not in its absolutist form.) "Neo-Reformation thinkers are unanimously opposed to anti-Semitism," he affirms. "Nevertheless, we are able to find statements which may contain seeds of *Judenhass,* even if this is not intentional." The examples Dr. Eckardt brings forward, however, are not very convincing. Surely we must allow the actions of the neo-Reformation Churches in Europe, especially in Holland, to stand as a practical exegesis of their theology.

The record of the Continental Church—the German and Dutch Churches in particular—receives critical consideration from Dr. Eckardt. The revolting idolatry of the German-Christian movement is bitterly excoriated; and the hesitant, uncertain, though finally triumphant course of the Confessional Church is very effectively described. Particularly interesting is the account of the tortured dialectic of those who, like Gerhard Kittel, tried to square their Evangelical tradition with their Nazi affirmations.

The German Confessional Church took its final stand only after much faltering and hesitation. But for the Dutch Church there never was any question as to the position it would take. It denounced antisemitism and the idolatrous pretensions of the Nazis in its very first pronouncement, and never budged thereafter. One's attitude to the Jews, it proclaimed soon after the Nazi invasion, would be the criterion of obedience to God: "He who stands up against Israel stands up against the God of Israel." The profound feeling of Dutch orthodoxy for the absolute claims of God and the chosenness of Israel stood it in good stead.

Religious relativism denies that a particular historical reality or belief, even the Christian Church and the Christian religion, can be equated with ultimate truth or attributed absolute value. This is well expressed in John Donne's pregnant saying" "Nothing hinders our own salvation more than to deny salvation to all but ourselves." It was Christian liberalism that first made relativism explicit. Dr. Eckardt does not fail to credit liberal Christianity with this achievement, just as he does not spare his criticism of its hopelessly inadequate theology. Rather too severely he scores the liberalist reduction of religion to ethics; but only incidentally does he touch upon the liberal's blindness to the irreducible element of evil and unreason in the nature of man, which is particularly pertinent in dealing with antisemitism.

Neo-reformation relativism is the position Dr. Eckardt himself takes, and I think it is one of profound appeal. Only God is absolute; everything else, literally everything else—society, institution, belief, or movement—is infected with relativity and stands under divine judgment. As Karl Barth holds, once we confess and acknowledge one God, everything which is not God is "criticized, limited and made relative." According to H. Richard Niebuhr, "The great source of evil in life is the absolutizing of the relative, which in Christianity takes the form of substituting religion, revelation, church or Christian morality for God." The power of this radical

God-centered relativism as a dynamic of social action is magnificently borne out in the theologically-grounded social philosophy of Reinhold Niebuhr. It is in terms of this Christocentric relativism that Dr. Eckardt develops his own theology of the "Jewish question." The line of thought, as he unfolds it, is impressive. Judaism and Christianity "stand in a dialectical relationship, each one presupposing the other." Judaism performs an indispensable function in the divine economy, "that of testifying against paganism on behalf of a universal God of justice." Dr. Eckardt asks: "Can the Christian Church supersede the Synagogue in the struggle against paganism? No, because the Church is itself subject to pagan distortions." And he quotes Paul Tillich: "The Church is always in danger of losing her prophetic spirit. Therefore the prophetic spirit included in the traditions of the Synagogue is needed as long as the gods of space are in power, and this means to the end of history."

Dr. Eckardt underlines Tillich's thesis thus:

> The demonic forces of pagan particularism are especially powerful in the Church simply because the Church is *accepted* and *established* in the local and national community . . . The Church is not as fitting a representative of the God of justice as are the Jews, "despised and rejected of men" . . . The Church worships the gods of space by attempting to limit divine grace to a particular historical reality, as for example a priestly class or sacrament or a particular book or denomination. Against all idolatries Judaism protests: "Hear, O Israel: the Lord our God is one Lord."

"Synagogue and Church," says Tillich, "should be united in our period in the struggle for the Lord of time . . . When all those who struggle for the Lord of history, for his justice and truth, are united under persecution and martyrdom, the eternal victory in the struggle between time and space will become visible, the victory of time and the one God who is the Lord of history." The Christian Church cannot therefore be said to have superseded Israel as God's Chosen People. "The Church is no more the successor of Israel," Dr. Eckardt believes, "than Israel is the successor of the Church . . . Even in the matter of the Messianic role of Israel and the Church, the Church cannot say unequivocally that it has succeeded Israel."

On this theological basis, Dr. Eckardt attempts an analysis of the ambiguity of Jewish existence, of the universal and particularist elements within it, of its ethnic and religious aspects, and thereby also of the meaning of Zionism. His discussion of these matters, informed and well meant, suffers, I think, from a double defect: (1) the author tends to forget his own warning that one cannot apply the category of "nation" to the Jews if that term is taken in its usual sense, and (2) he fails to follow out his own insight that the problem of Jewish universalism and particularity must ultimately be dealt with on a *theological* level if justice is to be done to the "mystery of Israel." On the whole, the section on Zionism is the weakest in the book.

Now what is the significance of Dr. Eckardt's theology of the "Jewish question" for the fight against antisemitism?

Since antisemitism is ultimately rooted in man's rebellion against God, it can cease only when that rebellion is broken—in principle, for every man through repentance and grace; in history, only with the coming of the Kingdom of God. Yet antisemitism must be fought on every level, since on every level there is always the possibility of achieving a better balance of justice and a greater measure of decency in human relations. The Kingdom of God transcends history; but, as Reinhold Niebuhr points out, "the *agapé* of the Kingdom of God is a resource for infinite develop-

ments towards a more perfect brotherhood in history."
Even though the final elimination of evil is not possible
in the life of man, yet, under judgment of God, man
must never rest so long as there is evil to be fought;
and what is antisemitism, theologically considered,
but the quintessence of evil? The tension between the
historical and the suprahistorical is here, as elsewhere,
the source of an unfailing dynamic of social action.
Judaism and Christianity, Dr. Eckardt tells us,
"stand in dialectical relationship, each one presupposing the other." And he continues: "It is the vocation of
Israel to proclaim and maintain the divine Law; it is
the vocation of the Church to preach the Christian
gospel of divine grace." For the believing Jew, however,
this dialectical reconciliation cannot be satisfactory.
Judaism cannot relinquish the gospel of grace.
    It is to be regretted that Dr. Eckardt did not extend
his researches to the writings of Franz Rosenzweig, for
there he would have found a viewpoint on the relation
between Judaism and Christianity well worth his
thought. Rosenzweig, too, in his profound insight,
regarded Judaism and Christianity as standing in
organic, dialectic relation to each other, but in a rather
different way and on a rather different level. His conclusions on many points are remarkably similar to
those reached by contemporary Christian theology.
The following quotations are from the summaries of
Rosenzweig's views compiled and documented by
Agus[3] and Glatzer:[4]

> [Both Judaism and Christianity] are divinely
> ordained . . . Judaism and Christianity to-
> gether constitute the "Überwelt"—that is, the
> stage of being which brings eternity into time
> and God into the world . . . Both are, in a real
> sense, revealed religions, and each one, in itself,
> is only part of the truth . . . In symbolic lan-
> guage, Rosenzweig calls Judaism "the eternal
> fire" and Christianity "the eternal rays." While
> Israel stays with God, Christianity constantly

marches toward Him, subduing the world on
His behalf . . . The Jew can bring the world to
God only through Christianity . . . Borrowing
the analogy of the medieval poet, Judah Halevi,
Rosenzweig compares historical revelation to a
seed, which, falling to the ground, draws the
necessary elements to itself, producing a tree,
in the fruit of which it reappears again. The
ground is the pagan world; the tree is Christianity; the seed is Judaism . . . Christianity
contains within itself the tension between
paganism and [God] . . . Christianity could not
long remain an effective force for redemption if
Israel did not remain in its midst . . . The ancient people of the Book persist and, through
persisting, continue to be to him [the Chris-
tian] a reminder of his duty as Christian.
Whenever the pagan in the Christian soul rises
in revolt against the yoke of the Cross, he vents
his fury on the Jew. Thus anti-Semitism cannot
be understood simply by an examination of
present-day conditions. It stems from the tension in the Christian mind between revelation
and paganism. "The fact of anti-Semitism, age-
old and ever-present though totally groundless,
can be understood only by the different functions which God has assigned to the two communities—Israel to represent in time the eternal Kingdom of God, Christianity to bring
itself and the world toward that goal." (Agus)

The two religions, or rather views of reality,
are treated as equal representations of the
truth—equal before God . . . In contrast to
Judaism as "the eternal life," Christianity is
presented as "the eternal way" . . . The Christian is sent out to conquer the unredeemed
world. He is, however, always in danger of lapsing into paganism . . . And the Christian Jew-
hatred (heir to the pagan Jew-hatred), directed
against the tacit critic, the Jew, is in reality self-
hatred, hatred of the Christian's own incompleteness, of his own "Not-Yet." (Glatzer)

To a believing Jew, who tries to see the meaning of history under God in its entirety, Christianity thus presents itself as the "Judaism of the Gentiles." The two are of one piece, are essentially *one* religious system: Judaism facing *inward* to the Jews, Christianity facing *outward* to the Gentiles, who through it are brought to the God of Israel. Between them there is the unity and tension of a dialectic that will be resolved only with the resolution of history.

Notes

[1] This essay by Herberg appeared originally as a review of Dr. A. Roy Eckardt's book *Christianity and the Children of Israel* (New York: King's Crown Press, 1948).

[2] Sigmund Freud, *Moses and Monotheism* (1939), pages 144–5.

[3] Jacob B. Agus, *Modern Philosophies of Judaism* (1941), chap. III, "Franz Rosenzweig."

[4] Nahum N. Glatzer, "Franz Rosenzweig," *Yivo Annual of Social Science,* vol. I (1947).

—10—

Anti-Semitism on the Left

WHAT DO THE PRAGUE TRIALS FORESHADOW? AN ANALYSIS AND SOME PROPOSALS FOR THE WEST.

(1953)

Communist purges are nothing new. Since the large-scale "liquidations" of the late 1930's, the world has become accustomed—perhaps too accustomed—to periodical bloodlettings in the Soviet Union, performed against the nightmare background of state-managed "trials" and "confessions." Nor is there anything particularly novel about the removal and elimination of high-placed leaders in the satellite countries. In the few brief years of Soviet domination, every satellite country of Eastern Europe has undergone a purge, some indeed two or three in succession. Such things are more or less taken for granted as part of the mechanics of Communist rule.

And yet the recent trials in Czechoslovakia, in which Rudolf Slansky and thirteen co-defendants, most of them veteran Communists of high rank, confessed to the most atrocious crimes and were sentenced to death or long terms of imprisonment, did send a spasm of horror through the Western world. For these trials were not just routine purge trials. A new element seemed to be present not hitherto associated with Communist purges. Eleven of the fourteen persons accused were Jews and the indictments as well as the whole course of proceedings emphasized that fact. Nor was their Jewishness merely an irrelevant detail. They were accused of being the agents and accomplices of a vast Jewish conspiracy to promote "American imperialism" and to undermine the Soviet Union, the Czechoslovak "People's Republic," and the "people's democracies" of the other satellite states. The world Zionist movement, anchored in the state of Israel, was presented as the instrument of this conspiracy, and John Foster Dulles, Henry Morgenthau, and David Ben Gurion—along with Konni Zilliacus, the British leftist!—were denounced as among the foreign ringleaders. Two Israeli citizens in Czechoslovakia, one of them a prominent member of the pro-Soviet Mapam, were charged with, and of course confessed, active participation in the conspiracy, while the Israeli envoy in Prague was accused of espionage and his recall demanded. The "confessions" of Slansky and the other defendants were lurid with details of this vast and worldwide Jewish-Zionist plot; the whole thing, in fact, took on the appearance of a horribly real stage production of the half-forgotten Protocols of the Elders of Zion, translated into the vocabulary of present-day Soviet Communism.

What can this new Soviet anti-semitism mean? What are its roots and sources? How indeed is a Communist anti-semitism possible; is not anti-semitism something that only the "extreme right" goes in for? And what do the Prague trials foreshadow as to the fate of the Jews behind the Iron Curtain and as to the course of Soviet policy in the coming period?

These questions go right to the heart of an understanding of contemporary Communism.

I t is important to realize that despite first appearances, there is nothing essentially new about the Prague trials except the crassness of the anti-semitism. Anti-semitism in more or less explicit form has for decades been an instrument of Communist strategy, and since the middle 1930's at least, increasingly part of the Soviet way of life. Peter Viereck has shown, in a valuable appendix to his *Conservatism Revisited,* how anti-semitism was used by Stalin as a political weapon as far back as 1907. He and others have also laid bare the Communists' frequent resort to anti-semitism in the course of the political struggles and inner-party conflicts of the late 1920's and 1930's, in Russia, in Germany, in France, even in America. In September 1929, for example, during some bloody conflicts in Palestine in which the Communists took the anti-Jewish side, the Yiddish-language organ of the Communist Party in this country, *Freiheit,* published a series of cartoons full of fat, hooknosed, grosslooking Jews, with dollar-signs all over their moneybags and bellies, shooting innocent Arabs or else brandishing the whip over poor undernourished working girls. The cartoons could easily have appeared, later on, in Streicher's anti-semitic gutter press.

But until the middle 1930's, this kind of thing was largely a matter of the unscrupulous utilization of an effective political weapon, although even then an undercurrent of authentic anti-semitic sentiment could be detected. But around 1936 or 1937, most students of Russian history would now agree, something new appeared that was to have fateful consequences: a vociferous Great Russian chauvinism emerged as part of the Communist party "line" and increasingly of official Soviet life and culture. Russification of the Ukraine, White Russia, and other non-Great Russian lands in the Soviet empire was carried through at great cost. Western orientation and Western connections came to be regarded with rabid suspicion and finally fell under official ban.

The Nazi-Soviet pact naturally intensified the anti-Western orientation; and even the war years, in which Russia was at least formally associated with the Western powers, did not seriously affect the basic attitudes. Great Russian chauvinism was maintained at a fever pitch during the war, and after the war, particularly with the onset of the "cold war," all stops were removed. Any "Westerners" who remained in Soviet public affairs were wiped out, and a Russian "nativism" of a most extravagant sort became the official ideology of Soviet life, tirelessly inculcated through every device of modern education and propaganda. Soviet writers and historians who so much as hinted that non-Great Russian traditions or achievements might have certain value were ruthlessly purged, while every great Russian figure, no matter how vile or atrocious, was exalted if only he could be shown to have contributed something to the glory of the Russian nation. We find the Soviet penchant for claiming every discovery and invention made on the face of the earth rather ludicrous, but we may be assured that the mood out of which such absurdities grow is anything but funny: it is something deeply sinister and laden with the most serious significance for the world.

In this upsurge of chauvinism, the Jew was inevitably the first and chosen victim. All signs of independent Jewish life in the Soviet Union were wiped out—press, literature, schools, the remnants of Jewish social and cultural institutions. Even Communist party papers published in Yiddish or intended for Jewish readers were eliminated. And the Jews themselves became the object of a savage state-organized campaign of hatred and suspicion. The public services, especially the military and the foreign branches, were purged of Jews. Jewish writers and minor officials, most of whom had almost succeeded in forgetting that they were Jews, were suddenly dragged out and pilloried as "homeless cosmopolitans" and "passportless intellectuals," and Jew-baiting became a recognized Soviet activity. Soviet anti-semitism has since passed through several phases, reflecting domestic and foreign developments, but no one can doubt that it is today an integral part of Soviet life and culture.

The Prague trials may therefore be properly considered as an extension of Soviet anti-semitism to the satellite countries of the Soviet orbit. For that very reason, a closer examination of the factors involved may prove instructive.

The common explanation in the West is that the Jews were again being cast in their immemorial role of "scapegoats." There is considerable truth in this view as far as it goes. When Ludwik Frejka, the author of the Czech Two and Five Year Plans, was made to confess, "I sabotaged in such a way that there is still rationing of electricity and food," or when others solemnly swore that they had diverted shipments intended for domestic use or the Soviet Union to the State of Israel, the point is pretty obvious. Scapegoats to take up popular resentment and to be saddled with the blame for destructive economic politics were clearly needed; but why the Jews, of whom there are only thirty-five thousand in all Czechoslovakia, and why the fantastic machinery of a vast "Zionist conspiracy?"

The fact of the matter seems to be that there exists a certain fear of Zionism among the Communist masters of Eastern Europe. To the beaten, crushed, and miserably oppressed Jewish masses of Romania, Hungary, Poland, Czechoslovakia, and Russia, Zionism comes as a revivifying gospel of hope and the State of Israel beckons with the promise of refuge.

In Russia, Zionism was outlawed in the first years of the new regime; in the satellite countries, its status was increasingly precarious, until there too it was outlawed. But the growing appeal of Zionism among the Jewish masses could not be held in check. The Soviet masters had a startling demonstration of this fact when in 1949 Golda Myerson came as the first Israeli ambassador to Moscow; the Jews of Moscow, braving the police, gave her an overwhelming spontaneous and unmistakably pro-Zionist ovation. There can be no doubt about it: this kind of primitive and unideological Zionism has become a real force among the Jews under the Soviet yoke and therefore an intolerable challenge to Communist totalitarianism. That is at least part of the reason for the fantastic structure of a worldwide "Zionist conspiracy" on which the Prague trials were erected.

By the same token, the Prague trials were unquestionably intended to play a part in the current Soviet intrigues in the Near and Middle East. For a brief period, Moscow supported the State of Israel, but informed observers pointed out at the time how short-lived this "pro-Zionist" orientation was bound to be. As far back as the spring of 1949, American Communists were denouncing the government of Israel as a "tool of American imperialism," and of course they were merely echoing Moscow's instructions.

Today the Soviet line is definitely anti-Israel; it is directed at stirring up large-scale violence on all fronts and at establishing "connections" with the leading forces in the Arab world. Obviously, the Prague trials can be turned to good use for these purposes. It is significant that the anti-semitic theme of these trials was highlighted most openly and crudely in the propaganda directed to the Arab lands. Reports from these areas indicate that these efforts have not been entirely without success.

T he current Soviet strategy in the Near and Middle East is linked with something considerably more far-reaching in its implications, and that is the new over-all Soviet line as it emerged in recent months. There seems to be every indication that alongside of a renewed Popular Front appeal where that can bring results, Soviet strategists are beginning to develop another kind of front, a front designed to embrace ultra-nationalist forces as well as politically active elements of pro-fascist background and orientation. The demonstrative Communist support given not only to Peron's rabid anti-Americanism but also to his economic program is an aspect of this policy, and so also is the systematic playing up to barely disguised Nazi hopes and ambitions in Eastern Germany. Moscow seems to be promoting a new kind of "national Communism" with a special appeal to reactionary, extreme nationalist elements, whose resentments make them anti-American and therefore fit partners for the Kremlin.

In this sinister game, anti-semitism can be a powerful weapon, and it is one that Stalin knows well how to use. It should not be forgotten that over large parts of Europe the anti-semitism which the Nazis fomented and exploited is very far indeed from being dead; it is this smoldering Jew-hatred that the masters of Soviet strategy are counting on arousing and utilizing for their own purposes.

But, as I have already suggested, it would be wrong and misleading to attempt to reduce the matter simply to deliberate and calculated strategy. Anti-semitism has become part of the Soviet Communist *ethos*, both in the "motherland" and in the satellite states. The elimination of every "alien infection" is, of course, a

corollary of the chauvinism that dominates official
Soviet life and that serves also as ideological preparation for a war with the West. "One by one, every group
[in the satellite states] with any kind of tie beyond the
Iron Curtain has been eliminated," James Reston reports in the *New York Times* for November 27, 1952.
"First, it was the politicians who had ties with the
West; then the intellectuals with their 'dangerous' notions of free inquiry; then the Roman Catholics with
their ties to the Vatican; and now it is the Jews. . . ."
Whenever any society falls to deifying itself—and that
is surely what totalitarianism, Soviet or Nazi, does to
a consummate degree—the Jew stands out as a challenge and reproach. The Jew bears this witness quite
apart from any views or desires of his own; he may be
eager to surrender everything and make his peace with
the regime on any terms—but he will not be permitted. Merely by being a Jew, merely by existing, he is an
affront to self-idolizing totalitarianism. "Inevitably,"
Roger Shinn notes in a perceptive study of religion and
history, "Hitler found in the Jews *(by their very existence)* and in faithful Christians (by their religious
protests) a reminder of the universalisms . . . he could
not tolerate"[1] [emphasis mine.—W.H.]—and what
Shinn says about Hitler is becoming increasingly true
about Stalin.

    To the Communist hierarchy intent upon "coordi-
nating" the bodies, minds, and spirits of the masses in
the Soviet Union and the satellite states of the Soviet
empire, the Jew is indeed an indigestible element: do
what he may, he cannot quite conform and lose himself in the idolatrous self-enclosed culture of the totalitarian state. Somehow he is *in,* but never entirely *of,*
the world in which he finds himself; somehow, for all
he may say or do, he cannot quite throw off the
shadow of the supra-national "ghost-people" to which
he belongs. He is an anomaly, an insufferable anomaly. Hitler felt this with all the insane passion of his
hatred, and Stalin has begun to feel it too. Hitler could

not understand it, nor does Stalin; nor for that matter do we, fully: it is part of the "mystery of Israel." But it is a fact, a hard and gritty fact, an intolerable fact for the totalitarian; and it is this fact that in the last analysis provides the clue to the weird phantasmagoria of the Prague trials.

What do the Prague trials portend for the Jews behind the Iron Curtain? There are, according to our best reckoning, some two and one half million of them—two million in the Soviet Union, two hundred fifty thousand in Romania, one hundred thousand in Hungary, eighty thousand in Poland, and thirty five thousand in Czechoslovakia. It seems only too likely that these are destined for a fate very like that which the Jews of Europe a decade ago met at the hands of Hitler. The tempo will be slower; above all, the way will be more devious; but except for those who can be rescued and the few able to lose themselves and somehow erase their Jewish identity, the end will be extinction. This is beginning to be sensed by the Jews behind the Iron Curtain; the wave of suicides reported among Jews in Czechoslovakia and Romania, and to some degree also in Hungary and Poland, painfully recalls memories of what happened in Germany when the true meaning of Nazi anti-semitism first began to dawn on the still incredulous Jews.

Czechoslovakia is first among the satellite states; why, it is hard to tell—perhaps the anti-semitic drive fell in with the desperately savage clique struggle among the top Communist leadership. But after Czechoslovakia will come the others. Ana Pauker, a bitterly self-hating Jew from an Orthodox Jewish family, is waiting her turn in Romania, and in Poland the Israeli minister has, like his colleague in Prague, been charged with espionage and expelled. The Budapest Communist press is repeating with monotonous ferocity, "Hungary too is plagued with Zionism," and incredibly enough similar officially-inspired outbursts are to be heard in East Germany, which one would think to be singularly free of the Jewish "taint." The demon of anti-semitism has been let loose once more; who can foretell the havoc it will work before it can be curbed again?

What can we of the outside world do? Frustratingly little, but that little is important. We must in the first place rouse ourselves out of the moral insensibility into which an endless succession of horrors has beaten us. For our own spiritual health if for no better reason, we ought to speak up and give expression to what remains of what was once known as the "conscience of mankind." This applies to all of us—to the government, to the churches, the schools and colleges, the professions, the labor movement, the civic organizations. There ought to be no group or institution in this country that does not make its voice heard.

If we are really aroused to the horror of the situation, we will be ready to give of our aid and resources to rescue whom we can from the slaughterhouse behind the Iron Curtain. This is a task of simple humanity: every Jew rescued is a human life saved.

Finally, the Prague trials and the whole situation which they reflect ought to teach us something about the enemy we face. The so-called "East-West" conflict is not simply an economic, political, military, or even ideological conflict, although it is all of these. It is above all a religious struggle, a struggle of vast spiritual forces, a conflict of ultimate loyalties. As we confront Communism, we are wrestling not merely with "flesh and blood," but also and above all with "principalities and powers," with the "world rulers of this darkness," with the "spiritual hosts of evil in the high places," to employ St. Paul's stirring terminology. And for this struggle it is just possible that we need other weapons and another spirit than those we have so far been able to muster.

Notes

[1] "Religious Faith and the Task of the Historian," Liberal Learning and Religion, ed. Amos N. Wilder (New York, 1951), p. 70.—"The Jew," says H. Sacher, "is always in a minority. He can hardly avoid putting a note of interrogation after every dogma or convention" ("Revenge on the Prophets: A Psychoanalysis of Antisemitism," Menorah Journal, Fall 1940).

—11—

Anti-Semitism Today

(1954)

Organized anti-Semitism is definitely on the wane in this country; even the "hidden" forms that make themselves felt in prejudice and discriminatory practices are in decline. According to the best information, overt anti-Semitism seems to have emerged on a national scale in the wake of the Nazi victory in Germany. In the middle thirties, hundreds of anti-Jewish groups, openly racist and pro-Hitler, sprang up throughout the country, and launched well-financed programs of incitement and rabble-rousing. These activities evoked a certain response, not only among German sympathizers in the big cities but also among smalltown Americans in the middle- and southwest, who still remembered the great stir the Klan had made a decade before. Anti-Semitic hate-mongering became something of a national problem for the first time in American history.

With Pearl Harbor, organized anti-Semitism went into eclipse, and the various anti-Jewish groups scurried for cover, remaining more or less hidden throughout the war. The war over, they emerged briefly, trying to stage a comeback by exploiting the disillusionment and revulsion of feeling they confidently expected to set in. The venture proved a failure, and by 1947, organized anti-Semitism had reached its lowest ebb. Since then, the manifestations have been too insignificant to permit any attempt to define a trend.

It may be noted, however, that there does not exist at the present time a single anti-Semitic organization of national scope; the local "hate" groups have declined in number (less than fifty today as against some one hundred and forty a dozen years ago), in membership, and in influence, and are showing signs of inner disintegration. Most of them have shifted the burden of their agitation away from overt anti-Semitism to "nationalist" issues of a political character, or even to local and municipal issues which they see some possibility of turning to account. There would seem to be no question that anti-Semitism, in its organized form at least, has virtually ceased to exist in American life.

It is not so easy to draw any firm conclusions as to the incidence and extent of anti-Semitism in its "hidden" forms, although here too all the evidence would seem to show that discrimination in such matters as employment, housing, public accommodations, and educational opportunities has markedly declined, though by no means altogether disappeared. By and large, it may be said that the country today is as free from anti-Semitism as it has been in living memory.

Just what it is that has made for this notable development is by no means clear. There are those who trace it in part to the continuing economic prosperity which this country has been enjoying in the decade since the end of the war; this prosperity, they say, has eased the tensions of life, at least on the economic level, and has made a large tolerance possible. Whatever projection of fear and insecurity is generated by the anxieties of our time, moreover, is today directed not so much against any group within the national community as against the Kremlin and its "fifth column." In a way, the reality of the peril in which the nation finds itself under threat of Communist totalitarianism has tended to make less necessary the nightmare elaboration of imaginary objects of hatred and fear on which anti-Semitism thrives, though it cannot be denied that anti-Communism here and there has itself tended to take on a tinge of this nightmarish quality.

Be this as it may, it is a fact that a profoundly significant change in public feeling has taken place during the past fifteen years: *Anti-Semitism, and racism generally, have become disreputable.* No one who has followed the cross currents of public sentiment in the twentieth century will be inclined to minimize the vast significance of this shift. Before 1933, overt anti-Semitism was, of course, frowned upon in respectable circles as something rather vulgar and uncultured, but (with rare exceptions) there was no intensity of feeling about it. Racism, particularly in the form of the "Nordic myth," was widespread and unashamed, and it had its explicit anti-Semitic overtones. Henry Adams' shocking outburst against the Jews did not prove so shocking to the cultured ladies and gentlemen in his circle a half-century ago. As for the mass of the people, a kind of traditional anti-Semitism at low tension prevailed; it did not lead to any serious outbreaks, but there could be no doubt that it was there. In the 1920's, this kind of anti-Semitism contributed something to the rise to power of the Ku Klux Klan in certain parts of the country, although it should be remembered that the Klan was primarily anti-Catholic and anti-Negro, rather than anti-Jewish. It was in the decade of the 1930's, as I have suggested, that anti-Semitism in virulent and organized form emerged, to be brought to an abrupt halt by America's entry into the war against Nazi Germany. Somehow as a consequence of the war and the immediate postwar years, public feeling underwent an extraordinary change. Racism had been part of the demonic ideology we were fighting, and racism, particularly anti-Semitism, now suddenly became *un-American.*

It is not necessary to insist that large numbers of Americans do not harbor racist or anti-Semitic feelings; of course they do. What is meant is that even they are reluctant to admit these sentiments to themselves and to others, and tend to disguise them in various ways. No military man of our time would dare issue an order such as Grant's notorious diatribe against the "Hebrew merchants" of Vicksburg, and overt anti-Semitism is today the mark of death in politics, as it was not, by and large, before the second World War. The great fact is: *it is no longer decent, respectable, or "American" to be anti-Semitic.* Even the frequent occurrence of "Jewish names" on the growing list of Communist spies, subversives, and "infiltrators" has not, so far as can be judged, had any real effect in stimulating a new anti-Semitism. The change in public feeling brought about by the war and the immediate postwar period seems to be deep and far-reaching.

Yet we cannot leave it at that. The problem of anti-Semitism in America is a problem that goes beyond shifts and fluctuations in public sentiment, no matter how profound. It is, in a real sense, the problem of the historical life of Western man, touching as it does, our society and culture at its every point. A serious attempt to assess the sources and prospects of anti-Semitism in this country would, in effect, amount to a diagnosis of American life. I shall not undertake any such project, but I think that certain considerations on this head might prove of interest and relevance.

Anti-semitism is obviously in some sense related to the status and role of the Jew in the non-Jewish world. *Sociologically, the Jew in the non-Jewish world is the very incarnation of marginality;* other groups there are which are marginal in this or that society, under such and such circumstances—but the Jew is marginal everywhere, at all times, under all circumstances. No matter how well-adjusted to his culture the Jew may strive to be, he remains marginal: *in* his world, but never quite *of* it. The American Jew is almost quintessentially American, or rather middle-class American; whatever it is that makes the middle-class American middle-class and American, the Jew is even more so. Yet this consummately middle-class American is never fully or entirely a part of middle-class America; there is something about him that forces him, to his own discomfort and often against his will, to stand "outside of" and "over against." Frequently he can make no sense of this anomaly, and would like nothing better than to be rid of it, but it is there and he knows it.

For in the last analysis, the Jew cannot really be totally adjusted to his environment, try as he might. He is the very embodiment of *non-adjustment*. He cannot so identify himself with any culture, society, or institution that he no longer lives in tension with it. There is a dimension of his Jewishness that forces him beyond the limitations of every particular society and culture: his very being as Jew is trans-national, trans-social, trans-cultural. He is therefore, no matter how sincerely he may regard his society and culture as his own, in a deeper sense an "outsider," and "alien," a man unadjusted and unadjustable. The description of the position of the early Christians given by the author of the Epistle to Diognetus fits the basic actuality of Jewish existence in the non-Jewish world with uncanny precision:

They dwell in all countries, but only as sojourners. As citizens, they share in all things with others and yet endure all things as if they were strangers. Every foreign land is to them as a native country, and every land of their birth as a land of strangers.

S ociologists and historians not blinded by doctrinaire formulas or get-rich-quick methodologies have long noted and documented this strange anomaly of Jewish existence, and the events of our generation have hammered it home into the consciousness of Jew and non-Jew alike. Sociologists and historians have also proffered "explanations," and these "explanations" have not been without their limited relevance; but it is becoming increasingly clear that the fact itself somehow escapes all empirical explanation and remains a "mystery," an aspect of the larger "mystery of Israel," "The Jewish people," sociologist Carl Mayer has pointed out, "represent a sociologically unique phenomenon and defy all attempts at general definition" ("Religious and Political Aspects of Anti-Judaism," *Jews in a Gentile World*). Theologians, Christian and Jewish alike, have related this "unique phenomenon" to the vocation of Israel in the divine purpose: "Like an alien body, . . . it gives the world no peace . . . so long as the world has not God" (Jacques Maritain, *A Christian Looks at the Jewish Question*). If we take this standpoint and attempt to see the problem from this angle, we may perhaps catch a glimpse of the ultimate significance of the marginality and unadjustability of the Jew under an aspect not open to sociological analysis, though immediately relevant to social life.

In any case, the fact itself cannot be ignored or denied. And it provides us with a fruitful approach to the problem of the sources and long-range prospects of anti-Semitism in this country.

I n the first place, it must be stated quite plainly that anti-Semitism is not something that can be eliminated through changes of culture, ideology, or social system. It is inherent in the "Jewish" situation, that is, in the projective reaction of the non-Jew (pagan, "Christian," or post-Christian) to the "offense" of Jewish existence. Anti-Semitism manifests itself in many and various forms, on many and various levels: it is sometimes virulent, sometimes latent; it makes use of this or that ideology; it expresses itself in terms of economic, social, cultural, political, or religious conflict, or some combination of these. But however it manifests itself, its manifestations do not constitute its "essence," its underlying continuity and enduring meaning. The "essence" of anti-Semitism is the obverse of the "mystery of Israel," and like the latter, it is both historical and trans-historical. Certain consequences, moreover, would seem to follow as to the incidence of anti-Semitism in the changing context of history. Because the Jew is inescapably an unadjustable "outsider," he is directly imperilled by any tendency towards a closed, totalistic society or institutional set-up, which in its very nature cannot tolerate any form of "outsideness" or non-adjustment. On the other hand, the Jew is most secure in a society that is loose, open, pluralistic, full of undefined, unregimented areas, with plenty of room for non-adjustment, and with a certain tolerance for dimensions of existence beyond nation, state or culture. Perhaps this point would be illumined, and made relevant to the Jew's continuing history, by thinking of the Jew as the embodiment of the "principle" of anti-idolatry. To the extent that any society or culture tends to absolutize itself into the all-in-all of human existence, it becomes idolatrous and is impelled to see in the Jew a threat and a challenge, an indigestible element, who, do what he may, can never quite conform and lose himself in the idolatrous whole.

All history bears witness to this fact. Whether it is the Hellenistic effort to establish a divinized world culture, or the medieval attempt to exalt Christendom as indeed the very City of God, or the Nazi and Communist ventures to erect a divinized total state in which all life would be absorbed: it is always the Jew who is the enemy to be singled out and destroyed. The Jew, by his very being, is at once an offense to, and the bad conscience of, an idolatrous, self-enclosed culture. He is the "eternal outsider" and therefore the "eternal scapegoat," the victim of every society whose unity is monolithic.

I n so far as these comments have any validity at all, they would seem to cast some light on the problem of anti-Semitism in the United States. In a very real sense, the position of the Jew in contemporary America is the most favorable that he has enjoyed in the long history of the Diaspora. He lives in a society as loose and pluralistic as is to be found in the world, a society in which he is completely enfranchised as citizen and in which cultural chauvinism (of the kind so pervasive in France) is almost unknown. Despite the calamity-howlers on the "right," the United States is the most unregimented country on the face of the earth; official institutions are only a part of the web of society, and all varieties of groups, "minorities," and associations jealous of governmental interference, flourish in disorderly freedom. No one expects a man's life to be totally encompassed in, or defined by, the official institutions of state, society, and culture; indeed, the very notion of such totalism is abhorrent to American tradition and the American "way of life." In such a situation, the Jew can feel really secure and at home, because the trans-national, trans-cultural, trans-political aspects of his Jewishness fall most naturally into the wide areas of "openness" which our society permits.

There is still another factor which renders present-day America a particularly favorable environment for the Jew. For American society is, almost literally before our eyes, being restructured from a land of ethnic-immigrant groups into a national community harboring within itself three sub-communities in terms of which almost every American identifies himself. These three sub-communities,which are increasingly coming to constitute the primary contexts of social location for the American of today, are the so-called "religious communities," Protestant, Catholic, and Jewish. These are American structures in the most literal sense of the term. For the American Jew, this sociological development means that his "separateness" as a Jew is no longer regarded as a mark of his foreignness, but rather as a sign of his Americanness. He is a Jew, and is everywhere recognized as legitimately a Jew, in the same sense in which his neighbor is a Protestant or a Catholic. Unlike Europe, America knows no national or cultural separateness ("minorities"), except as a transitional immigrant phenomenon pending full Americanization; it knows racial separateness unfortunately only in terms of inequality and discrimination. But it does know, and approve of, diversity and separateness of religion as something permanent and equal.

The Jew who identifies himself as a Jew in terms of his religious community is therefore doing something that every "right-thinking" American understands and applauds. Jews in the past were often granted the possibility of Jewish existence, but only at the price of exclusion from the larger society and culture. With the emancipation, the Jew as a human being was enfranchised and given equal status, this time, however, at the price of his Jewishness and Jewish identity. In present-day America almost for the first time, the Jew can find his assured and equal status in American society not despite, but *because* of, his identification with the "Jewish community." This is all so new that we still do not fully appreciate its tremendous significance for American life.

I do not think any one at all conversant with American reality will care to deny that the conditions of Jewish life in this country are indeed extraordinarily favorable. Yet there are darker sides to the picture as well, and it is necessary to examine them along with the others. American society is still loose, open, and pluralistic, remarkably immune to nationalism and chauvinism as the Old World knows them. But this kind of society has hitherto been closely associated with America's favored position of security and self-confidence. This position is now being seriously undermined by world developments. Objectively, America has lost its security—it finds itself in extreme and unprecedented peril as it confronts the Communist world in Europe and the Far East—and this development has already begun seriously to affect the basic consciousness of the American people. There is an anxiety and tension today unknown since the days of the Civil War; it is manifesting itself in all sorts of disturbing ways. In other words, the openness and looseness of American society, upon which everything depends, is being threatened by the course of history; a certain constriction is beginning to set in, perhaps inevitably, but not without its ominous overtones for the Jewish future.

There is another factor, operating much more subtly, but likely to turn out in the long run to be of even greater significance, and that is the growth of "other-direction" in American life. I here employ the terminology and categories developed by David Riesman in his important work, *The Lonely Crowd*. Riesman, it will be recalled, distinguished three types of character structure—tradition-directed, inner-directed, and other-directed—which he finds predominating at different times in different societies, and yet also entering in different degrees into the characterological picture of a society such as ours. Tradition-direction, so characteristic of primitive and stable peasant societies, implies the transmission from generation to generation, and the internalization by each succeeding generation, of a fairly fixed pattern of folkways as a code of behavior. Inner-direction is something very different; in inner-direction, what is internalized by each succeeding generation is not a traditional pattern of folkways but a set of "principles" or "goals," together with an inner drive ("conscience") that keeps the individual true to them: the inner-directed man operates with a kind of built-in gyroscope, which keeps him steadily on his course, driving ahead for the fulfillment of his purposes.

In our society, tradition-direction has disappeared, if indeed it ever existed; inner-direction is dominant, but a new character type is emerging, the type designated as *other-directed*. Instead of possessing a built-in gyroscope which keeps him true to his course, the other-directed man operates with a kind of built-in radar apparatus, which is ceaselessly at work receiving signals from the person's "peer group" and adjusting him to the situation indicated by those signals. The greatest horror of the other-directed man, that which renders him so acutely uncomfortable, is to feel "unadjusted" or "unsociable," at odds with his environment. The "morality" of the inner-directed type becomes "morale" for the other-directed; "character" becomes "personality"; moral indignation and intolerance give way to a kind of all-embracing tolerance—of a very curious kind. The large tolerance of the other-directed man has its limitations: it is tolerant of everything except inner-direction and non-adjustment, which it brands as "anti-social" and which it finds to be both unhealthy and sinister.

Now the Jew is almost by definition the inner-directed man; almost by definition, too, he is the unadjusted and unadjustable. What can the bland, friendly, tolerant, and sophisticated suburbanite junior executive and his wife, who so largely compose the other-directed group in our society, make of this?

Anti-Semitic in the crude old sense of the term they cannot be; they are far too tolerant and sophisticated for that. But on the other hand, they are emotionally repelled and disturbed by the inadjustability of the Jew, by what they must regard as his self-assertiveness and restlessness. To the man whose supreme law of life is adjustment and conformity, and that is essentially the kind of man the other-directed type is, the Jew, who by virtue of his Jewishness "gives the world no peace," must appear, as I have said, to be something unhealthy and sinister. He has nothing against the Jew, this other-directed man, he really hasn't; but the Jew must give up his Jewishness, not his "religion," of course—every decent person has his "religion"—but his being "different." Yet how can a Jew help being "different"? That is what his Jewishness means.

It is this invisible, almost undefinable spread of other-direction, and not the "McCarthyism" with which liberals love to make our flesh creep, that is the primary factor making for conformity in our society. The threat of a stifling conformity is real, but it is much more subtle and insidious than a largely imaginary political terrorism. Political terrorism, where it exists, we can take care of, but how are we to deal with the spread of the cult of "adjustment"? This constitutes a real problem for our entire American culture, but above all for the American Jew, who would necessarily be the first victim of a culture in which other-directed conformism allowed no room for "eccentricity," individuality, and non-adjustment.

This, I think, is a fair picture of the situation as it confronts us today. The situation is complex and intricate; it does not lend itself to simple black-and-white formulation. Anti-Semitism in the United States is not, or is only minimally, a problem of the lunatic-fringe "hate" groups, which have never been so weak as they

184 FROM MARXISM TO JUDAISM

are today. Anti-Semitism in the United States is basically a problem of the inner dynamics of our society and culture. If we can preserve our loose, pluralistic, open society against the constricting forces, political and cultural, that history and social development have unleashed, then we need not be unduly disturbed about the danger of anti-Semitism in this country. "Every age," Solomon Schechter once said, "has its own idolatry, and the Jew is always the chosen victim of the Moloch in fashion." If we can somehow manage to preserve our society and culture from falling into the idolatries of totalism and worshiping the Moloch of total "adjustment," we will be able to look with some assurance to the future of the Jew in America and to the future of our American hope. For better or for worse, the future of the Jew in America is bound up with America's future.

Part IV

RELIGION AND PUBLIC LIFE

—12—

The Sectarian Conflict Over Church & State

A DIVISIVE THREAT TO OUR DEMOCRACY?

(1952)

More than once in 1952, Rabbi Philip S. Bernstein has had occasion to note with concern the marked deterioration of Protestant-Catholic relations in this country and to warn Jews against exacerbating these tensions. Indeed, the widening conflict within the Christian community may well constitute a major problem far overshadowing in its immediacy the more familiar problem of Jewish-Christian relations. Many thoughtful observers, Catholics, Protestants, and Jews, are disturbed over the cleavage, but few display any real conception of the gravity of the threat which this increasing divisiveness holds for democracy; and fewer still show any clarity on the fundamental issues involved. Some sober, searching thinking seems to be called for if a sharpening of the conflict is to be avoided.

I

Although it would be a mistake to see the situation primarily in terms of isolated issues, it is still worth noting that the most persistent occasion for Protestant-Catholic conflict in recent years has been the issue of church and state in education. Even in this problem many aspects are intertwined. There is first the question of basic attitude to the public schools, particularly in connection with the religious day schools which the Catholic Church and some Protestant denominations are conducting. But there is also the question of the role of religion in the public school pattern, and finally the most hotly debated issue of governmental assistance to non-public schools. Each of these questions, moreover, is loaded with all sorts of implications that range far beyond the particular points of conflict.

We must remind ourselves that the American public school system is preeminently the creation of American Protestantism. It was established because of the deep Protestant concern for popular education and assumed its characteristic "secular" form because of the American Protestant distaste for ecclesiastical control. This was particularly true of the Congregationalists in New England and of the Baptists and Methodists in the more outlying parts of the expanding nation. To this very day, these groups feel a deep emotional—one might even say, proprietary—interest in the public school, despite the vast changes that have taken place in the inner character of public education in the course of the past half-century. And yet American Protestantism, for all its strongly affirmative attitude to the public schools, has in the past two decades become increasingly troubled over certain developments in public education and has been trying, though not very successfully, to understand and deal with the problems that these developments have created.

When the public school system first came into being in this country, it was nonsectarian rather than nonreligious. And nonsectarian in those days meant all-Protestant, since non-Protestant groups were of relatively little social or cultural importance in most parts of the nation. It was taken for granted that religion, in the generalized Protestant sense, was the foundation of education, though the schools were not of course to be used to favor one Protestant denomination over another. In its *ethos,* the public school, as well as the community at large, was Christian and Protestant.

To a minor extent, this is still the case in some parts of the country. But by and large, under the impact of newly emerging social and cultural forces, the public school system has become something very different from what it was three-quarters or even half a century ago. By the end of the great immigration the country had ceased to be almost entirely Protestant; Catholics now make up a large part of the population, and so do Jews in certain urban centers. For these and like reasons, nonsectarian may no longer be equated with a generalized Protestantism; indeed, it has rapidly come to mean dissociation from religion as such. An important contributing factor has been the very considerable secularization of the Protestant consciousness itself in recent years. Administratively, public education today reflects the changing structure of the American community, with Catholics and Jews occupying positions of influence side by side with Protestants. But even more striking is the change in the *spirit* of public school education, which today is no longer religious, neither Catholic, nor Protestant, nor Jewish; it is, by and large, *secularist,* even militantly so. (I use this term to signify an outlook on life in which man is held to be sufficient unto himself and God disappears as an unnecessary, outmoded concept.) The most influential educational philosophies and centers of teachers' training are self-consciously secularist, and so is educational practice in almost every part of the country.

From non-sectarian, the public school has become "neutral" in matters of religion. As a matter of fact, many charge that this neutrality is no neutrality at all, that in effect our schools positively indoctrinate a substitute faith, arguing: "If you teach no religion at all, you are teaching a new cult, secularism."

It would be a mistake to think that most Protestants in this country have such a picture of the situation. Most of them take the "neutrality" of the public school at its face value, and indeed see little difference between what emerges from this "neutrality" and their own "liberal" Protestantism, which (I use the words of a well-known Protestant teacher) is "sometimes not to be distinguished from humanism or mere ethical culture." But many important Protestant leaders are deeply concerned, even alarmed. This concern, however, has resulted in very little, in part because of a confusion of counsel, but primarily because Protestant concern about the schools has been thoroughly bedeviled by an all-absorbing preoccupation with the Catholic "menace."

Catholics, on their part, never took the American public school to their hearts as did the Protestants. It was not of their creation, and did not in the beginning, any more than it does today, accord with their philosophy of education. Catholics cannot see any proper education for Catholic children that is not religiously grounded and religiously oriented, and that of course means grounded and oriented in Catholic faith. For the Catholic, therefore, the only really acceptable educational institution, particularly on the lower levels, is the church school, usually parochial in structure and administration. Indeed, probably half of the Catholic children of public school age in this country attend parochial schools; in 1947–48, there were 2,305,000 students in elementary church schools, 482,000 in secondary schools, and nearly 300,000 in more advanced institutions. The total number of Catholic schools was 10,900. The goal has never changed: "A seat in a Catholic school for every Catholic child." This is not a matter of varying "opinion"; it is a matter of conscience and canon law.

Increasingly, certain Protestant groups, alarmed at the effects of public school "neutralism," have moved in the same direction. Protestant religious day schools are by no means new to this country; in 1830, there were some 400 Lutheran schools in the United States, but these schools were motivated as much by ethnic cultural reasons (to preserve the German "language and heritage") as by religious; and to an extent, this is still true of the "Continental" churches in this country, though decreasingly so. The present-day movement toward religious day schools under Protestant auspices is predominantly of a religious character. Compared to the vast Catholic structure, the Protestant day schools still amount to very little: in 1951–52, the over-all figure was 2,904 schools, almost entirely elementary, with about 190,000 pupils.[1] But this represented a 61 per cent increase over 1937, and the movement is definitely gaining momentum. Its philosophy is well expressed in the recent pronouncement of President Henry Van Dusen of Union Theological Seminary: "Unless religious instruction can be included in the program of the public school, church leaders will be driven increasingly to the expedient of the church-sponsored school." The Protestant position, even where it favors church schools, is by no means so categorical as the Catholic. On the whole, Protestants regard the church school not as something desirable in itself, but as something which they may some day have to accept because of the "religious failure" of the public school. Protestantism is still "for" the public school, but no longer without reservations.

The spread of the religious day school has brought to the fore the problem of the relation of the government to such schools. This problem cannot be solved simply by repeating the hallowed formula of the "separation of church and state." It is agreed on all sides that the First Amendment definitely prohibits the *establishment* of an official religion, or government action in any way *favoring* one religious denomination over another. But does it bar any and every governmental action extending aid *on an equal basis* to all religious groups? To this there is no unequivocal answer. In the McCollum case (1948), the Supreme Court seemed to say yes, but that is not what it said four years later in the New York released-time case. We may leave the exegesis of Supreme Court decisions to the proper authorities; it is, however, a matter of historical fact that neither in the minds of the Founding Fathers nor in the thinking of the American people through the 19th and into the 20th century, did the "separation of church and state" imply unconcern with, much less hostility to, religion on the part of the government. Indeed, the promotion of religion was always held to be one of the prime objects of public education. The Northwest Ordinance, a classical expression of early national concern with education, laid it down that: "Religion, morality, and knowledge being necessary to good government and the happiness of mankind, schools and the means of education shall forever be encouraged. . . ." And Jefferson himself, writing thirty-one years after the ratification of the First Amendment, stated in a discussion of public education: "It was not, however, to be understood that instruction in religious opinion and duties was meant to be precluded by the public authorities, as indifferent to the interests of society. On the contrary, the relations which exist between Man and his Maker, and the duties resulting from those relations, are the most interesting and important to every human being, and the most incumbent on his study and investigation." Public education in this country generally operated on this principle during the earlier part of its history.

It is simply not true, despite the widespread notion to the contrary, that there exists or has ever existed in the United States a "high and impregnable wall of separation between church and state" (Justice Black's words). The federal government has always given, and continues to this very day to give, direct aid to religious bodies, though of course on an equal and nondiscriminatory basis. It pays the salaries of chaplains, religious functionaries selected by their churches and assigned to the various branches of the armed services; it has appropriated and spent money, at various times and in various ways, to spread Christianity among the Indians; it exempts churches and church institutions from taxation. As for church schools, provided they meet the specified educational standards, they are fully recognized and protected by law (Oregon case, 1925); their certificates and credentials are received on a par with those of public institutions; they are the recipients of considerable financial assistance from the public authorities (textbooks, Cochran case, 1930; bus transportation, Everson case, 1947; school lunches, National School Lunch Act, 1946). The question, therefore, is not so much *whether* church schools may be aided by public authorities, as *in what way* and *to what extent* they may be so aided; this question, however, cannot be answered with abstract formulas; there is, moreover, wide disagreement on it, not only among but within the various denominations.

The position of the Catholic Church is that church schools (of all denominations, of course) are morally entitled to receive aid from public funds on a par with the public schools because they too perform a public educational function. In addition to religious instruction, which is itself of public concern, these schools, it is contended, carry on a program of general education specified by public authority and accepted as fulfilling a public requirement under the compulsory school laws. Catholic parents complain that they are saddled with a double burden, being obliged to support the schools which their children attend as well as the public schools of which they cannot in conscience make use. Catholic spokesmen are emphatic in denying that they are "against" the public schools. They are quite ready to support them for the use of those who find them acceptable; they do, however, ask that their own schools, which they say occupy a "semi-public" status, should also be supported.

This attitude is more or less in line with the practice prevailing today in Canada, Great Britain, and other countries, where denominational schools regularly receive support from the public funds. And it has been advocated in this country by many non-Catholics, by some even who are devoid of any religious concern but are moved by considerations of what they take to be equity and the public welfare. I recall a surprisingly large number of people with whom I discussed the matter, people of all shades of opinion, who, "off the record" and "in principle," substantially endorsed the Catholic claim, but hastened to add that it was out of the question to advocate it in public at this time. And indeed it is, as Catholics themselves acknowledge. As a matter of immediate strategy, therefore, Catholics have concentrated on federal legislation to supply the so-called "auxiliary" services (social services, textbooks, transportation, etc.) to parochial school children along with those in the public schools.

Here they have come into conflict with much of official Protestant opinion. Protestants have tended to denounce all proposals to extend auxiliary services to church school children on the ground that they are merely disguised forms of "direct aid," thus constituting a breach in the "wall" that is alleged to separate church and state. Some Protestants are so conscientiously committed to this view that they specifically include their own institutions among those which they demand should be barred from public aid; Baptist leaders have protested against government assistance to their own church hospitals, and there have even been voices raised against the public maintenance of military and prison chaplains. But on the whole, the crusade for the preservation of the "wall of separation" between church and state in education as elsewhere is conceived by Protestants as a defensive campaign against Catholic "aggression."

This feeling, which most Protestants seem to share, is the key to the current embitterment of Protestant-Catholic relations. "The nub of the whole matter," comments the *Information Service* of the Federal (now National) Council of Churches in its September 10, 1949 issue, "clearly seems to be the fear on the part of non-Catholics of the political power and purposes of the Roman Church." This defensive psychology appears to be rapidly permeating American Protestantism. Practically every Protestant leader with whom I discussed the matter referred in vague but disturbed terms to the "ominous growth" of the Catholic Church in this country and expressed grave concern over what the future might bring. One, in fact, called my attention to the "portent" of a Catholic majority (52 per cent, he said) in Holland, a classic land of Protestantism. "In another generation," he exclaimed almost in anguish, "we'll be a minority; America too will be Catholic."

This fear of Catholic domination of the United States would at first hardly seem to be borne out by statistics. In the twenty-four-year period from 1926 to 1950, church membership in this country increased by 59.8 per cent, as against a 28.6 per cent increase in population. The Catholic Church grew by 53.9 per cent, but in the same period Protestantism increased by 63.7 per cent. Most of this increase, however, was accounted for by the expansion of the Baptists, especially the Southern Baptists. The churches affiliated with the National Council, the authoritative national federation of Protestant (and some Eastern Orthodox) churches, grew only by 47.7 per cent, falling short of the total increase as well as of the comparable Roman Catholic growth. It cannot be denied that in those parts of the country in which Protestants and Catholics come into direct contact, particularly in the urban centers, the Catholic Church has been making notable headway.

More important even than the numerical growth is the comparatively vigorous institutional and cultural life of the Catholic Church, its really amazing skill in presenting itself attractively to the public, and the intellectual prestige it has lately acquired from the work of a number of artists, philosophers, and writers, mostly European. Catholic churches are full, where Protestant churches so frequently remain half empty. Catholic thinking, at least as seen from the outside, is aggressive and self-confident, whereas so much of American Protestant thinking, except on the very highest seminary levels, is thoroughly enfeebled by the abstractions of "liberalism" and "humanism." Catholic religiosity has "substance" and numinous power, while—here one can cite ample testimony from Protestant self-evaluation—much of American Protestantism is little more than an emotionalized ethic and gospel of social service. And finally, Catholicism possesses unity and a fighting front, while Protestantism is fragmented, divided, and apparently incapable of any positive cohesion. Protestantism, in short, has lost the initiative; it has been thrown on the defensive, and what is worse, it has developed a defensive minority-group psychology in which it sees itself threatened on all sides. All this is not my own judgment, although I would not disagree with it; it is substantially the analysis presented to me by a distinguished Protestant theologian, who expressed himself more concerned over the "loss of morale" in Protestantism than over the plots the Catholic Church might be hatching.

Not that there is no ground whatever for concern over Catholic power in the United States. Catholic power does constitute a problem for American democracy. It constitutes a problem first in the sense in which every potent special-interest group makes the workings of the democratic government more complex. Beyond that, it is a problem because the traditionally formulated political and social aims of the Catholic Church sometimes run counter to what most Americans hold to be the democratic way of life. The claims and pretensions of the Church to legal primacy, if not monopoly, in religion, education, and family relations, seem to many, as they do to me, incompatible, in their authoritarianism, with the liberal, pluralistic foundations of American democracy. Equally disturbing is the Church's tendency to confuse, or rather to equate, the spiritual interests of Christianity with the political and social, even economic, interests of the Vatican, the hierarchy, and the Church establishment. Catholics in America have sometimes employed the preponderance of power that has fallen to them in certain localities and states in ways that have given much offense to other citizens.

All this may be granted. And yet the Protestant reaction has surely been far out of proportion to any conceivable threat or provocation. There has been, in ordinary Protestant thinking on the Catholic issue, little or no sense of the relativities of politics, little or no sense of the very considerable gap that often separates the phrases of a creed from the actualities of a concrete situation. Everything is painted in the strongest colors without discrimination or mitigation, so that the resulting picture is often grossly false even when some of the details are in themselves not very far from the truth. "Most American non-Catholics," Reinhold Niebuhr points out, "have a very inaccurate concept of Roman Catholic political thought and life. In this concept, it is assumed that if Catholics anywhere had their way, they would at once build a political structure as much like Spain's as possible. . . . Some forms of deduction proceed on the assumption that on any and every question a religious group's political attitude is dictated by its basic creed. Others do not even bother to start with the group's actual basic tenets but with the tenets which the group is imagined to hold." ("Catholics and Politics: Some Misconceptions," *The Reporter*, January 22, 1952.)

Consider the vast excitement over the "Vatican appointment." Whatever may be thought of the wisdom or the timeliness of President Truman's proposal to appoint an envoy to the Vatican, only by the wildest stretch of the imagination can it be regarded as unconstitutional or a threat to the religious liberties of any group of Americans. Yet American Protestantism reacted to this proposal with a violence and fury that have given thoughtful Protestants pause. The only unity of which American Protestantism seems capable, it has been sadly noted, is unity against Rome. The major "Vatican lesson," *Social Action* (Congregational) for May 1952 ruefully points out, is that "the psychological basis of much of American Protestantism lies in a negative rejection of Roman Catholicism. . . . The one emotional loyalty that of a certainty binds us together as Protestants . . . is the battle against Rome."

It is this Protestant negativism and defensiveness that has opened the way for the strange alliance between a considerable section of American Protestantism and the forces of militant secularism, an alliance organizationally represented by the Protestants and Other Americans United for the Separation of

Church and State (POAU), launched some years ago under the auspices of *Christian Century* and a number of high Protestant dignitaries. It is this negativism and defensiveness that has made possible the "similarity" which a Federal Council of Churches report notes "between official Protestant pronouncements and the typical secularist position on all points discussed [in relation to religion, education, and the schools]." It is this that has driven American Protestants to interpret the separation of church and state to mean the abdication by religion of its responsibilities in large areas of social life and the abandonment of those areas to non- and anti-religious influences and control. American Protestantism has, in fact, conceded the primary secularist claim that religion is strictly a "private affair" and that culture and social life are to be built on humanistic foundations. But humanism and secular autonomy are now on the wane in many quarters, and so, by an astounding reversal of intention, American Protestantism, itself more religiously concerned today, has withdrawn as a religious influence in many areas, and thus has actually left the field free to the Catholic Church, which has naturally not failed to take full advantage.

This anomalous situation is very well illustrated in the attitude adopted toward public education. The theory behind public education is traditionally very different in the United States and Great Britain from what it is on the Continent, and the difference is instructive. In Britain and America, the government engages in public education because experience has shown that this is the only way to provide adequate educational opportunities for the mass of the people; the government is obliged to do what individual and group effort has not been able to do. But wherever individuals or groups (non-governmental agencies) can offer the proper facilities, they

200 FROM MARXISM TO JUDAISM

have the clear right to compete with the government and are entitled to recognition and encouragement by the public authorities. In other words, the Anglo-American system is pluralistic. In France and in other Continental countries, however, the concept of public education, at least as propounded by its accredited spokesmen, is something altogether different. Public education is there looked upon not as a device for making up the inadequacies of individual or group effort, but as a "natural" activity of the state designed primarily to inculcate a common doctrine and create a uniform mentality among the citizens. From this point of view, private individuals and non-state institutions (churches, for example) really have no business in the field of education; they are rivals of the state and such rivalry is held to be intrinsically "antisocial," even though under the circumstances it may have to be grudgingly tolerated. Of late, we have become increasingly aware that this doctrine, despite its popularity among Continental liberals and socialists, and its spread in this country, has a marked authoritarian, even totalitarian, potential.

The Supreme Court decision in the celebrated Oregon case (*Pierce v. The Society of Sisters,* 1925) made explicit the fundamental American doctrine on the question: ". . . the right of parents to direct the rearing and education of their children, free from any general power of the state to standardize children by forcing them to accept instruction from public school teachers only." To this may be added a reference to a more recent decision (*Prince v. Massachusetts,* 1944) in which the Supreme Court declared: "It is cardinal with us that the custody, care, and nurture of the child reside first in the parents, whose primary function and freedom include preparation for obligations the state can neither supply nor hinder." This is a doctrine that goes beyond particular Supreme Court decisions since it lies at the foundation of any tenable conception of constitutional democracy and the limited-power state.

American secularist educators are by no means rec-

onciled to this doctrine. They still feel that the public
school is the only "proper" educational institution
which all children should somehow be required to
attend in order that they might be protected against
"divisive cultural influences" and helped to acquire a
"common outlook." These educators are constantly
on the watch for some way of circumventing the intent
of the Oregon decision. "A more satisfactory compulsory education law," Professor John L. Childs of
Teachers College, Columbia, has suggested, "might be
one in which the state would require each child to
spent at least one half of the compulsory school period
in the common, or public, schools. Many Americans
hope that states will pioneer in legislation of this sort."
Max Lerner is even more forthright. He has declared
that "the first step [in breaking down the separation
principle] was taken when the Supreme Court decided
that a religious group could not be compelled to send
its children to the public schools, and it could run its
own schools at its own expense."

I n a way, of course, Max Lerner is right. State
recognition, toleration, and protection of religious
schools *is* a breach in any *absolute* separation of
church and state. But such absolute separation was
never contemplated by the Founding Fathers, is not
written into the Constitution, and has never been the
policy or practice of the federal or state governments;
it is simply the eager dream of those who have no
patience with the traditional faiths and desire them
replaced by their own non- or anti-religious faith. The
startling thing is that so much of Protestant opinion in
recent decades has tended to go along with this concept of separation, to the point indeed of applauding
Paul Blanshard when he denounces Catholics for affirming that they would disobey a law banning religious schools and compelling them to send their children to the public schools. Surely it needs very little
unbiased consideration to recognize that this attitude,

even though held by Catholics, is thoroughly in line with the best of democratic tradition, which has always tended to check pretensions of the state to a monopoly of social and cultural life.

The fact of the matter seems to be that in its inordinate preoccupation with defending itself and America against Catholic aggression, American Protestantism has surrendered intellectual leadership to non-religious forces and has been fighting the battle for the separation of church and state under essentially secularist slogans. In making "Blanshardism" its semi-official philosophy, it has done no service to Protestantism, to Christianity, or to the cause of religion in general.

Nor has it done any service to democracy. For "Blanshardism," or rather the anti-Catholic animus it articulates, seems to me to constitute a much more serious threat to our democracy than any of the horrendous Romanist plots that Paul Blanshard has been so fond of conjuring up to make our flesh creep.

"This kind of reasoning," says Reinhold Niebuhr, who has never hesitated to criticize Catholic teaching and practice, "is highly damaging to the mutual understanding upon which a democracy must rest. Democracy requires more careful and discriminate judgments about friend and foe, particularly since a political foe upon one issue in a vast welter of issues may be a friend on another." American Catholicism is not without its share of responsibility for what Milton Konvitz has called the "frightening growth of Protestant-Catholic tensions," but the major share, it seems to me, must be laid at the door of Protestantism, which has permitted itself to be maneuvered into an unreal, contradictory, and panicky position.

II

What has been the Jewish position on these questions? Strictly speaking, of course, there is no single Jewish position, even less so than there is a single Protestant position. But there are the pronouncements of responsible Jewish leaders and institutions, and the stand taken in particular cases by accredited Jewish agencies, from which a "Jewish position" is often inferred by other religious groups and the public at large. Insofar as such a "Jewish position" may be thus inferred, it is one that, in my opinion, should give grave concern to every American Jew.

It can hardly be denied that the intervention of most Jewish bodies in the current church and state controversy has generally not tended to allay the sharpening religious cleavage in American life. It has often operated on principles in some ways even more extreme and basically secular than those of the Protestant guardians of the "wall of separation." It has shown little understanding of the realities of the educational and cultural situation as it confronts the religious parents, Christian or Jewish, who take their faith seriously as the substance of life.

Religious leaders, lay educators, and parent groups have in recent years become increasingly disturbed over the religious vacuum in public education, which is felt to have serious moral and spiritual consequences. With due consideration to constitutional limitations, a number of ways have been proposed to strengthen the foundations of the public school by compensating for the religious emptiness that is devitalizing it. President Van Dusen of Union Theological Seminary and former Dean Weigle of Yale have suggested a "common core" program of religious education; others have looked to various schemes of dismissed or released time to provide a partial remedy. All of these suggestions are animated by the desire to preserve the public school for its undoubted merits as a vehicle of cultural unification and to obviate the necessity of establishing separate church schools.

How has the most vocal Jewish opinion reacted to these proposals? Almost entirely in the negative, and often violently: spokesmen representing a broad segment of organized Jewish community life applauded the Supreme Court's invalidation of released time in the McCollum case, joined in the opposition to the New York released-time program and criticized the Supreme Court's validation of it, opposed Bible readings in schools, opposed the New York Board of Regents' suggestion of a daily prayer, and of course opposed every variety of aid, direct or indirect, to religious schools. I am not trying to make a case for any of these plans or programs; they may all be very properly criticized as impracticable and ineffective. Indeed, it may even be contended, with considerable show of reason, that under present-day American conditions, with the bewildering diversity of cult that characterizes our "pluralistic" society, the practical difficulties in the way of any acceptable program of religion in the schools are quite insuperable. Perhaps that is so; nevertheless, all of the plans and suggestions, however impracticable in themselves, do point to a problem that cannot be ignored, especially by those who are so much concerned with repelling attacks on the public schools.

What answer have Jewish spokesmen had for parents and educators? Only this: school and religion must be kept rigorously apart; no religion in the school or in any conceivable association with it; let the schools inculcate in the children "basic moral principles" and "social ideals," the place for "religion" is the home and the church. Leaving aside the psychological unreality of this kind of mechanical division of labor, which flies in the face of any view of personality held by modern educators themselves, how can such a reliance upon secularism to do the work of moral education be supported? It is, in fact, not supported. It is simply taken for granted that "basic moral principles" and "social ideals" are autonomous, and can and should be established, validated, and inculcated without reference to religion. Nor is any consideration given to the actual realities of the American situation. Many argue that the literally god-less education the child receives in the typical public school can be supplemented by religious teaching in home and church. But is it not usually the school, where the child spends so much of his waking day, that exerts the primary formative influence on his mind, so that whatever reactive influence there is, is likely to proceed from school to home, rather than the reverse? The school establishes the priority and prestige of ideas, and the child who becomes habituated in the school to thinking about things exclusively in secular and naturalistic terms is more than likely to regard the religious ideas he finds floating around in the average home or church with indifference and contempt. Even if the home could "compete" with the school for the soul of the child, the very idea of such competition is somehow shocking.

I am not suggesting that all parents feel this way or that the school is exclusively guilty in what has been called the "religious illiteracy" of the American child. On the contrary, many parents, including many Jew-ish parents, see no place for religion in education, or for that matter in life, and are quite happy at the extrusion of religion from the schools. Even those parents who have a religious interest only too easily tend to overlook their own failure and the failure of the church in their readiness to blame everything on the school. This must be admitted, and yet it remains a fact that to large numbers of our citizens the present pattern seems increasingly questionable. For it operates to make the schools into instruments acting toward and sanctioning the rejection of religion, whereas we Americans are, as the Supreme Court put it in its opinion on the recent New York released-time case, "a religious people whose institutions presup-pose a Supreme Being." Need we recall that while the propaganda of atheism is protected under the Constitution, non- or anti-religion has never enjoyed and does not now enjoy the same public status as religion? Anyone who doubts this might try proposing that the federal government commission atheist or "humanist" chaplains on a par with Jewish and Christian! The public school system, in effect, reverses this relation, and makes non- or anti-religion the established "religion" in public education. No wonder that dissatisfaction with the public school has been growing.

Operating under a concept of the separation of church and state more rigid and absolute than even that held by doctrinaire Protestants, most Jewish community leaders have paid little heed to these realities of the situation. A few, however, particularly among the Orthodox, have attempted something positive. Feeling it undesirable or impossible to change the character of the public schools, and realizing the feebleness of most after-school religious education, they have undertaken to set up religious day schools. The movement is not yet very extensive. In 1945, there were perhaps 75 such schools throughout the country; today, there may be over 150, almost all operating on the elementary or pre-elementary levels; attendance has increased rather more than proportionately. Some Jewish religious leaders outside the Orthodox camp have endorsed the idea, but lay opinion seems generally opposed. Significant too is the line taken by some of its religious advocates in justifying it. In a recent article defending Jewish day schools, the Orthodox author was very much concerned to point out that after all Jewish day schools were utterly different from analogous Catholic institutions because the latter, the Catholic schools, employed their own religiously oriented textbooks, while the Jewish schools used the regulation public school texts and curricula, merely adding a program of "Jewish knowledge." Note how the "separation of church and state" is now duplicated *within* the Jewish school: all subjects of everyday, worldly concern, presumably not only mathematics, but also history, the social sciences, literature, and the humanities, are taught from the same textbooks and in the same secular spirit as in the public schools; to this is added some "Jewish instruction," which must in the nature of the case be peripheral and irrelevant. So far has the spirit of secularism permeated Jewish thinking, even that which considers itself strongly religious.

It is worthwhile to pause at this point. I think no informed observer will care to deny that of all comparable groups in this country Jewish community leaders, including leaders in the synagogue, appear most secular-minded in their public attitude on matters of church and state. In what other American religious community, for example, could the proposal be advanced by respected *religious* leaders—out-Blansharding Blanshard—that American democracy be made the vehicle of a "common American faith" to be inculcated in the public schools with all the paraphernalia of a religious cult? Yet that is substantially the idea that a number of influential Jewish religious leaders have been advocating for years. By and large, those who speak for the American Jewish community, whether they be rabbis or laymen, religious individuals or men and women avowedly secular-minded, judging by their public expressions, seem to share the basic secularist presupposition that religion is a "private matter"—in the minimizing sense of "merely private"—and therefore peripheral to the vital areas of social life and culture, which latter are held to have non-religious foundations. Jewish religion, if it is affirmed at all, is affirmed as something to be *added to* the common life, not as something that pervades and is inextricably involved in every aspect of it. Separation of church and state is thus at bottom advocated as only one phase of the separation of religion from life.

How has this come about? How could this isolation of religion from life have arisen in a group with whom religion has traditionally been conceived as coterminous with life? Basically, it seems to me, it is due to the conviction, widely held though rarely articulated, that because the Western Jew achieved emancipation with the secularization of society, he can preserve his free and equal status only so long as culture and society remain secular. Let but religion regain a central place in the everyday life of the community, and the Jew, because he is outside the bounds of the dominant religion, will once again be relegated to the margins of society, displaced, disfranchised culturally if not politically, shorn of rights and opportunities. And it is well to note that by "religion" in this context, it is Christianity that is meant, and by Christianity primarily Catholicism. The Catholic Church still remains in Jewish eyes the standard form of Christianity and the prime symbol of Christian persecution. Deep down, it is Catholic domination that is feared. Such are the anxieties that beset many American Jews, and it cannot be denied that they have much justification. Religion has so often with good conscience been turned into an instrument of exclusive privilege that one can well understand the feeling of those who believe that democracy requires the eviction of religion from public life and the thorough secularization of society.

Yet in the long run such a view is short-sighted and self-defeating. Jewish survival is ultimately conceivable only in religious terms; and when its *raison d'être* is whittled down to a few "supplemental" factors, survival itself loses much of its meaning. Furthermore, a thoroughly "de-religionized" society would make Jewish existence impossible. But a "de-religionized" society is itself for long impossible. Ultimately, man finds the autonomy which secularism offers him an intolerable burden, and he tends to throw it off in favor of some new heteronomy of race or nation, of party or state, that the idolatrous substitute faiths of the time hold out to him. In such idolatrous cultures, the Jew is inevitably the chosen victim; the lesson of history and contemporary experience seems clear on this head. The way of the Jew in the world is not and never will be easy; it will certainly not be made any the easier by his throwing in his lot with an increasingly total secularism, which both invites and is helpless to withstand the demonic idolatries of our time. The American Jew must have sufficient confidence in the capacity of democracy to preserve its pluralistic libertarian character without any *absolute* wall of separation between religion and public life. After all, the Jew is no less free in Britain, where church and state are more closely linked.

The fear felt by Jewish leaders of the possible consequences of a restoration of religion to a vital place in public life is what throws them into an alliance with the secularists and helps make their own thinking so thoroughly secular. They feel the problem primarily in terms of the Jew's status as member of a minority group. The minority-group defensiveness, which we noted in contemporary Protestantism, is of course far more intense among Jews; indeed, it may probably be said to be the most influential determinant of the policy and activities of many leading Jewish groups in this country. Public assistance to religious schools, it is felt, would mean overwhelmingly aid to Christian, primarily Catholic schools, with Jewish schools sharing to a relatively insignificant extent. Released or dismissed time, in most communities, would mean the invidious isolation of a handful of Jewish children amidst large numbers of their Protestant and Catholic schoolmates.[2] Reading the Bible would necessarily mean reading the "Christian" Bible, that is, the King James version, even if only Old Testament passages were read.† And so on. In every case, the "intrusion" of religion into public life, it is feared, would result in situations in which Jews would find themselves at some disadvantage—greater isolation, higher "visibility," an accentuation of minority status. Uneasy memories of past persecution and oppression are stirred up. The most elementary defensive strategy would seem to dictate keeping religion out of public life at all costs; hence the passionate attachment of American Jews to the secularist-Protestant interpretation of the principle of separation of church and state. It is a question, however, whether defensive strategy is, after all, the highest wisdom of Jewish existence and survival.

Another factor in the situation must be mentioned, as it applies to both Protestants and Jews. It is perhaps best formulated in the brilliant *mot* of Peter Viereck: *"Catholic-baiting is the anti-Semitism of the liberals."* How true this is anyone can see by scanning the week's supply of "liberal" literature. For some such "liberals," Catholic-baiting is a clever device of anti-anti-Communism. Of course, Communism is a menace, they tell us, *but*—the "of course-*but*" sequence is characteristic—*but* there is "also" the Vatican, the "center of world reaction." To many more, anti-Catholicism is simply a syllogism of liberal logic, hallowed by decades of liberal tradition; after all, didn't the Pope "endorse" fascism, and isn't McCarthy a Catholic? It matters little that the facts are quite otherwise, that the Catholic labor and social program in America, for example, is as advanced as anything the country can show; that the Catholic Church is one of the most important forces fighting Communist totalitarianism on a world scale; and that the attempt to equate the two as like perils to American democracy on the ground that both alike are authoritarian systems is dangerous nonsense and could lead to disaster, should it ever come to influence national policy. Stereotyped "liberal" slogans seem far more appealing than the most obvious facts can ever be, especially when they permit one to work off one's fears, prejudices, and aggressions in an approved fashion. How else account for the great popularity of Mr. Blanshard's extremist *Communism, Democracy, and Catholic Power,* among so many "liberal" Jews and Protestants? And so, through a combination of historical memories and fears, the negativism of minority-group defensiveness, and the insidious operations of the "liberal" equivalent of anti-Semitism, it has come about that Jewish intervention in the current controversies over church and state has only too often tended to strengthen the forces of secularism and to intensify the friction between Catholics and Protestants. Here we would do well to heed Rabbi Bernstein: "Do not take any satisfaction from the current Catholic-Protestant frictions. . . . A poisoned atmosphere of divisiveness and distrust will engulf us." (*Time,* May 5, 1952.)

III

The interests of religion, of democracy, and of sound community relations without which American democracy cannot survive, demand a rethinking of the whole situation. America is predominantly a land of minorities; that is its uniqueness, its strength, but to a degree also its weakness. Some way must be found in which these minorities within the national community may each freely pursue its own particular concerns without impairing the over-all unity of American life. Because American minorities— and in a real sense, the Protestants too constitute a minority, as well as Catholics and Jews—are many of them religious in character, or at least religiously tinged, the problem immediately becomes one of the relation of church and state. It is in this area that we need our most serious and creative rethinking.

On the basis of my own observation, and the many discussions I have had with men and women of all creeds directly involved in the interfaith situation, I may perhaps venture some suggestions.

American Catholics must come to realize the deep suspicion with which their every move is regarded by a large segment of the American people, and admit, at least to themselves, that there is considerable historical justification for such suspicion. They should complete and clarify the reorientation on matters of church and state that is currently under way in authoritative Catholic circles in this country and is reflected in the sharp rebuke recently administered by American Jesuits to Cardinal Segura of Seville on the occasion of the latter's attack on religious freedom. There *is* a new Catholic attitude, and it would be well if the public knew more about it. The Catholic Church in America would also be well advised to moderate its demands in the field of education, to curb exhibitions of ecclesiastical power in politics, and in general to do what it can to avoid inflaming the non-Catholic mind, today in an extremely nervous state.

American Protestants should make a fresh effort to overcome the defensive psychology that seems to dominate them. Such negativism is good neither for them nor for the country as a whole. They should cease making Rome the inverse criterion of everything they think or do, and above all they should rid themselves of the defeatism that has led them to surrender large areas of public life, including education in and out of the public school, to secularism. Surely Protestantism has more to offer than an intransigent determination to prevent Catholic parochial school children from using public buses.

American Jews even more than Protestants, must rid themselves of the narrow and crippling minority-group defensiveness. Just because Jews in this country occupy such a curious "third" position between Protestants and Catholics, their responsibilities are great. We must rethink the problem of church and state, of religion and life, as it affects the Jew and as it affects the entire nation. We must be ready to abandon ancient fears and prejudices if they no longer conform to reality, and we must be ready to strike out boldly in new directions required by the times. There is no need for—indeed there is every need to abandon—the anxious search for injuries and grievances which has characterized so much of the Jewish "defense" psychology. On the question of aid to religious schools, I do not believe we have much to fear from any of the proposals thus far suggested. On the question of teaching religion in the public schools, I have yet to see a plan that seems to me wise or practicable, and perhaps there is none. But these questions will continue to be raised by many citizens seriously concerned with the problem, and we owe it to ourselves and to them to give fair and sober thought and discussion to their point of view, without attempting to throw it out of court in advance. Should not our community leadership more openly reflect the genuine religious interest of Jews and their concern over the religio-ethical education of their children, which has always been strong, however confused by the felt pressures and demands (often misunderstood) of the new American environment—a concern that every observer reports at high and rising tide in the present decade? That the question of public and private schools, and of church and state in education, can be discussed from the Jewish point of view in a sober, constructive, unprejudiced manner may be seen from Hayim Greenberg's exploratory article last year in the *Yiddisher Kemfer*. We urgently need more of such thinking.

Finally all of us, Catholics, Protestants, Jews, and secularists too, must realize the seriousness of the present tensions and our responsibility to do everything in our power to allay them, certainly not to exacerbate them.

Milton Konvitz is one of our best-known champions of a more rigid interpretation of the principle of the separation of church and state; he probably would not agree with much of what I have said in this article. But I think all of us might take to heart his warning, published in *Congress Weekly* of March 3, 1952, about the dangers of religious controversy:

"Whatever strengthens this principle [of the separation between church and state] serves the interests of American democracy; but one ought to feel grave concern over the cost Americans are paying for the achievement of this value—for little by little, as the wall of separation between church and state is being built up, there goes up also a wall of separation between Catholic and Protestant. While one wall strengthens the structure of American democracy, the other wall creates prejudice, misunderstanding, suspicion, and even enmity—religious conflict which can ultimately poison the wellsprings of American democracy.

"The conflict, as one sees it developing slowly but surely before our eyes, bodes ill for our society. The situation is one that calls for heart-searching and the highest reaches of statesmanship. . . . Ways must be found to maintain the separation between church and state which would not intensify religious divisions. . . . Only statesmanship and charity will lead to the discovery of such ways."

Notes

[1] It is significant that nearly a majority of the schools (1,410) are Lutheran. Seventh Day Adventists run a close second with 919. The great denominations of a pietistic cast—Methodists and Baptists—are almost unrepresented: 15 schools are listed for the latter, none for the former.

[2] It has even been contended that religious instruction in public schools might be psychologically harmful to children of minority groups. However, Dr. Samuel H. Flowerman of Teachers College, Columbia, reporting on the results of a detailed study to a conference on religion in public education arranged by the Reform rabbinical association, stated that "he believed the effects were not harmful except when parents passed on an anxiety about it to their children."

† Thus it is that the People of the Book so often find themselves in the false position of appearing to be "against the Bible."

—13—

Religion and
Public Life

(1962)

With its decisions in the *Engel* case (1961) and the *Schempp* and *Murray* cases (1962), the United States Supreme Court has precipitated the problem of religious symbols and ceremonies in public life into a compelling issue of public policy. I hope to deal with some of the constitutional and political aspects of this problem in a later article. For the present, I want to address myself to a point that seems to me to need more careful consideration than it has received, since it touches the theological evaluation of these Supreme Court decisions and the trend they represent.

Every newspaper reader will remember, perhaps to his bewilderment, that the Supreme Court actions outlawing the New York State Regents' prayer a year ago, and enjoining Bible readings and the Lord's Prayer in public schools earlier this year, were greeted with approval by a considerable number of Protestant theologians, and by some Catholic publicists, mostly laymen. These were men of acute mind and deep religious faith, men I know and respect. Yet they welcomed the "separationist" decisions of the Supreme Court, and, in effect, asked for more. What was their argument? What *is* their argument?—for they are still pressing it in resolutions, articles, and books. . .

Their argument, brushing aside certain irrelevancies, is essentially a *religious* one. Whatever may have been the case some centuries ago, they say, religious symbols and ceremonies in public life today, considering the advance of secularism in our culture, are becoming a mockery, a travesty of religion, a superficial routinization that, in its tendency to trivialize faith, is worse than an honest and outright secularism. Let the movement toward the "de-religionization" of our public life, so powerfully promoted by the recent Supreme Court decisions, go on, they say, and go on to the bitter end. Then, perhaps, the real religious situation in this country will become apparent; and seriously concerned men and women will turn in the only direction in which a renascence of authentic faith could be expected—to the home and the church.

A Higher Majesty

There is some truth in this argument. After all, what can the routine repetition of a prayer mean in the religious life of a child when all the rest of what goes on in school is so utterly religionless? Is not the child more likely to receive an impression of the marginal place of religion in life than of its central importance? Perhaps. But the argument of these religious advocates of a public secularism remains profoundly and dangerously wrong; for, as we should understand from our theological and political traditions, a society, and the state through which it is organized politically, remain "legitimate," "righteous" and "lawful" *only insofar as they recognize a higher majesty beyond themselves,* limiting and judging their pretensions. Once the state forgets or denies this, once it sets itself up as its own highest majesty, beyond which there is nothing, it becomes *totalitarian* in effect, it divinizes itself, and thereby ceases to be a "legitimate" state in the theological understanding of the term. Therefore the "established order"—the state, above all—ought to include within itself signs, symbols, and ceremonials constantly reminding itself and the people that it *is* subject to a majesty beyond all earthly majesties. That is the indispensable function of religious symbols and ceremonials in public life, one that no responsible theologian, however resentful he may be of trivialization and superficiality in religion, can afford to forget.

Children in American schools, public and private, generally salute the flag every school day, and pledge their allegiance to the United States. This pledge now includes the Lincolnian phrase, "this nation, *under God*"; and the child who takes this pledge of allegiance, if he is encouraged to pay attention to what he is saying, will know that the American state and nation are not absolute; that they stand under the scrutiny and judgment of a higher power. With this phrase "under God" removed, as it might well be removed by a sequential Supreme Court decision pursuing the "separationist" line, the child repeating the pledge of allegiance every day at school would have no reminder of a majesty beyond all earthly majesties, and would naturally be prone to see the state and nation as the supreme reality demanding his highest allegiance. The Founding Fathers, whether "conservative" or "radical," well understood this principle as the presupposition of our constitutional system. "Before any man can be considered a member of civil society," James Madison once declared, "he must be considered a subject of the Governor of the universe." It is to remind us, and especially the rising generation, that we are, first and foremost, "subjects of the Governor of the universe," that we need religious symbols and ceremonials in public life.

The Protestant theologians who applaud the Supreme Court decision, and even want to go beyond, seem for the most part to have overlooked the consequences of the "de-religionizing" movement for our political order, a political order which makes no sense except in terms of a higher majesty, a higher allegiance, and a higher law. This appears to be a failure of responsibility. And it is a failure of responsibility not unconnected with a deficient understanding of the religious task in America today, pursuing, as it does, a kind of "back to the catacombs" outlook. But of this, as of the constitutional aspects of the Supreme Court decisions, I hope to write at greater length at a later time.

The crucial passage in Justice Clark's majority opinion in the *Schempp* and *Murray* (Lord's Prayer and Bible reading) cases, is no doubt the following:

> . . . to withstand the strictures of the establishment clause [of the First Amendment] there must be a secular legislative purpose and a primary effect that neither enhances nor inhibits religion.

This passage well reflects the strange incoherence of the majority opinion as a whole. For the second part of the criterion it offers ("neither enhances nor inhibits religion") not only does not follow from the first ("secular legislative purpose"), but stands in obvious logical and historical contradiction to it.

The Federal Government is indeed restricted to "secular" purposes. That is because it is a state, not a church; and, in our Western tradition, the jurisdiction and activities of the state have almost always been understood as limited to the promotion of the common good in the civil order, which (I presume) is what Justice Clark means by "secular purpose." Note well that this restriction of the state to the civil ("secular") order is not a peculiarly American "separationist" notion derived from the First Amendment; it is, as I have said, deeply rooted in our Western tradition, and rests upon the primary distinction between State and Church, which was at least as clear to Augustine and

Thomas Aquinas as it is to the justices of the Supreme Court. With this part of Justice Clark's criterion, there can be no quarreling; it deserves all the emphasis it can get.

But the second part of Justice Clark's test of constitutionality does not follow from the first; rather it contradicts it. *For the promotion of religion may well be seen as a major "secular" purpose of the state in its furtherance of the common good of the* civil *order.* This was the almost universal conviction of Americans at the time of the adoption of the federal Constitution; and it has remained the conviction of the American people, and the practice of federal and state government to this very day, despite the confusion introduced by recent Court decisions.

The Northwest Ordinance of 1787 is widely recognized as a significant reflection of the best mind of the American people at the outset of their career as a nation. Perhaps the most celebrated article of this ordinance is Article 3, which reads as follows:

> Religion, morality, and knowledge being necessary to *good government* and the happiness of mankind, schools and the means of education shall forever be encouraged [my emphasis].

Two years before, in 1785, what was probably the first state university in this country, the University of Georgia, was established. The charter of the university—adopted, let us remember, not in "theocratic" New England but in "Jeffersonian" Georgia—included the following paragraph:

> When the minds of the people in general are viciously disposed and unprincipled, and their conduct disorderly, a free government will be attended with greater confusion, with evils more horrid, than the wild, uncultivated state of nature. It can only be happy when the public

principles and opinions are properly directed, and their manners regulated. This is an influence beyond the sketch of laws and punishments, and can be claimed only by religion and education. It should therefore be among the first objects of those who wish well to the *national prosperity,* to encourage and support the principles of religion and morality . . . [my emphasis].

Documentation could be multiplied; but the point, I think, is clear: the promotion of religion, along with the promotion of morality and education, is understood as a legitimate, indeed an imperative purpose of the state *in the promotion of "good government" and "national prosperity."* This was a recognized principle at the time of the emergence of the new nation.

The very first Congress, which ratified the First Amendment, also assigned certain funds to subsidize Christian missionaries among the Indians; and, in one case at least, if my memory serves, the missionary thus subsidized was a Roman Catholic. This action, which must shock and outrage every conscientious "separationist," was hardly taken out of a deep concern for the Christian religion, and emphatically not out of a predilection for the Roman Catholic Church. It was taken because it was obvious to all thinking people that religion (in this case, of course, Christianity) was "necessary to good government"; and the promotion of religion among the Indians—even, where expediency dictated, the Roman Catholic version of religion—was important for the national welfare. It was with this *"secular"* motive that the Congress moved, thus acting upon a well-established principle.

This principle has not changed either in theory or in practice, despite the protests of a few doctrinaires. Why do we exempt religious, along with educational and charitable institutions, from the burden of taxation which might otherwise crush them? Because we recognize that religious institutions along with the others, perform an indispensable *public* ("secular") service. Why do we support an extensive chaplaincy system in the armed forces? Because we recognize that the chaplain in the armed forces performs an indispensable *public* ("secular") service essential to the national welfare. If, as Justice Douglas said some years ago in the majority opinion in the *Zorach* case, "we are a religious people whose institutions presuppose a Supreme Being," it would seem to be stultifying to prohibit the government from *in any way* promoting the activities of religion serving to strengthen our social institutions by strengthening their "presupposition"? And, in fact, the government has not been so inhibited, as we all know.

Theologians may very well have their qualms about a religion that is thus converted into an instrument for strengthening the secular order of society. This aspect of the problem I hope to discuss in a later article. Here, however, my point is something quite different. My point is that, within the meaning of our political tradition and political practice, the promotion has been, and continues to be, a part of the very legitimate "secular" purpose of the state. Whatever the "neutrality" of the state in matters of religion may be, it cannot be a neutrality between religion and no-religion, any more than (to recall the language of the Northwest Ordinance) it could be a neutrality between morality and no-morality, knowledge and no-knowledge. All three, in our American conviction, are necessary to "good government" and "national prosperity"; and all three fall within the legitimate scope of the friendly assistance of the state.

Part V

RELIGION IN AMERICA: TRENDS AND DEVELOPMENTS

—14—

The Postwar Revival of the Synagogue

DOES IT REFLECT A RELIGIOUS REAWAKENING?

(1950)

There is a religious revival under way among American Jews today. On this fact all informed persons whom I had the opportunity of consulting in recent months seem to be agreed, although each hastens to qualify and interpret the situation in a somewhat different way. The outward signs are obvious enough. Hundreds of synagogues and religious educational institutions are engaged in building-expansion programs; one exceptionally well-informed source put the figure close to a thousand. Synagogue membership is probably at a record level. Many synagogues, indeed, have been compelled to close their books and establish waiting lists, while others have set up subsidiaries or have helped found entirely new institutions to take care of the overflow. Attendance is also markedly on the increase, not only during the High Holidays, but even at the regular Friday night or Saturday morning services. Hebrew and religious schools, particularly day schools, are making notable gains. As for higher education, the Jewish Theological

Seminary reported the largest freshman class in its history last year. Both the Hebrew Union College-Jewish Institute of Religion and the Yeshiva University, the other two leading seminaries, are extending their scope and activities, and scores of small yeshivas of varying pretensions have sprung up in the larger Jewish centers.

Not only have synagogue affiliation and attendance been growing, but, according to my informants, the members of the congregations—even of the Orthodox—are no longer primarily older people and immigrants. On the contrary, they are in good part American born and bred, young men and women in their twenties and thirties, with a sizable proportion of youngsters in their teens. Veterans have in many instances been active in initiating and building synagogues, and there is hardly a new housing project in any of the larger cities without its congregation. Reaching to some extent even beyond the circle of synagogue affiliation, the practice of certain Jewish observances in the home has been growing—particularly the blessing over the candles and the *kiddush* on the Sabbath eve and the fixing of the *mezuzah* to the doorpost. This is the general picture, and although not all of my informants would agree on every detail, it fairly well represents the consensus of experts.

But questions immediately arise. With all its gains, the synagogue still represents only a minority of American Jews. This minority is divided into a number of competing "movements," each striving to become *the* religious community. And over and above everything else, there are qualms concerning the real character of the current revival. Virtually every one of the rabbis, teachers, scholars, and publicists whom I consulted, after detailing the evidence of expansion, paused to add reflectively: But how much *religion* is there in all that, I wonder?" A big element in the "boom," they thought, was the war and postwar prosperity, which gave many congregations the resources to get done what had long needed doing. Another important factor, in the view of many, was the urge to impress the "outside" world; this is what Paul Blanshard has, with undue severity, called the "technique of denominational display." But in every explanation offered of the rise of synagogue affiliation and attendance, the new urge to Jewish self-affirmation was mentioned first.

It is, of course, a commonplace that the events of the past two decades—the shattering experience of demonic anti-Semitism at one pole and the triumphant emergence of the State of Israel at the other—have helped reverse the trend toward assimilation that was once so rampant among American Jews. Today, the great mass of Jews in this country, even the younger generation, think of themselves as Jews, "accept" themselves as Jews. This new Jewish "pride" was particularly evident among soldiers in the late war. Rabbi Isaac Klein, in his very instructive report on the experiences of a Jewish chaplain,[1] tells of asking a young Jewish soldier his reason for showing such interest in religious services. The soldier's reply was that "since he had come into contact with so many non-Jewish soldiers, his Jewish pride demanded some expression, and the only way in the army was to come every Friday evening to services." Similarly with a number of Jewish doctors whom he interrogated: "They gave me the same answer. They felt that Jews had to identify themselves somehow, and going to services on Friday night was the only way."

Another factor, ranking in importance with this powerful need for self-identification, and in a sense an aspect of it, is the desire of parents, often themselves quite indifferent to religion to give their children a "Jewish education." For most American Jews today, a

"Jewish education" means an education with some Hebrew in it and at least peripherally religious. Hence it usually involves a bond with the synagogue.

To what degree is this concern for self-identification as a Jew religious? And why has the synagogue become the chosen means of Jewish self-identification? At other times and places, other means—political, social, and cultural—quite remote from religion and the synagogue, were found to satisfy the same desire. Why the new emphasis on the synagogue?

One explanation may well be that, under American conditions, it is very difficult for the Jew to know himself as a Jew except in some sort of religious terms. As Rabbi Jacob Agus has persuasively argued,[2] America knows no national minorities except as temporary and transitional phenomena. But America does know a free variety and plurality of religions, and it is as a member of a religious group that the great mass of Americans understand the status of the Jew in this country. Rabbi Agus voices the thinking of many in his conclusion that "Jews can be satisfactorily integrated within the American nation only as a religious community"—with the qualification, however, that it is a "religious community" broad enough somehow to include even those Jews who are indifferent or hostile to religion. And in fact, the average American Jew—I mean the Jew who is acculturated to America—if he thinks of himself as a Jew at all, tends almost automatically to think of himself as belonging to a kind of religious community, even if he himself does not happen to be religious. In the Vilna of the 1920's it was possible for a militantly anti-religious Jewish doctor to assert himself as a Jew by sending his children to a secular Yiddish school, and for some time the same pattern was familiar among Jewish immigrants in this country. Here in the United States, it has been possible to "be a Jew" through philanthrophy and, more recently, through political Zionism. But today, if the American Jew is to feel himself a Jew, and is to be regarded by his Gentile friends and neighbors as a Jew, some religious association would seem to be indicated, however vague. The importance of religion for the continuation of the Jewish people, which was once so self-evident and then so violently denied, has been tremendously reinforced by the social and spiritual upheavals of the past thirty years. I know of no better way of making this point clear than by quoting the words of a distinguished Jewish scholar of thoroughly secularist outlook: "Jewish religion has proved itself to be the most stormproof aspect of Jewish existence. It is the only force that can preserve the Jews as a group." Almost the same words were used by another informant of mine, a radical Socialist and Zionist of long standing.

The "survivalist" utility of Jewish religion has made a deep impression on people who only yesterday thought of religion as something they had dispensed with once and for all. And so, without seriously modifying their own indifference and skepticism, they are ready to adopt what might be called a *pro-religious attitude*. They are ready to associate themselves with a synagogue, give their children a "Jewish education," and perhaps even adopt certain of the traditional ritual observances in the home. With some, this "survivalist" attitude is a conscious and well-articulated ideology; for the most part, however, it is little more than a vague sentiment, though surely a very influential one.

What does this add up to? Not necessarily to the assertion that religion is actually becoming an important concern of life or that the synagogue as a religious institution is on the way to regaining the preeminence it once enjoyed; on the contrary, as we shall see, the tendency may well be the other way. What it does imply is some sort of general feeling that religion is a "good thing" for the continuation of the Jewish group in the present-day world and so ought to be "encouraged."

I do not, of course, mean to minimize the influence of truly religious need in bringing about the current synagogue revival. "Suffering," as Silone says, "has carved out new dimensions in our souls, of which we were unaware in 1919," and these new dimensions are undeniably religious. Certainly a high regard for Jewish religion merely as an effective instrument of group survival is worlds apart from authentic religious conviction and may even stand in direct opposition to it. Yet we must not ignore the "new dimensions in our souls," nor, for that matter, can we refuse some measure of religious value even to the impulse to group survival, since in the Jewish scheme of things the mere existence of the people Israel is of religious significance. In any case, motives are compounded on many levels, and the problem is a complicated and many-sided one. While every serious observer of the present situation will be cautious about simply identifying building programs and increased synagogue membership with an authentic awakening of religious life, he will by no means exclude the latter as a factor in the total situation.

T he three main groups into which the synagogue in America is divided—Orthodox, Conservative, and Reform—have all benefited, though to varying degrees, from the expansion of recent years.

The nature of these divisions in the American synagogue is a perplexing problem to sociologist and theologian alike. They are not sects or denominations in the usual sense, for they do not differ significantly as bodies in creed, rite, liturgy, or corporate government. Indeed differences in these respects among American Jews today cut across all group lines. Solomon Schechter called them "parties," thus implying that each had its legitimate place in the totality of Israel. Their character has, however, changed rather markedly in the last generation.

The early Jewish communities in this country were mainly Sephardic and were, of course, Orthodox. Before the middle of the 19th century, the first signs of the Reform movement began to show themselves, partly under the influence of German Reform and partly as a parallel development on American soil. American Reform leaders were sufficiently far from the traditional norm to make their development as a separate tendency inevitable. The chief Reform institutions, established in the 1870's and 1880's, were originally meant to be all-inclusive, but they soon became almost entirely partisan in character, and so they have remained.

Meanwhile, in the older Jewish communities, a moderate reform movement was emerging with a program that stressed change of very limited scope in synagogue procedure and liturgy. It did not, like Reform, challenge the traditional concept of *halachah* as law (rather than as folkways) but instead merely insisted that this law be regarded as essentially historical and subject to change with changing conditions. In many ways, this tendency was akin to the Historical Judaism of Zechariah Frankel in Europe, and indeed the two streams later coalesced to form the modern Conservative movement.

With the "new" immigration towards the end of the century, Orthodoxy of the East European type was transplanted into this country and soon began to vie with the older tendencies. Both the Reform and the Conservative movements recruited heavily from its ranks, especially with advancing Americanization. Very soon, East European immigrants became the largest numerical group in most Jewish centers.

By the time of the First World War, the three tendencies were fairly well defined. Orthodoxy, however, still had a major transformation to undergo. For with the shutting off of immigration and the emergence of a new generation of American-born Jews of Orthodox leanings, differentiation rapidly developed in Orthodox ranks between the foreign-oriented immigrant group and a new "modern" or "American" Orthodoxy. In many ways, the latter began to approach the Conservative pattern in organization and activities.

Thus we have today in the United States a Conservative and a Reform group, each with its own seminary, rabbinical association, and synagogal union, and then an Orthodox tendency, in which the older immigrant and the newer American elements are separately organized. In addition, there are the Sephardim, who maintain institutions of their own.

As the American wing of Orthodoxy has become less "orthodox," in the older European sense, so has the Reform movement grown more traditional, especially in very recent years. The radical Reformism of earlier days is no longer dominant, although it is still not unknown in some sections of the country. "The spirit of self-criticism and dissatisfaction with the extreme departure of Reformism is common among the Reform rabbinate," reports Abraham G. Duker.[3] "Reform Judaism [is] retracing its steps to the middle ground in Judaism, so much so that it is difficult to distinguish between some Conservative synagogues and Reform temples. . . ." It is also, the same observer notes, "frequently difficult to distinguish between an Orthodox and a 'right-wing' Conservative synagogue or institution." Thus the old distinctions, rooted in historical, cultural, and even ethnic factors, and sometimes associated with important theological issues, are tending to disappear.

That does not mean that there are no differences in belief or practice in the American synagogue, but these differences, as I have suggested, cut across group lines and are not essentially "party" differences. It is true that fundamentalism is more common among the Orthodox and modernism more at home in the Reform camp. But Jewish religious life in this country is theologically so feeble that this doctrinal distinction is of little practical relevance. Most Conservative rabbis would agree with the Orthodox position on *halachah* as law, although insisting on its changing historical character, whereas most Reform rabbis show little interest in the matter. But in each camp there are plenty who differ with the majority view.

As to the general level of observance, it is hard to speak with any authority, but it is worth noting that an Orthodox publicist, Dr. Weiss-Rosmarin, quotes a member of an Orthodox synagogue as saying: "There is no difference in ritual observance [between the Orthodox and the non-Orthodox], except that they don't care if their rabbi, too, isn't observant, whereas we want the rabbi to eat kosher and keep Shabbes."[4] Conservative and Orthodox men cover the head during prayer and worship; Reform makes it "optional." The old-line Orthodox forbid, and the "modern" Orthodox still feel uneasy about, organs and mixed pews, whereas many Conservatives and almost all Reform people are accustomed to them. It would be hard to carry the list of differences much further. Even the earlier social and cultural distinctions have virtually disappeared, at least so far as the American groups are concerned. In education, outlook, economic position, and social standing, the membership of a "modern" Orthodox synagogue looks very much like the membership of a Conservative synagogue in the same locality and neither differs markedly from the membership of the Reform temple, although some observers insist that the Reform group at least in the older centers, retains vestiges of its former social preeminence.

The revival of religious concern among American Jews appears to have benefited the Conservative group most, for this group not only allows a wide range of variation but also seems best able to combine a considerable degree of traditionalism in the forms of religion with a modern and "American" outlook in everything else. It is undoubtedly significant that the younger generation of Jews who turn to religion are attracted not so much by religious modernism as by a certain amount of Orthodoxy in belief and practice, especially in liturgy, within the framework of a modern outlook. Conservatism seems well designed to meet this demand, which may be related to the feeling that a more distinctive Jewish observance better satisfies the need for self-identification.

The "modern" wing of Orthodoxy has also been making impressive headway. Its appeal is very much the same as that of Conservatism, and it has a rather greater attraction for young people brought up in Orthodox homes and accustomed to Orthodox ways. The Reform group appears not to have kept pace with the others, although there is some evidence that its recent shift in outlook on Zionism and ritual matters has strengthened its position.

Even the old-line immigrant Orthodoxy has been doing fairly well. But, by and large, it seems likely that whatever progress Orthodoxy is to make in this country in the future will be made by its "American" wing.

Meanwhile, the aims and purposes of the various groups are growing increasingly similar. Each of the three major divisions—the immigrant wing of Orthodoxy hardly comes into the picture here—is today essentially committed to a program of creating an indigenous pattern for all American Jews along its own lines, with "the ultimate goal of becoming not, as formerly, the major party in American Judaism, but American Judaism itself."[5] The favorable conditions of recent years have encouraged these ambitions.

Religious statistics relating to American Jews are notoriously hard to obtain and largely inaccurate. The best information would seem to indicate that in 1949 the Conservative United Synagogue of America had

365 synagogues affiliated with it, the Reform Union of American Hebrew Congregations had 392, and the Union of Orthodox Jewish Congregations 500, with an unknown number of congregations, largely Orthodox, unaffiliated. (Each of these groups claims and is credited with a varying influence beyond its circle of affiliates.) What these figures mean in terms of individuals is merely a guess, since the congregations differ greatly in size. Dr. Davis states "the total estimated congregational membership based on family affiliations" to be "about 1,500,000 individual Jews," but this probably includes scores of thousands whose connection with the synagogue is limited to attendance on the High Holidays. It is generally agreed that the actual figure would be considerably lower.

Even the most cursory survey is bound to raise questions as to the reason and justification for the maintenance of existing "party" lines. The original historical causes are virtually gone, no new ones of a compelling character appear to have arisen, and yet the division persists. There are, of course, a number of all-inclusive bodies, such as the Jewish Welfare Board, which was formed in 1917 to minister to the religious and social needs of Jewish soldiers and has since performed a variety of other functions; the Synagogue Council of America, set up in 1926 as a delegate body of the three "parties" for their common religious interests; and a few local joint rabbinical associations (New York, Philadelphia, Boston, Chicago, etc.). But these are all agencies for specific purposes and are vested with very limited powers; they do not bring American Jewry much nearer to the religious unity that every one professes to desire. The situation is particularly anomalous since in the armed forces during World War II, where the official "party" lines could not be preserved and Jewish chaplains had to serve their people simply as Jews, a common pattern—essentially Conservative—quickly developed that overrode the distinctions which loom so large in civilian life.[6]

To be sure, considerable talk about unity has been heard in recent years. Rabbi Morris Lieberman, in his address at the exercises opening the seventy-fifth academic year of Hebrew Union College in Cincinnati on October 15, 1949, called for the merger of the Reform and Conservative groups, asserting that the differences between them were "chronological, quantitative, and personal, not ideological." But Rabbi Lieberman apparently saw no possibility of union with the Orthodox wing. From the Orthodox side have come more ambitious plans. The emergence of the State of Israel, in which the Orthodox Chief Rabbinate enjoys exclusive jurisdiction in religious matters, seems to have fanned the hope in Orthodox circles of overcoming the division in the American synagogue by uniting it in obedience to the Chief Rabbinate in Jerusalem, very much, to use the analogy of Chief Rabbi Herzog's secretary, as Roman Catholics are united in their obedience to the Pope. Rabbi Israel Tabak, head of the Orthodox Rabbinical Council of America, President Samuel Belkin of the Yeshiva University, and others have endorsed this project, but it has naturally not commended itself to Reform and Conservative circles. Indeed, it does not appear that even the Orthodox element in this country is of one mind. Chief Rabbi Herzog's official contacts in the United States seem to be limited to the "modern" Orthodox group, so that the old-line Orthodox rabbis have been moved to lodge vehement protests against the "recognition" thus granted their "American" colleagues.

The most serious plea for a rapprochement of the three "parties" in American Jewry was made, in my opinion, by the Jewish chaplains. The first national convention of their association, meeting in New York in 1947, adopted a resolution that deserves to be remembered:

"We, chaplains who served in this last war, alumni of the three major rabbinic seminaries and representatives of the Orthodox, Conservative, and Reform ideologies within American Judaism, unanimously affirm that the mutuality, fellowship, and comradeship which united us in our common service of God and country proved a most enriching spiritual experience which we aim to apply in our civilian ministry. To expand and extend the blessings of this creative fellowship, we urge upon the three rabbinic bodies to project plans for their respective national conventions in a manner that would provide, once every three years, a simultaneous session of the three bodies."

But even this modest request has met with little encouragement. As far back as 1943, indeed, a joint session of the Conservative and Reform rabbinical conventions was held in New York, but this precedent has not been followed. Nor has it proved possible to form local or regional synagogue councils, patterned after the national Synagogue Council, even for the most limited purposes.

As far as official action is concerned, the religious unification of American Jewry is as remote as ever, despite the impressive evidence of the war experience that the "party" differences are not fundamental and can be overcome where the need and pressure are great enough.

W hat is it that perpetuates the "party" separatism and stands in the way of a rapprochement? We should not, of course, ignore official "philosophies" and platforms or such factors as "differences of temper and temperament, of training and surroundings," to which Schechter referred. But neither should institutional considerations be overlooked. Institutions and movements have a logic of their own. Once they get under way, corporate interest becomes a consideration in its own right, and appropriate loyalties, ideologies, and prejudices do not delay in making their appearance. And it is surely no ground for surprise that an institution with a history of useful work will go ahead doing its work with a clear conscience, without considering the possibility that this work might be done as well or perhaps even better if its own institutional identity were absorbed in a larger whole. Nor is it much to be wondered at that it will tend to exaggerate its special points of difference to the proportions where they can serve as a satisfactory *raison d'être*. Such things are not unknown in the life of organizations and rabbinical or synagogal organizations are organizations like any other. In my discussions with Jewish leaders of various shades of opinion, there was usually some connection discernible between one's attitude towards the problem of religious unity and the estimate of the prospects of one's own "party." It is not altogether accidental perhaps that Conservative spokesmen have done the least talking on this question. After all, most observers agree with Duker that the "unmistakable trend" is towards the "middle ground," which is precisely the ground occupied by Conservatism.

All in all, the outlook for the organizational unification of the three movements into one united synagogue cannot be said to be very promising. But the problem will not down, for a situation in which the religious community is divided into rival and competing groups, each trying to create its own "movement" but unable to establish fellowship with the others, is certainly not something that can be accepted with complacency or indifference.[7] A number of my informants thought they discerned a new type of religious Jew emerging in America, a Jew to whom the beliefs and traditions of Judaism are not merely inherited routine but something new, personal, and exciting. To this type of "new" Jew—and there may be more of them than we suspect, especially among the younger people—the old distinctions and divisions appear rather remote and artificial, as they seemed to so many in the army. Whatever kind of synagogue they join, they are really independents who transcend "party" lines. Perhaps this type of Jew will have something to say about the fashioning of synagogue life in America.

But the divisions within the synagogue, however large they may loom when seen from the inside, are trifling compared to the great gulf that to-day separates the synagogue as a whole from the vital areas of Jewish life. Let it not be forgotten, in the first place, that out of the close to five million Jews in this country, no more than one and a half million—or less than a third—have even the remotest connection with the synagogue. Public-opinion surveys some years ago indicated that hardly eighteen per cent of American Jews attended religious services at least once a month. In the army, according to Rabbi Klein, the figure rose to thirty-one per cent, but it is certain that army conditions were not carried over to civilian life at the end of the war. Some increase there has been, as we have seen, but when all is allowed for, it must be admitted that only a minority of American Jews are in any important way associated with the synagogue.

Even the minority of Jews who do belong to the synagogue do not as a rule find it the center of their interest as men and as Jews. Other concerns— Zionism, labor unionism, philanthropy, social service, "anti-defamation"—seem closer and more deeply related to the immediacies of life and the core of personal emotion; and with these concerns religion and the synagogue appear to have very little to do. Religion is, in fact, often regarded as a kind of leisure-time, supplemental activity, and the synagogue as something you belong to because you "happen" to be a Jew.

This strikes us as so natural that we rarely pause to think what it really means. Most synagogue leaders, if I am to judge by those with whom I have discussed the matter, simply take the situation for granted. After all, they say, there are so many things demanding attention in the modern world; the synagogue is just one of the many institutions in Jewish life; it may be too bad, but that's how things are. What is not sufficiently appreciated is that, however natural it may appear to us, the present position of the synagogue in relation to Jewish life represents probably the sharpest break with fundamental Jewish tradition that modern history has witnessed. It represents the fragmentation of Jewish existence, and the secularization of Jewish institutions and activities.

Until the 19th century, all Jewish activities—work, education, philanthropy—were in some sense religious activities, and the synagogue was at the heart of Jewish life. But new interests began to arise for which the traditional Jewish community was either unwilling or unable to find a place. Chief among these new interests were Zionism, labor socialism, and modern learning. It has been said that the Jewish labor-socialist movement in East Europe emerged as a veritable schism in the Jewish community, the first of any importance since Karaism. This is profoundly true, and the same may be said, with some qualification, of the rise of Zionism at the end of the 19th century or even of the *haskalah* somewhat earlier. They could not develop within the established Jewish community and so they broke through its limits and set themselves up as autonomous interests. Jewish life lost its unity and, for increasing numbers, the synagogue became an altogether secondary institution. Actually, the labor-socialist movement, and to some extent Zionism too, came into being not simply outside the sphere of the synagogue but in bitter hostility to it. They were, in fact, anti-religious movements, though not always ready to avow themselves as such.

I t would be pointless, at this stage, to try to assess and distribute responsibility for this development which destroyed the integral pattern of Jewish community life. After all, very much the same thing had been going on for some centuries in Christian Europe. It was part of the emergence of the modern world. Modernity came late to the Jewish communities in Central and Eastern Europe, but for that very reason its impact proved especially devastating. Within one or two generations, the greater part of European Jewry passed directly from the Middle Ages to modern secularism. The organic Jewish community was shattered and the fragments, flying apart, began to establish themselves as independent centers of Jewish life.

Today, almost everything that is vital in American Jewish life is carried on outside the sphere of influence of religion. The estrangement of most Jews from the synagogue, as well as the disunity within it, seem to render this state of affairs inevitable and may even give it the appearance of normality but it is a normality that spells defeat for the synagogue. Jewish religious leaders are frequently so busy equipping their particular "movement" to take over American Judaism that they do not see what is happening before their very eyes.

The failure of the synagogue is reflected in its relation to the Jewish workers. The workers are, of course, not the only group of American Jews remote from the synagogue, but their case is perhaps most symptomatic. By its social conservatism and lack of concern for the problems of the working class, the European synagogue contributed to the bitter anti-religious fixation with which the Jewish labor-socialist movement was born and which it brought with it to this country. Here in the United States, Jewish labor developed a rich community life of its own from which religion and the synagogue were rigorously excluded. Even today, when much of the earlier bitterness has been dissipated by time and circumstance and Jewish labor leaders are beginning to look upon religion as a "good thing," the essential alienation of the organized Jewish industrial worker from religion and the synagogue remains a conspicuous fact. The Jewish worker no longer goes out of his way to flaunt his contempt for religion; he does something much more disturbing; he ignores it as irrelevant. He is often actively involved in Jewish affairs (Zionism, philanthropy and relief, activity against anti-Semitism), as well as in the affairs of his trade and union, but frankly, he just doesn't see where religion and the synagogue have any bearing on these matters. This is usually just as true of trade unionists who happen to be affiliated with the synagogue as of those who, like the older generation of Jewish labor leaders, still remain remote from it.

Nowhere in the course of my inquiries among religious leaders did I find much concern with this situation. By and large, the Jewish worker, and especially the Jewish unionist, has been written off, and the synagogue is content to remain a middle-class institution. It quiets its social conscience by passing all kinds of radical resolutions at the annual conferences, but these resolutions bear no relation to the actualities of its institutional life or to the lives of its members. Thus is one of the largest and socially most significant sections of American Jewry virtually given up as far as the synagogue is concerned. And what is true of Jewish labor is true of other groups of American Jews as well—intellectuals, particularly—though perhaps not to the same degree.

While the synagogue is in this way being relegated to the periphery of Jewish life, it is undergoing a certain inner decay as well, and indeed, its own kind of secularization. To put it plainly, the synagogue in America no longer represents a community of believers. Nothing in the way of belief or practice—not even the belief in God or the practice of the most elementary *mitzvot*—may be taken for granted among synagogue members. This is basically just as true of the Orthodox group as of the Conservative or Reform. I was amazed at the indifference of many religious leaders in the face of this situation. Some told me that "after all, we Jews don't go in for dogmas," and others simply shrugged their shoulders in resignation. The fact itself virtually no one felt it possible to deny. This means that, in a very basic respect, the synagogue of today is no longer the synagogue of the entire Jewish past. There have always been unbelievers and there have always been those who paid little attention to religious belief and observance, but in former times these people were relatively few, and, what is more important, they were held in reproach by themselves and their fellow-Jews. Only since the last century, and perhaps only in the past generation or two, has it become "normal" for Jews, and even for synagogue members, to believe in and observe nothing in particular. This is surely something portentous.

Building expansion, the growth of the synagogue in membership and attendance, as well as the other aspects of the current revival, are undeniable and important facts; but they must not be permitted to obscure our understanding of certain deeper processes that are surely more fateful for the future of Judaism in America. On the one hand, the Jewish community is broken into bits, with each fragment an independent entity competing for total allegiance at the expense of the synagogue. On the other hand, the synagogue itself has ceased to be a community of believers in the traditional or any other sense. It is becoming an institution in which religion is no longer indispensable.

What could be done about this situation, even if there were a desire to do anything about it, is not clear. Vital religion is not something that can be brought into being by campaigns and propaganda. We cannot, nor do most of us want to, undo the effects of Emancipation and bring back the Jewish community of a hundred and fifty years ago. If the renovation of the synagogue and the Jewish community is to be effected at all, it will have to be effected in accordance with the conditions of modern life.

There are those who think that they can rebuild the Jewish community by shifting its base from religion to some secular concern—Zionism, "national culture," and the like—on the ground that the modern Jew is incorrigibly secular-minded. But such programs are bound to prove vain and delusive. It is difficult to see how any merely secular Jewish community can in the long run prove viable, in the modern world any more than in earlier times. Collective Jewish existence has always been and is, by its very nature, essentially and inherently religious. Saadya said the last word on the subject when he stated: "Our people are a people only by virtue of its Torah." It can be taken as a conclusion warranted by all history and experience that if the Jewish people is to survive in the modern world, above all in America, it can only do so as a religious community, and that means a community in which the synagogue as a *religious* institution is restored to central place.

Linking the adjective "religious" to the noun "synagogue" is not in our day a mere redundancy. Many rabbinical spokesmen and educators who proclaim the need for a synagogue-centered community seem to think of the synagogue as just another institution absorbed in the round of institutional affairs. But it would surely be no gain to Judaism for the synagogue to become central in community life if the synagogue itself is so busy with other things that it has but little concern for trying to develop the power of religion as a transforming force in the lives of its members. Even granting that a *secular* synagogue could compete successfully with or dominate other secular institutions, which is by no means certain, mere hegemony without the bond of faith and commitment would only tend to repeat in a somewhat different form the 19th-century experience—the very experience out of which the contemporary crisis in the synagogue has grown.

But the power of faith is a power for life, and religious concern cannot mean withdrawal from the

ongoing affairs of existence. If the "secular" synagogue merely touches the externals of life, the "spiritual" synagogue that abjures the world, or ministers
only to one side of the personal life of the Jew, can
never be more than a peripheral institution without
vital significance. Jewish faith knows no such separation between religion and the world: all of the affairs
of life stand under divine law and divine judgment,
and all are therefore the concern of religion. To the
extent that it has tended to accept a departmentaliza-
tion of life in one form or the other, the modern
American synagogue—Orthodox, Conservative, and
Reform alike—has broken with one of the central
affirmations of Jewish religion. For, in the Jewish view,
religion is not just a phase or area of life, however
important; nor is it a collection of external activities
invested with a "religious" aura. In the Jewish view,
religion irradiates the totality of life—but life in its
ultimate concern.

Judaism counted so greatly for Jews in the past
because it served the deep need of human beings for
some vision to give meaning to everything they did and
were and to relate their individual daily acts and the
destiny of the historic community of which they were
members to some great design in line with external
values and purposes. In view of all that the present
generation of Jews has seen and suffered, who can
gainsay that many who are today turning to the synagogue may be seeking a similar faith?

Two main trends, we have said, seem compounded in the current revival of religion
among American Jews. On the one side is the
"survivalist" urge to individual self-identification and
the enhancement of the Jewish communal position in
the pattern of American life. On the other, perhaps less
prevalent but undoubtedly widespread, is the search
for a saving faith, a total existential commitment, in

terms of which one's life may be related significantly to ultimate reality. The two are often fused in motivation and expression. Synagogue building and institutional growth may more obviously reflect the one, and mounting interest in religious thinking the other, but the distinction is relative and cannot be pushed beyond a certain point.

Let us not be misled by labels. Some of my non-rabbinical informants made a point of emphasizing, and I think with some justice, that ostensibly "secular" activities outside the synagogue might in fact be serving as a more genuine vehicle of religious commitment and values than certain activities currently associated with the synagogue. A man may throw himself into Jewish philanthropic or "defense" work, or even fundraising, because he has acquired a keen sense of vocation, while on the other hand, religious affiliation may often turn out to be motivated by little more than a desire to overcome one's sense of isolation from the larger group through self-identification as a Jew. Similarly it is important, I think, to recognize the authentic religious significance of much of the new thinking going on in Jewish intellectual circles today, even though such thinking is carried on largely outside the sphere of the synagogue. As a matter of fact, in comparison with the deeply religious concern that seems to pervade some of this thinking, it is the synagogue that often strikes one as secular in its orientation and interests. Indeed, is there not some warrant for the assertion, often made, that many a synagogue has become so completely secularized that it is neither a center for teaching, study, and worship, nor a community of believers, but simply a large institution entangled in a multiplicity of external activities without religious content or meaning? Such activities may seem to compensate for the growing estrangement of the synagogue from the deeper concerns of human existence; actually they but aggravate the emptiness and unreality of so much of conventional religion. I call to mind the distinguished rabbi who rather impatiently complained that Jewish intellectuals were "unhealthily" absorbed in "mystical questions," instead of being "active" in the synagogue. It seems to me—and here I find support in the comments made by one or two of the more thoughtful religious leaders whom I consulted—that the reconstitution of the synagogue into a force capable of playing in our time the same central role it played in the best periods of Jewish history demands a return to religious essentials. For this, the first step is a fresh, unprejudiced approach; a readiness to detect and to cherish every sign of authentic religious concern, however unfamiliar or conventionally "unreligious" it may seem. It calls—to employ the cabalistic figure—for an earnest effort to seek out and gather the sparks of faith hidden among the fragments of contemporary Jewish existence. It involves the return of the rabbi from his present functions as administrator, political leader, and popular lecturer, to his earlier and more authentic role of religious teacher and counselor. Most of all it implies a synagogue interested primarily not in making itself dominant as an organization but in helping to make Judaism operative in the hearts and lives of the Jews whom it reaches.

Notes

1 *Yivo Bleter*, volume xxvii, pages 186–194.

2 "The Status of American Israel," *Conservative Judaism*, February 1946.

3 "On Religious Trends in American Jewish Life," *Yivo Annual IV* (1949).

4 "From a Lecturer's Notebook," *Jewish Spectator*, April 1945.

5 Moshe Davis, "Jewish Religious Life and Institutions in America," *The Jews*, ed. by Louis Finkelstein.

6 See Philip Bernstein, "Jewish Chaplains in World War II," *American Jewish Year Book*, vol. 47 (1945–6).

7 Various current plans proposed by religious leaders to unify the Jewish community around the primacy of the synagogue are placed in a doubtful light, a number of observers comment, by the inability of the chief

religious groups to find enough accord among themselves to cooperate upon anything beyond the most limited objectives. If they show so little capacity for unity among themselves, how, it is queried, can religious leadership hope to be the chief force for ending divisiveness and disunity in Jewish community life?

—15—

The Religion of Americans and American Religion

(1955)

What do Americans believe? Most emphatically, they "believe in God": 97 per cent according to one survey, 96 per cent according to another, 95 per cent according to a third.[1] About 75 per cent of them, as we have seen, regard themselves as members of churches, and a sizable proportion attend divine services with some frequency and regularity.[2] They believe in prayer: about 90 per cent say they pray on various occasions.[3] They believe in life after death, even in heaven and hell.[4] They think well of the church and of ministers.[5] They hold the Bible to be an inspired book, the "word of God."[6] By a large majority, they think children should be given religious instruction and raised as church members.[7] By a large majority, too, they hold religion to be of very great importance.[8] In all of these respects their attitudes are as religious as those of any people today, or, for that matter, as those of any Western people in recent history.

Yet these indications are after all relatively superficial; they tell us what Americans say (and no doubt believe) about themselves and their religious views;

they do not tell us what in actuality these religious views are. Nowhere are surface appearances more deceptive, nowhere is it more necessary to try to penetrate beyond mere assertions of belief than in such ultimate matters as religion.

W e do penetrate a little deeper, it would seem, when we take note of certain curious discrepancies the surveys reveal in the responses people make to questions about their religion. Thus, according to one trustworthy source, 73 per cent said they believed in an afterlife, with God as judge, but "only 5 per cent [had] any fear, not to say expectation, of going [to hell]."[9] Indeed, about 80 per cent, according to another source, admitted that what they were "most serious about" was not the life after death in which they said they believed, but in trying to live as comfortably in this life as possible.[10] And in their opinion they were not doing so badly even from the point of view of the divine judgment: 91 per cent felt that they could honestly say that they were trying to lead a good life, and 78 per cent felt no hesitation in saying that they more than half measured up to their own standards of goodness, over 50 per cent asserting that they were in fact following the rule of loving one's neighbor as oneself "all the way"![11] This amazingly high valuation that most Americans appear to place on their own virtue would seem to offer a better insight into the basic religion of the American people than any figures as to their formal beliefs can provide, however important in themselves these figures may be.

But perhaps the most significant discrepancy in the assertions Americans make about their religious views is to be found in another area. When asked, "Would you say your religious beliefs have any effect on your ideas of politics and business?", a majority of the same Americans who had testified that they regarded religion as something "very important" answered that their religious beliefs had no real effect on their ideas or conduct in these decisive areas of everyday life; specifically, 54 per cent said no, 39 per cent said yes, and 7 per cent refused to reply or didn't know.[12] This disconcerting confession of the irrelevance of religion to business and politics was attributed by those who appraised the results of the survey as pointing to a calamitous divorce between the "private" and the "public" realms in the religious thinking of Americans.[13] There is certainly a great deal of truth in this opinion, and we shall have occasion to explore it in a different context, but in the present connection it would seem that another aspect of the matter is more immediately pertinent. *Some* ideas and standards undeniably govern the conduct of Americans in their affairs of business and politics; if they are not ideas and standards associated with the teachings of religion, what are they? It will not do to say that people just act "selfishly" without reference to moral standards of any kind. All people act "selfishly," of course; but it is no less true of all people, Americans included, that their "selfishness" is controlled, mitigated, or, at worst, justified by some sort of moral commitment, by some sort of belief in a system of values beyond immediate self-interest. The fact that more than half the people openly admit that their religious beliefs have no effect on their ideas of politics and business would seem to indicate very strongly that, over and above conventional religion, there is to be found among Americans some sort of faith or belief or set of convictions, not generally designated as religion but definitely operative as such in their lives in the sense of providing them with some fundamental context of normativity and meaning. What this unacknowledged "religion" of the American people is, and how it manages to coexist with their formal religious affirmations and affiliations, it is now our task to investigate.

II

E very functioning society," Robin M. Williams, Jr. points out, "has to an important degree a *common* religion. The possession of a common set of ideas, rituals, and symbols can supply an overarching sense of unity even in a society riddled with conflicts."[14] What is this "common religion" of American society, the "common set of ideas, rituals, and symbols" that give it its "overarching sense of unity"? Williams provides us with a further clue when he suggests that "men are always likely to be intolerant of opposition to their central ultimate values."[15] What are these "central ultimate values" about which Americans are "intolerant"? No one who knows anything about the religious situation in this country would be likely to suggest that the things Americans are "intolerant" about are the beliefs, standards, or teachings of the religions they "officially" acknowledge as theirs. Americans are proud of their tolerance in matters of religion: one is expected to "believe in God," but otherwise religion is not supposed to be a ground of "discrimination." This is, no doubt, admirable, but is it not "at least in part, a sign that the crucial values of the system are no longer couched in a religious framework"?[16]

What, then, is the "framework" in which they *are* couched? What, to return to our original question, is the "common religion" of the American people, as it may be inferred not only from their words but also from their behavior?

It seems to me that a realistic appraisal of the values, ideas, and behavior of the American people leads to the conclusion that Americans, by and large, do have their "common religion" and that that "religion" is the system familiarly known as the American Way of Life. It is the American Way of Life that supplies American society with an "overarching sense of unity" amid conflict. It is the American Way of Life about which Americans are admittedly and unashamedly "intolerant." It is the American Way of Life that provides the framework in terms of which the crucial values of American existence are couched. By every realistic criterion the American Way of Life is the operative faith of the American people.

It would be the crudest kind of misunderstanding to dismiss the American Way of Life as no more than a political formula or propagandist slogan, or to regard it as simply an expression of the "materialistic" impulses of the American people. Americans are "materialistic," no doubt, but surely not more so than other people, than the French peasant or petty bourgeois, for example. All such labels are irrelevant, if not meaningless. The American Way of Life is, at bottom, a spiritual structure, a structure of ideas and ideals, of aspirations and values, of beliefs and standards; it synthesizes all that commends itself to the American as the right, the good, and the true in actual life. It embraces such seemingly incongruous elements as sanitary plumbing and freedom of opportunity, Coca-Cola and an intense faith in education—all felt as moral questions relating to the proper way of life.[17] The very expression "way of life" points to its religious essence, for one's ultimate, over-all way of life in one's religion.

The American Way of Life is, of course, conceived as the corporate "way" of the American people, but it has its implications for the American as an individual as well. It is something really operative in his actual life. When in the *Ladies' Home Journal* poll, Americans were asked "to look within [themselves] and state honestly whether [they] thought [they] really obeyed the law of love under certain special conditions," 90 per cent said yes and 5 per cent no when the one to be "loved" was a person belonging to a different religion; 80 per cent said yes and 12 per cent no when it was the case of a member of a different race; 78 per cent said yes and 10 per cent no when it concerned a business competitor—but only 27 per cent said yes and 57 per cent no in the case of "a member of a political party that you think is dangerous," while 25 per cent said yes and 63 per cent no when it concerned an enemy of the nation.[18] These figures are most illuminating, first because of the incredible self-assurance they reveal with which the average American believes he fulfills the "impossible" law of love, but also because of the light they cast on the differential impact of the violation of this law on the American conscience. For it is obvious that the figures reflect not so much the actual behavior of the American people—no people on earth ever loved their neighbors as themselves as much as the American people say they do—as how seriously Americans take transgressions against the law of love in various cases. Americans feel they *ought* to love their fellow men despite differences of race or creed or business interest; that is what the American Way of Life emphatically prescribes.[19] But the American Way of Life almost explicitly sanctions hating a member of a "dangerous" political party (Communists and fascists are obviously meant here) or an enemy of one's country, and therefore an overwhelming majority avow their hate. In both situations, while the Jewish-Christian law of love is formally acknowledged, the truly operative factor is the value system embodied in the American Way of Life. Where the American Way of Life approves of love of one's fellow man, most Americans confidently assert that they practice such love; where the American Way of Life disapproves, the great mass of Americans do not hesitate to confess that they do not practice it, and apparently feel very little guilt for their failure. No better pragmatic test as to what the operative religion of the American people actually is could be desired.[20]

It is not suggested here that the ideals Americans feel to be indicated in the American Way of Life are scrupulously observed in the practice of Americans; they are in fact constantly violated, often grossly. But violated or not, they are felt to be normative and relevant to "business and politics" in a way that the formal tenets of "official" religion are not. That is what makes the American Way of Life the "common religion" of American society in the sense here intended.

It should be clear that what is being designated under the American Way of Life is not the so-called "common denominator" religion; it is not a synthetic system composed of beliefs to be found in all or in a group of religions. It is an organic structure of ideas, values, and beliefs that constitutes a faith common to Americans and genuinely operative in their lives, a faith that markedly influences, and is influenced by, the "official" religions of American society. Sociologically, anthropologically, if one pleases, it is the characteristic American religion, undergirding American life and overarching American society despite all indubitable differences of region, section, culture, and class.

Yet qualifications are immediately in order. Not for all Americans is this American religion, this "common religion" of American society, equally operative; some indeed explicitly repudiate it as religion. By and large, it would seem that what is resistive in contemporary American society to the American Way of Life as religion may be understood under three heads. First, there are the churches of immigrant-ethnic background that still cherish their traditional creeds and confessions as a sign of their distinctive origin and are unwilling to let these be dissolved into an over-all "American religion"; certain Lutheran and Reformed churches in this country[21] as well as sections of the Catholic Church would fall into this classification. Then there are groups, not large but increasing, that have an explicit and conscious theological concern, whether it be "orthodox," "neo-orthodox," or "liberal"; in varying degrees, they find their theologies at odds with the implied "theology" of the American

Way of Life. Finally, there are the ill-defined, though by all accounts numerous and influential, "religions of the disinherited," the many "holiness," pentecostal, and millenarian sects of the socially and culturally submerged segments of our society;[22] for them, their "peculiar" religion is frequently still too vital and all-absorbing to be easily subordinated to some "common faith." All of these cases, it will be noted, constitute "hold outs" against the sweep of religious Americanism; in each case there is an element of alienation which generates a certain amount of tension in social life.

What is this American Way of Life that we have said constitutes the "common religion" of American society? An adequate description and analysis of what is implied in this phrase still remains to be attempted, and certainly it will not be ventured here; but some indications may not be out of place.

The American Way of Life is the symbol by which Americans define themselves and establish their unity. German unity, it would seem, is felt to be largely racial-folkish, French unity largely cultural; but neither of these ways is open to the American people, the most diverse in racial and cultural origins of any in the world. As American unity has emerged, it has emerged more and more clearly as a unity embodied in, and symbolized by the complex structure known as the American Way of Life.

If the American Way of Life had to be defined in one word, "democracy" would undoubtedly be the word, but democracy in a peculiarly American sense. On its political side it means the Constitution; on its economic side, "free enterprise"; on its social side, an equalitarianism which is not only compatible with but indeed actually implies vigorous economic competition and high mobility. Spiritually, the American Way of Life is best expressed in a certain kind of "idealism" which has come to be recognized as characteristically American. It is a faith that has its symbols and its rituals, its holidays and its liturgy, its saints and its sancta;[23] and it is a faith that every American, to the degree that he is an American, knows and understands.

The American Way of Life is individualistic, dynamic, pragmatic. It affirms the supreme value and dignity of the individual; it stresses incessant activity on his part, for he is never to rest but is always to be striving to "get ahead"; it defines an ethic of self-reliance, merit, and character, and judges by achievement: "deeds, not creeds" are what count. The American Way of Life is humanitarian, "forward looking," optimistic. Americans are easily the most generous and philanthropic people in the world, in terms of their ready and unstinting response to suffering anywhere on the globe. The American believes in progress, in self-improvement, and quite fanatically in education. But above all, the American is idealistic. Americans cannot go on making money or achieving worldly success simply on its own merits; such "materialistic" things must, in the American mind, be justified in "higher" terms, in terms of "service" or "stewardship" or "general welfare." Because Americans are so idealistic, they tend to confuse espousing an ideal with fulfilling it and are always tempted to regard themselves as good as the ideals they entertain: hence the amazingly high valuation most Americans quite sincerely place on their own virtue. And because they are so idealistic, Americans tend to be moralistic: they are inclined to see all issues as plain and simple, black and white, issues of morality. Every struggle in which they are seriously engaged becomes a "crusade." To Mr. Eisenhower, who in many ways exemplifies American religion in a particularly representative way, the second world war was a "crusade" (as was the first to Woodrow Wilson); so was his campaign for the presidency ("I am engaged in a crusade . . . to substitute good government for what we most earnestly believe has been bad government"); and so is his administration—a "battle for the republic" against "godless Communism" abroad and against "corruption and materialism" at home. It was Woodrow Wilson who once said, "Sometimes people call me an idealist. Well, that is the way I know I'm an American: America is the most idealistic nation in the world"; Eisenhower was but saying the same thing when he solemnly affirmed: "The things that make us proud to be Americans are of the soul and of the spirit."[24]

The American Way of Life is, of course, anchored in the American's vision of America. The Puritan's dream of a new "Israel" and a new "Promised Land" in the New World, the *"novus ordo seclorum"* on the Great Seal of the United States reflect the perennial American conviction that in the New World a new beginning has been made, a new order of things established, vastly different from and superior to the decadent institutions of the Old World. This conviction, emerging out of the earliest reality of American history, was continuously nourished through the many decades of immigration into the present century by the residual hopes and expectations of the immigrants, for whom the New World had to be really something new if it was to be anything at all. And this conviction still remains pervasive in American life, hardly shaken by the new shape of the world and the challenge of the "new orders" of the twentieth century, Nazism and Communism. It is the secret of what outsiders must take to be the incredible self-righteousness of the American people, who tend to see the world divided into an innocent, virtuous America confronted with a corrupt, devious, and guileful Europe and Asia. The self-righteousness, however, if self-righteousness it be, is by no means simple, if only because virtually all Americans are themselves derived from the foreign parts they so distrust. In any case, this feeling about

America as really and truly the "new order" of things at last established is the heart of the outlook defined by the American Way of Life.[25]

In her *Vermont Tradition,* Dorothy Canfield Fisher lists as that tradition's principal ingredients: individual freedom, personal independence, human dignity, community responsibility, social and political democracy, sincerity, restraint in outward conduct, and thrift.[26] With some amplification—particularly emphasis on the uniqueness of the American "order" and the great importance assigned to religion—this may be taken as a pretty fair summary of some of the "values" embodied in the American Way of Life. It will not escape the reader that this account is essentially an idealized description of the middle-class ethos. And, indeed, that is just what it is. The American Way of Life is a middle-class way, just as the American people in their entire outlook and feeling are a middle-class people.[27] But the American Way of Life as it has come down to us is not merely middle-class; it is emphatically inner-directed. Indeed, it is probably one of the best expressions of inner-direction in history. As such, it now seems to be undergoing some degree of modification—perhaps at certain points disintegration—under the impact of the spread of other-direction in our society. For the foreseeable future, however, we may with some confidence expect the continuance in strength of the American Way of Life as both the tradition and the "common faith" of the American people.[28]

III

The American Way of Life as the "common faith" of American society has coexisted for some centuries with the historic faiths of the American people, and the two have influenced each other in many profound and subtle ways. The influence has been complex and reciprocal, to the point where casual priority becomes impossible to assign if indeed it does not become altogether meaningless. From the very beginning the American Way of Life was shaped by the contours of American Protestantism; it may, indeed, best be understood as a kind of secularized Puritanism, a Puritanism without transcendence, without sense of sin or judgment. The Puritan's vision of a new "Promised Land" in the wilderness of the New World has become, as we have suggested, the American's deep sense of the newness and uniqueness of things in the Western Hemisphere. The Puritan's sense of vocation and "inner-worldly asceticism" can still be detected in the American's gospel of action and service, and his consciousness of high responsibility before God in the American's "idealism." The Puritan's abiding awareness of the ambiguity of all human motivations and his insight into the corruptions of inordinate power have left their mark not only on the basic structure of our constitutional system but also on the entire social philosophy of the American people.[29] Nor have other strands of early American Protestantism been without their effect. There can be little doubt that Pietism co-operated with frontier revivalism in breaking down the earlier concern with dogma and doctrine, so that the slogan, "deeds, not creeds," soon became the hallmark both of American religion and of the American Way of Life.[30] These are but aspects of an influence that is often easier to see than to define.

The reciprocal action of the American Way of Life in shaping and reshaping the historic faiths of Christianity and Judaism on American soil is perhaps more readily discerned. By and large, we may say that these historic religions have all tended to become "Americanized" under the pervasive influence of the American environment. This "Americanization" has been the product not so much of conscious direction as of a "diffuse convergence" operating spontaneously in the context of the totality of American life. What it has brought, however, is none the less clear: "religious groupings throughout [American] society [have been] stamped with recognizably 'American' qualities,"[31] to an extent indeed where foreign observers sometimes find the various American religions more like each other than they are like their European counterparts.[32]

Under the influence of the American environment the historic Jewish and Christian faiths have tended to become secularized in the sense of becoming integrated as parts within a larger whole defined by the American Way of Life. "There is a marked tendency," Williams writes in his discussion of the relations of religion to other institutions in the United States, "to regard religion as a good because it is useful in furthering other major values—in other words, to reverse the ends-means relation implied in the conception of religion as an ultimate value."[33] In this reversal the Christian and Jewish faiths tend to be prized because they help promote ideals and standards that all Americans are expected to share on a deeper level than merely "official" religion. Insofar as any reference is made to the God in whom all Americans "believe" and of whom the "official" religions speak, it is primarily as sanction and underpinning for the supreme values of the faith embodied in the American Way of Life. Secularization of religion could hardly go further.

As a consequence, in some cases of its own origins, but primarily of the widespread influence of the American environment, religion in America has tended toward a marked disparagement of "forms," whether theological or liturgical. Even the highly liturgical and theological churches have felt the effects of this spirit to the degree that they have become thoroughly acculturated. Indeed, the anti-theological, anti-liturgical bias is still pervasive despite the recent upsurge of theological concern and despite the greater interest being shown in liturgy because of its psychological power and "emotional richness."

American religion is (within the limits set by the particular traditions of the churches) non-theological and non-liturgical; it is activistic and occupied with the things of the world to a degree that has become a byword among European churchmen. With this activism has gone a certain "latitudinarianism," associated with the de-emphasis of theology and doctrine: Americans tend to believe that "ethical behavior and a good life, rather than adherence to a specific creed, [will] earn a share in the heavenly kingdom."[34] The activism of American religion has manifested itself in many forms throughout our history: in the Puritan concern for the total life of the community; in the passionate championing of all sorts of reform causes by the evangelical movements of the first half of the nineteenth century; in the "social gospel" of more recent times; in the ill-starred Prohibition "crusade"; in the advanced "progressive" attitudes on social questions taken by the National Council of Churches, the National Catholic Welfare Conference, and the various rabbinical associations; in the strong social emphasis of American Protestant "neo-orthodoxy." This activism, which many Europeans seem to regard as the distinguishing feature of American religion, both reflects the dynamic temper of the American Way of Life and has been a principal factor in its development.

It is hardly necessary to continue this analysis much farther along these general lines. The optimism, moralism, and idealism of Jewish and Christian faith in America are plain evidence of the profound effect of the American outlook on American religion. Indeed, such evidence is amply provided by any tabulation of the distinctive features of religion in America,[35] and needs no special emphasis at this point.

What is perhaps of crucial importance, and requires a more detailed examination, is the new attitude toward religion and the new conception of the church that have emerged in America.[36]

Americans believe in religion in a way that perhaps no other people do. It may indeed be said that the primary religious affirmation of the American people, in harmony with the American Way of Life, is that religion is a "good thing," a supremely "good thing," for the individual and the community. And "religion" here means not so much any particular religion, but religion as such, religion-in-general. "Our government makes no sense," President Eisenhower recently declared, "unless it is founded in a deeply felt religious faith—*and I don't care what it is*" (emphasis added).[37] In saying this, the President was saying something that almost any American could understand and approve, but which must seem like a deplorable heresey to the European churchman. Every American could understand, first, that Mr. Eisenhower's apparent indifferentism ("and I don't care what it is") was not indifferentism at all, but the expression of the conviction that at bottom the "three great faiths" were really "saying the same thing" in affirming the "spiritual ideals" and "moral values" of the American Way of Life. Every American, moreover, could understand that what Mr. Eisenhower was emphasizing so vehemently was the indispensability of religion as the foundation of society. This is one aspect of what Americans mean when they say that they "believe in religion." The object of devotion of this kind of religion, however, is "not God but 'religion.' . . . The faith is not in God but in faith; we worship not God but our own worshiping."[38] When Americans think of themselves as a profoundly religious people, whose "first allegiance" is "reserved . . . to the kingdom of the spirit,"[39] this is, by and large, what they mean, and not any commitment to the doctrines or traditions of the historic faiths.

With this view of religion is associated a closely analogous view of the church. For America, the celebrated dichotomy of "church" and "sect,"[40] however pertinent it may be to European conditions, has only a secondary significance. The concept of the church as the nation religiously organized, established socially, if not always legally, has only an oblique relevance to American reality; and though America does know sects in the sense of "fringe" groups of the "disinherited," it does not understand these groups and their relation to the more conventional churches the way Europe does. An entirely new conception of church and church institutions has emerged in America.

It must be remembered that in America the variety and multiplicity of churches did not, as in Europe, come with the breakdown of a single established national church; in America, taking the nation as a whole, the variety and multiplicity of churches was almost the original condition and coeval with the emergence of the new society. In America religious pluralism is thus not merely a historical and political fact; it is, in the mind of the American, the primordial condition of things, an essential aspect of the American Way of Life, and therefore in itself an aspect of religious belief.[41] Americans, in other words, believe that the plurality of religious groups is a proper and legitimate condition. However much he may be attached to his own church, however dimly he may regard the beliefs and practices of other churches, the American tends to feel rather strongly that total religious uniformity, even with his own church benefiting thereby, would be something undesirable and wrong, indeed scarcely conceivable. Pluralism of religions and churches is something quite axiomatic to the American. This feeling, more than anything else, is the foundation of the American doctrine of the "separation of church and state," for it is the heart of this doctrine that the government may not do anything that implies the preeminence or superior legitimacy of one church over another.

This means that outside the Old World distinction

of church and sect America has given birth to a new type of religious structure—the denomination.[42] The denomination as we know it is a stable, settled church, enjoying a legitimate and recognized place in a larger aggregate of churches, each recognizing the proper status of the others.[43] The denomination is the "nonconformist sect" become central and normative. It differs from the church in the European understanding of the term in that it would never dream of claiming to be *the* national ecclesiastical institution; it differs from the sect in that it is socially established, thoroughly institutionalized, and nuclear to the society in which it is found. The European dichotomy becomes meaningless, and instead we have the nuclear denomination on the one side, and the peripheral sect on the way to becoming a denomination on the other. So firmly entrenched is this denominational idea in the mind of the American that even American Catholics have come to think in such terms; theologically the Catholic Church of course continues to regard itself as the one true church, but in their actual social attitudes American Catholics, hardly less than American Protestants or Jews, tend to think of their church as a denomination existing side by side with other denominations in a pluralistic harmony that is felt to be somehow of the texture of American life.[44]

Denominational pluralism, as the American idea of the church may be called, obviously implies that no church can look to the state for its members or support. Voluntarism and evangelism are thus the immediate consequences of the American idea: for their maintenance, for their very existence, churches must depend on the voluntary adherence of their members, and they are therefore moved to pursue a vigorous evangelistic work to win people to their ranks. The accommodation of the church to American reality extends even to its inner polity. "As the polity of the Roman church followed the pattern of the Roman empire," H. Richard Niebuhr points out, "so the

American churches incline to organize themselves [along representative lines] in conformity with the system of state and national legislatures and executives."[45] Even the Roman Catholic Church, with its fixed hierarchical structure, has not been totally immune to American influence of this kind.[46]

The denominational idea is fundamental to American thinking about religion, but it is not the last word. Americans think of their various churches as denominations, but they also feel that somehow the denominations fall into larger wholes which we have called religious communities. This kind of denominational aggregation is, of course, something that pertains primarily to Protestantism and to a lesser degree to Judaism; both have more or less organized denominations which, taken together, form the religious communities. Catholicism, on the other hand, has no such overt inner divisions, but American Catholics readily understand the phenomenon when they see it among Protestants and Jews. Denominations are felt to be somehow a matter of individual preference, and movement between denominations is not uncommon; the religious community, on the other hand, is taken as something more objective and given, something in which, by and large, one is born, lives, and dies, something that (to recall our earlier analysis) identifies and defines one's position in American society.[47] Since the religious community in its present form is a recent social emergent, its relations to the denominations properly so-called are still relatively fluid and undefined but the main lines of development would seem to be fairly clear.

When the plurality of denominations comprehended in religious communities is seen from the standpoint of the "common faith" of American society, what emerges is the conception of the three "communions"—Protestantism, Catholicism, Judaism—as three diverse, but equally legitimate, equally American, expressions of an over-all American religion, standing for essentially the same "moral ideals" and "spiritual values." This conception, whatever may be thought of it theologically, is in fact held, though hardly in explicit form, by many devout and religiously sophisticated Americans. It would seem to be the obvious meaning of the title, *The Religions of Democracy,* given to a recent authoritative statement of the Protestant, Catholic, and Jewish positions.[48] "Democracy" apparently has its religions which fall under it as species fall under the genus of which they are part. And in this usage "democracy" is obviously a synonym for the American Way of Life.

It is but one more step, though a most fateful one, to proceed from "the religions of democracy" to "democracy as religion" and consciously to erect "democracy" into a super-faith above and embracing the three recognized religions. This step has been taken by a number of thinkers in recent years. Thus, Professor J. Paul Williams has been urging a program of religious reconstruction in which he insists that: "Americans must come to look on the democratic ideal (not necessarily the American practice of it) as the Will of God, or if they please, of Nature. . . . Americans must be brought to the conviction that democracy is the very Law of Life. . . . The state must be brought into the picture; governmental agencies must teach the democratic ideal *as religion* . . . primary responsibility for teaching democracy as religion must be given to the public school, for instance . . ."[49]

Professor Horace M. Kallen reaches very much the same conclusion from another direction. "For the communicants of the democratic faith," he writes, "it is the religion *of* and *for* religions. . . . [It is] the religion of religions, all may freely come together in it."[50]

It is not our purpose, at this point, to draw the theological implications of this super-religion of "democracy" as the "religion of religions"; it is only necessary to point out that it marks a radical break with the fundamental presuppositions of both Judaism and Christianity, to which it must appear as a particularly insidious kind of idolatry. What is merely implicit and perhaps never intended in the acceptance of the American Way of Life as the "common religion" of American society is here brought to its logical conclusion and made to reveal its true inner meaning.

By and large, the "common faith" of American society remains implicit and is never carried to the logical conclusion to which a few ideologists have pushed it. By the great mass of the American people the American Way of Life is not avowed as a super-faith above and embracing the historic religions. It operates as a "common faith" at deeper levels, through its pervasive influence on the patterns of American thought and feeling. It makes no pretensions to override or supplant the recognized religions, to which it assigns a place of great eminence and honor in the American scheme of things. But all the implications are there . . .

IV

The "common faith" of American society is not merely a civic religion to celebrate the values and convictions of the American people as a corporate entity. It has its inner, personal aspects as well; or rather, side by side and in intimate relation with the civic religion of the American Way of Life, there has developed, primarily through a devitalization of the historic faiths, an inner, personal religion that promises salvation to the disoriented, tormented souls of a society in crisis.

This inner, personal religion is based on the American's *faith in faith*. We have seen that a primary religious affirmation of the American is his belief in religion. The American believes that religion is something very important for the community; he also believes that "faith," or what we may call religiosity, is a

kind of "miracle drug" that can cure all the ailments of
the spirit. It is not faith in *anything* that is so powerful,
just faith, the "magic of believing." "It was back in
those days," a prominent American churchman
writes, recalling his early years, "that I formed a habit
that I have never broken. I began saying in the morning
two words, 'I believe.' Those two words *with nothing
added* . . . gave me a running start for my day, and for
every day" (emphasis not in original).[51]

The cult of faith takes two forms, which we might
designate as introvert and extrovert. In its introvert
form faith is trusted to bring mental health and "peace
of mind," to dissipate anxiety and guilt, and to translate the soul to the blessed land of "normality" and
"self-acceptance." In earlier times this cult of faith was
quite literally a cult of "faith healing," best expressed
in what H. Richard Niebuhr has described as the
"man-centered, this-worldly, lift-yourselves-by-your-
own-bootstraps doctrine of New Thought and Christian Science."[52] Latterly it has come to vest itself in the
fashionable vocabulary of psychoanalysis and is offering a synthesis of religion and psychiatry.[53] But at
bottom it is the same cult of faith in faith, the same
promise that through "those two words, 'I believe,'
with nothing added," all our troubles will be dissipated and inner peace and harmony restored.

The cult of faith has also its extrovert form, and that
is known as "positive thinking." "Positive thinking,"
thinking that is "affirmative" and avoids the corrosions of "negativity" and "skepticism," thinking that
"has faith," is recommended as a powerful force in the
world of struggle and achievement.[54] Here again it is
not so much faith in anything, certainly not the theocentric faith of the historic religions, that is supposed
to confer this power—but just faith, the psychological
attitude of having faith, so to speak. And here too the
cult is largely the product of the inner disintegration
and enfeeblement of the historic religions; the familiar
words are retained, but the old meaning is voided.

"Have faith," "don't lose faith," and the like, were once injunctions to preserve one's unwavering trust in the God from Whom comes both the power to live and the "peace that passeth understanding." Gradually these phrases have come to be an appeal to maintain a "positive" attitude to life and not to lose confidence in oneself and one's activities. "To believe in yourself and in everything you do": such, at bottom, is the meaning of the contemporary cult of faith, whether it is proclaimed by devout men from distinguished pulpits or offered as the "secret of success" by self-styled psychologists who claim to have discovered the "hidden powers" of man.[55] What is important is faith, faith in faith. Even where the classical symbols and formulas are still retained, that is very often what is meant and what is understood.

Such are some major aspects of the social, cultural, and spiritual environment in which religion in America moves and has its being. And religion in America means the three great religious communities, the Protestant, the Catholic, and the Jewish. These three religious communities must now be examined and the main features characterizing each of them in turn described.

Notes

[1] *Belief in God:* 97 per cent—"Do Americans Believe in God?", *The Catholic Digest,* November 1952; 96 per cent—Gallup poll, *Public Opinion News Service,* December 18, 1954; 95 per cent—Lincoln Barnett, "God and the American People," *Ladies' Home Journal,* November 1948, p. 37. According to the *Catholic Digest* poll 89 per cent of Americans believe in the Trinity ("How Many in the U.S. Believe in the Trinity?", *The Catholic Digest,* July 1953) and 80 per cent think of Christ as divine ("What We Americans Think of Our Lord," *The Catholic Digest,* August 1953).

[2] *Church membership and attendance:* see above, chap. iv, pp. 47–50.

3 *Prayer:* 92 per cent answer yes to the question, "Do you ever pray to God?" ("Americans and Prayer," *The Catholic Digest,* November 1953); 90 per cent say they pray, 56 per cent "frequently"—Barnett, "God and the American People," *Ladies' Home Journal,* November 1948, p. 37.

4 *Life after death:* 77 per cent believe in afterlife, 7 per cent don't, 16 per cent don't know—"What Do Americans Think of Heaven and Hell?", *The Catholic Digest,* March 1953; 76 per cent say yes, 13 per cent no, 11 per cent don't know—Gallup poll, *Public Opinion News Service,* December 11, 1944; 73 per cent say yes, 15 per cent no, 12 per cent no opinion—Barnett, "God and the American People," *Ladies' Home Journal,* November 1948, pp. 230–31; 74 per cent believe in life after death—Gallup poll, *Public Opinion News Service,* April 19, 1957.

Heaven and Hell: 72 per cent believe in heaven, 58 per cent in hell— *The Catholic Digest,* as above; 52 per cent think that "life after death is divided into heaven and hell," though heaven looms larger in their minds than hell—Barnett, "God and the American People," *Ladies' Home Journal,* November 1948, p. 231; 61 per cent believe there is a devil— Gallup poll, *Public Opinion News Service,* April 19, 1957.

5 *Opinion about church and clergymen:* 75 per cent deny the allegation that the church is too much concerned about money—"Is the Church Too Much Concerned About Money?", *The Catholic Digest,* March 1954; 68 per cent regard clergymen as "very understanding," 21 per cent as "fairly understanding"—"How Understanding Are Clergymen?", *The Catholic Digest,* December 1953; clergymen rank at the top in the scale of those who "do most good"—see above, chap. iv, p. 51.

6 *Bible:* 86 per cent regard it as divinely inspired, the "word of God"— "What Do Americans Think of the Bible?", *The Catholic Digest,* May 1954; a survey conducted by the *British Weekly* gives the figure for Americans who regard the Bible as divinely inspired as 86.5 per cent (see *Information Service* [National Council of Churches of Christ], December 27, 1952).

7 *Religious instruction:* 98 per cent say yes—"Do Americans Want Their Children to Receive Religious Instruction?", *The Catholic Digest,* September 1953. *Children raised as church members:* 72 per cent say yes— "How Important Is Religion to Americans?", *The Catholic Digest,* February 1953.

8 *Importance of religion:* 75 per cent regard it as "very important," 20 per cent as "fairly important"—"How Important Is Religion to Americans?", *The Catholic Digest,* February 1953; 69 per cent think that the influence of religion is increasing and 81 per cent believe that religion can answer "most of today's problems"—Gallup poll, *Public Opinion News Service,* April 21, 1957. The religiosity of the American people appears even more striking when it is contrasted with the much more "skeptical" views held by the British; see the series of comparative

surveys conducted by the Gallup organization, *Public Opinion News Service,* April 16, 17, 18, 19, 21, 1957.

[9] Barnett, "God and the American People," *Ladies' Home Journal,* November 1948, p. 234.

[10] "What the U. S. Thinks of Life Here and Hereafter," *The Catholic Digest,* May 1953.

[11] Barnett, "God and the American People," *Ladies' Home Journal,* November 1948, pp. 233, 234, 235.

[12] Barnett, "God and the American People," *Ladies' Home Journal,* November 1948, p. 234.

[13] See particularly the statement of Father George B. Ford, in Barnett, "God and the American People," *Ladies' Home Journal,* November 1948, p. 237.

[14] Robin M. Williams, Jr., *American Society: A Sociological Interpretation* (Knopf, 1951), p. 312.

[15] Williams, *American Society,* p. 320 n.

[16] Williams, *American Society,* p. 344.

[17] When an American tourist comes upon the inadequate sanitary arrangements in certain parts of Europe and discovers what seems to him the careless attitude of the inhabitants in matters of personal hygiene, he is inclined to feel what he experiences not simply as a shortcoming in modern living conveniences but as a *moral defect,* on a par with irreligion, caste rigidity, and the absence of American representative democracy. Cp. the following placard displayed by many restaurants in the midwest: "Sanitation is a way of life. As a way of life, it must be nourished from within and grow as an ideal in human relations."

[18] Barnett, "God and the American People," *Ladies' Home Journal,* November 1948, pp. 235–36.

[19] Where this "principle" of the American Way of Life is flagrantly violated by local prescription, as in the case of racial attitudes in the south and elsewhere, festering "bad conscience" and a destructive defensive aggressiveness are the result.

[20] "Differences in religion make a difference in social conduct" (Williams, *American Society,* p. 311). Investigating belief-systems from this angle would seem to be a good way of discovering what the "religion" of an individual or a group really is.

[21] Discussing the European background of such churches, H. Richard

Niebuhr writes: "These churches are doctrinal and liturgical in character, regarding conformity to creed and ritual as the essential requirements of Christianity" (*The Social Sources of Denominationalism* [Holt, 1929], p. 126).

22 For a discussion of the "religions of the disinherited," see below, chap. vi, pp. 122–23, chap. ix, pp. 216–19.

23 See the illuminating account of Memorial Day as an "American sacred ceremony" in W. Lloyd Warner, *Structure of American Life* (Edinburgh, 1952), chap. x. Warner writes: "The Memorial Day ceremonies and subsidiary rites, such as those of Armistice Day, of today, yesterday, and tomorrow, are rituals which are a sacred symbol system which functions periodically to integrate the whole community, with its conflicting symbols and its opposing autonomous churches and associations. . . . Memorial Day is a cult of the dead which organizes and integrates the various faiths, ethnic and class groups, into a sacred unity" (p. 214). As to the "saints" of the American Way of Life, Warner quotes a Memorial Day orator: "No character except the Carpenter of Nazareth has ever been honored the way Washington and Lincoln have been in New England. Virtue, freedom from sin, and righteousness were qualities possessed by Washington and Lincoln, and in possessing these qualities both were true Americans, and we would do well to emulate them. Let us first be true Americans" (p. 220). The theological implications of this statement are sensational: Washington and Lincoln, as "true Americans," are credited with the moral and spiritual qualities ("virtue, freedom from sin, and righteousness") traditionally associated with Christ, and we are all urged to "emulate" them!

24 For the quotations, as well as a general account of Mr. Eisenhower's religion, see Paul Hutchinson, "The President's Religious Faith," *The Christian Century,* March 24, 1954. For a sharp critique, see William Lee Miller, "Piety Along the Potomac," *The Reporter,* August 17, 1954.

25 For a penetrating examination of the sources and expressions of the American conviction of a "new order of things" in the New World, see Reinhold Niebuhr, *The Irony of American History* (Scribner's, 1952).

26 Dorothy Canfield Fisher, *Vermont Tradition* (Little, Brown, 1953). For a comprehensive survey of American life, see Max Lerner, *America as a Civilization: Life and Thought in the United States Today* (Simon and Schuster, 1957); see also Elting E. Morison, ed., *The American Style: Essays in Value and Performance* (Harper, 1958).

27 "America is a middle-class country, and the middle-class values and styles of perception reach into all levels except perhaps the fringes at the very top and the very bottom" (David Riesman, *Individualism Reconsidered* [Free Press, 1954], p. 499).

28 Riesman sees the immigrant generations as an important source of

replenishment of old-line middle-class inner-directedness in American society (*Individualism Reconsidered,* pp. 289, 290).

29 See H. Richard Niebuhr, *The Kingdom of God in America* (Willett, Clark, 1937), pp. 76–83.

30 See F. E. Mayer, *The Religious Bodies of America* (Concordia, 1954), pp. 352–53, 354, 378 n.

31 Williams, *American Society,* p. 319. See also Roy F. Nichols, *Religion and American Democracy* (Louisiana State University Press, 1959) and William Lee Miller, "Religion and the American Way of Life," in *Religion and the Free Society* (Fund for the Republic, 1958).

32 "European visitors are able to detect better than we ourselves the emergence of a 'typically American' form of Christian worship" (Herbert Wallace Schneider, *Religion in 20th Century America* [Harvard, 1952], p. 170). "As many have noticed, the Protestant churches in America, even though brought from Europe, show more qualities in common than any one retains with its European stem. And they feel that in America, the synagogue is no longer an alien. Even the Catholic Church in America acquires a tone unlike Catholicism in Europe" (Perry Miller, "The Location of American Religious Freedom," in *Religion and Freedom of Thought* [Doubleday, 1954], p. 21).

33 Williams, *American Society,* p. 337. Something of the shift involved in this secularization of Jewish-Christian faith is suggested by Ralph Barton Perry in his apologia for Protestant "liberalism": "If it does not stress the love of God, it does at least embrace the love of neighbor. If it neglects the fatherhood of God, it at any rate proclaims the fraternity of men. If it disparages the church along with other corporate entities, it is because it is so insistent on the finality of the human person. The independence of this moral ideal in no way argues *against* theism . . ." (Ralph Barton Perry, *Characteristically American* [Knopf, 1949], p. 117).

34 Oscar Handlin, *The Uprooted* (Little, Brown, 1951), p. 128.

35 See, e.g., the section, "Relatively Distinctive Features of American Religious Institutions," in Williams, *American Society,* pp. 315–51.

36 Two recent studies of contemporary American religion are of major importance: A. Roy Eckardt, *The Surge of American Piety* (Association Press, 1958) and Martin E. Marty, *The New Shape of American Religion* (Harper, 1959). See also Lerner, *America as a Civilization,* chap. x, sec. 1, "God and the Churches" (pp. 703–17) and William H. Whyte, Jr., *The Organization Man* (Simon and Schuster, 1956), Part VII, chap. 26, "The Church of Suburbia" (pp. 365–81).

37 *The New York Times,* December 23, 1952; see also G. Elson Ruff, *The Dilemma of Church and State* (Muhlenberg, 1954), p. 85. Cp. the

very similar sentiment expressed by Robert C. Ruark: "Although I am not a practicing religionist, I have a great respect for organized religion, no matter what shape it takes" ("Scoff-religious," *New York World Telegram,* October 10, 1955).

38 Miller, "Piety Along the Potomac," *The Reporter,* August 17, 1954. Mr. Miller continues: "If the object of devotion is not God but 'religion' . . . then the resulting religiosity may become simply the instrument of more substantial commitments." The most "substantial" commitment of the American people, to which their "religiosity" is instrumental, is the American Way of Life. Once more to quote Mr. Eisenhower: "I am the most intensely religious man I know. Nobody goes through six years of war without faith. A democracy cannot exist without a religious base. I believe in democracy" (*New York Times,* May 4, 1948).

39 Dwight D. Eisenhower, quoted in Paul Hutchinson, "The President's Religious Faith," *The Christian Century,* March 24, 1954.

40 See Ernst Troeltsch, *The Social Teaching of the Christian Churches* (1911; tr. by Olive Wyon, Macmillan, 1931), Vol. I, pp. 331–49, Vol. II, pp. 691–728; also J. Milton Yinger, *Religion in the Struggle for Power* (Duke, 1946), pp. 16–50.

41 Williams speaks of a "value-consensus in which religious differences are subsidiary to the values of religious liberty" (*American Society,* p. 345).

42 "The Mormons, the Orthodox Jews, and a few small religious communities are religiously organized peoples, but almost all other religious bodies in the United States, including the Roman Catholic Church, are neither national churches nor sects; they are commonly known as denominations or 'communions' " (Schneider, *Religion in 20th Century America,* p. 22). Even the groups Schneider mentions as exceptions, insofar as they have become acculturated to American life, would seem to fall into the same pattern.

43 Since most American denominations emerged from earlier sects, denominations have sometimes been defined as "simply sects in an advanced stage of development and adjustment to each other and the secular world" (Leopold von Wiese, *Systematic Sociology,* adapted and amplified by Howard Becker [Wiley, 1932], p. 626). There is, of course, a good deal of truth in this definition; its defect, however, is that it regards the denonination as essentially transitional between sect and church, which is emphatically not the case with denominations in the American sense. American denominations have indeed, by and large, developed out of sects, but they represent the final stage of development, rather than a transitional stage to something else ("church" in the European sense). For a more general discussion, see Joachim Wach, *Types of Religious Experience* (Routledge and Kegan Paul, 1951), chap. ix, "Church, Denomination, and Sect."

44 In a number of European countries (Germany, Holland, Switzerland), Protestant and Catholic churches have reached a kind of balance in which neither can pretend to be "the" national church. But where this is the case, it is simply a social and historical fact, not the proper and normative condition. In America, on the other hand, the plurality of churches is held to be proper and normative; in this the American situation differs fundamentally from the European, even where the latter seems to resemble it most.

45 H. Richard Niebuhr, *The Social Sources of Denominationalism*, p. 207. "The Church in our time, like the Church in any place at any time, is deeply influenced in its institutional forms by the political and economic society with which it lives in conjunction. As the polity of all the churches, whether they are episcopal, presbyterian, or congregational by tradition, has been modified in the direction of the political structure of Canada and the United States, so the institutional status and authority of the ministry are being modified in the direction of the democratic type of political, educational, and economic executive or managerial authority" (H. Richard Niebuhr, *The Purpose of the Church and Its Ministry* [Harper, 1956], p. 90). Cf. the statement of Franklin Clark Fry, president of the United Lutheran Church of America: "The polity of our church as a whole is frankly constructed on a secular model. Its prototype is the government of the United States" (quoted in H.E.F., "Lutherans Centralize," *The Christian Century*, October 27, 1954).

46 Thus McAvoy speaks of the "practical and parochial character of American Catholicism"; the "parochial" character he relates to the "American tradition of disestablishment," while for the "practical" aspect of American Catholicism, he notes that "some observers have claimed that [it] is the product of the puritanism dominant in American Protestantism" (Thomas T. McAvoy, "The Catholic Church in the United States," in Waldemar Gurian and M. A. Fitzsimons, *The Catholic Church in World Affairs* [Notre Dame, 1954], pp. 361, 364).

47 Despite all the instability of American life, fully 96 percent of Americans were found in 1955 still belonging to the religious community of their birth (see *Public Opinion News Service*, March 20, 1955).

48 Louis Finkelstein, J. Elliot Ross, and William Adams Brown, *The Religions of Democracy: Judaism, Catholicism, and Protestantism in Creed and Life* (Devin-Adair, 1946). One of the clearest expressions of this conception by a layman was voiced by Admiral William F. Halsey, principal speaker at the fifth annual "four chaplains award dinner." "This picture," Admiral Halsey declared, "is symbolic of our national life. Protestant, Catholic, and Jew, each group has given, when called upon, the full measure of devotion in defense of our [American democratic] way of life" (*The New York Times*, February 6, 1955).

49 J. Paul Williams, *What Americans Believe and How They Worship* (Harper, 1952), pp. 71, 78, 368, 374; see the critical review of this book

by J. H. Nichols, *The Christian Century*, September 3, 1952. (A strong tendency toward this kind of "religion of democracy" is to be found in Jewish Reconstructionism; see Ira Eisenstein and Eugene Kohn, *Mordecai M. Kaplan: An Evaluation* [Jewish Reconstructionist Foundation, 1952], p. 259). "The religion of the American majority is democracy. . . . In fact, the religion of public education is a more powerful factor in American life today than that of the churches. The only religion with which the great majority of American youth have ever come in contact is the religion of public education" (Conrad Moehlman, *School and Church: The American Way* [Harper, 1944], pp. ix, x). David Riesman speaks of "new ways of using the school as a kind of community center, as the chapel of a secular religion perhaps" (*Individualism Reconsidered*, p. 211).

50 H. M. Kallen, "Democracy's True Religion," *Saturday Review of Literature*, July 28, 1951.

51 Daniel A. Poling, "A Running Start for Every Day," *Parade: The Sunday Picture Magazine*, September 19, 1954.

52 H. Richard Niebuhr, *The Social Sources of Denominationalism*, P. 104. Niebuhr thus describes this type of religiosity in which the old Puritan spirituality has terminated: "In its final phase, the development of this religious movement exhibits the complete enervation of the once virile force . . . the problem of evil [has been] simplified out of existence, and for the mysterious will of the Sovereign of life and death and sin and salvation [has been substituted] the sweet benevolence of a Father-Mother God or the vague goodness of the All. Here the concern for self has been secularized to its last degree; the conflicts of sick souls have been replaced by the struggles of sick minds and bodies; the Puritan passion for perfection has become a seeking after the kingdom of health and mental peace and its comforts" (p. 105).

53 The most celebrated effort along these lines is undoubtedly Joshua Loth Liebman, *Peace of Mind* (Simon and Schuster, 1946).

54 Norman Vincent Peale, *The Power of Positive Thinking* (Prentice-Hall, 1952). For a careful study of American religious literature reflecting both the "peace of mind" and the "positive thinking" gospels, see Louis Schneider and Sanford M. Dornbusch, *Popular Religion: Inspirational Books in America* (University of Chicago Press, 1958).

55 A salesman writes to Norman Vincent Peale in the latter's regular question page in *Look*: "I have lost my faith and enthusiasm. How can I get them back?" To which Dr. Peale replies: "Every morning, give thanks for the new day and its opportunities. Think outgoingly of every prospect you will call on. . . . Affirm aloud that you are going to have a great day. Flush out all depressing, negative, and tired thoughts. Start thinking faith, enthusiasm and joy . . ." ("Norman Vincent Peale Answers Your Questions," *Look*, August 10, 1954). This may be compared with an

advertisement for a quite "secular" self-help book in *The New York Times Magazine* for May 8, 1949:

DON'T WORRY
If you don't acknowledge it,
it isn't so!
Develop the Art of Adaptability

—16—

America's Civil Religion: What It Is and Whence It Comes

(1974)

We get our notion of civil religion from the world of classical antiquity. In the world of ancient Athens and Rome, "the state and religion were so completely identified that it was impossible even to distinguish the one from the other. . . . Every city had its city religion; a city was a little church, all complete, with its gods, its dogmas, and its worship."[1] In recent years, many observers of American life have come to the conclusion that this country, too, has its civil religion, though not generally recognized as such, but fully operative in the familiar way, with its creed, cult, code, and community, like every other religion. On this there is wide agreement; but there are considerable differences among historians, sociologists, and theologians as to the sources of America's civil religion, its manifestations, and its evaluation in cultural and religious terms. These are precisely the matters I should like to discuss in the following paragraphs, with the hope of reaching some tentative conclusions on the subject.

"Every functioning society," says Robin Williams, in his influential work, *American Society: A Sociological Interpretation* (1951), "has, to an important degree, a common religion. The possession of a common set of ideas, [ideals], rituals, and symbols can supply an overarching sense of unity even in a society otherwise riddled with conflict."[2] This we might call the *operative* religion of a society, the system of norms, values, and allegiances actually functioning as such in the ongoing social life of the community. And, of course, the operative religion of a society emerges out of, and reflects, the history of that society as well as the structural forms that give it its shape and character. If we ask ourselves what is this system of "ideas, [ideals], rituals, and symbols" that serve as the "common religion" of Americans, providing them with an "overarching sense of unity," it is obvious that it cannot be any of the professed faiths of Americans, however sincerely held; I mean Protestantism, Catholicism, or Judaism, or any of the many denominations into which American Protestantism is fragmented. What is it, then, that does serve that all-important function? What is it in and through which Americans recognize their basic unity with other Americans as Americans? What is it that provides that "overarching sense of unity," expressed in the system of allegiances, norms, and values functioning in actual life, without which no society can long endure? It seems to me that a realistic appraisal of the values, ideas, and behavior of the American people leads to the conclusion that Americans, by and large, find this "common religion" in the system familiarly known as the American Way of Life. It is the American Way of Life that supplies American society with its "overarching sense of unity" amid conflict. It is the American Way of Life to which they are devoted. It is the American Way of Life that Americans are admittedly and unashamedly intolerant

about. It is the American Way of Life that provides the
framework in terms of which the crucial values of
American existence are couched. By every realistic
criterion, the American Way of Life is the operative
religion of the American people.

This is the civil religion of Americans. In it we
have—slightly modifying Fustel de Coulanges's classic
formulation—religion and national life so completely
identified that it is impossible to distinguish the one
from the other. I want to make it clear that when I
designate the American Way of Life as America's civil
religion, I am not thinking of it as a so-called com-
mon-denominator religion; it is not a synthetic system
composed of beliefs to be found in all or in a group of
religions. It is an organic structure of ideas, values,
and beliefs that constitutes a faith common to Americans as Americans, and is genuinely operative in their
lives; a faith that markedly influences, and is influenced by, the professed religions of Americans. Sociologically, anthropologically, it is *the* American religion, undergirding American national life and
overarching American society, despite all indubitable
differences of ethnicity, religion, section, culture, and
class. And it is a civil religion in the strictest sense of
the term, for, in it, national life is apotheosized, national values are religionized, national heroes are divinized, national history is experienced as a
Heilsgeschichte, as a redemptive history. All these aspects of the American Way as America's civil religion I
will illustrate and document. But, first, I want to call
attention to the notable difference in structure and
content between America's civil religion and the civil
religion of classical antiquity, or even the civil religion
as conceived of by Jean-Jacques Rousseau. It is a difference that reflects not only the vast difference in
historical context, but especially the separation between the culture of pre-Christian antiquity and the
culture of Western Christendom, especially America,
so thoroughly permeated with Jewish-Christian vi-

sions of redemptive history, messianism, and messianic fulfillment.

Let us try to look at the American Way of Life as
America's civil religion in the same objective way, in
the same detached yet not unfriendly way that an
anthropologist looks upon the religion and culture of
the primitive society he is studying. I say, let us try; it is
a question whether we, as Americans, can really scru-
tinize ourselves, as Americans, with any very high
degree of objectivity. For that, we may need another
de Tocqueville, though preferably not another
Frenchman.

America's civil religion has its spiritual side, of
course. I should include under this head, first, belief in
a Supreme Being, in which Americans are virtually
unanimous, proportionately far ahead of any other
nation in the Western world. Then I should mention
idealism and moralism: for Americans, every serious
national effort is a "crusade" and every serious national position a high moral issue. Among Americans,
the supreme value of the individual takes its place high
in the spiritual vision of America's civil religion: and,
with it, in principle, if not in practice—and, of course,
principle and practice frequently come into conflict in
every religion—the "brotherhood" of Americans:
"After all, we're all Americans!" is the familiar invocation. Above all, there is the extraordinarily high valuation Americans place on religion. The basic ethos of
America's civil religion is quite familiar: the American
Way is dynamic; optimistic; pragmatic; individualistic; egalitarian, in the sense of feeling uneasy at any
overtly manifested mark of the inequalities endemic in
our society as in every other society; and pluralistic, in
the sense of being impatient with the attempt of any
movement, cause, or institution to take in "too much
ground," as the familiar phrase has it. Culturally, the
American Way exhibits an intense faith in education,
significantly coupled with a disparagement of culture
in the aesthetic sense; and, characteristically, an extra-

ordinarily high moral valuation of—sanitation! This is a good example of how what would appear to be rather ordinary matter-of-fact values become thoroughly religionized in the American Way as civil religion. A printed placard displayed in hundreds, perhaps thousands, of restaurants all over the country reads: "Sanitation is a way of life. As a way of life, it must be nourished from within and grow as a spiritual ideal in human relations." Here cleanliness is not merely next to godliness; it is virtually on the same level, as a kind of equivalent.

But, of course, it is the politico-economic aspect of the American Way as America's civil religion that is most familiar to us, as, indeed, in its own way, it was in the civil religions of the ancient world. If America's civil religion had to be defined in one phrase, the "religion of democracy" would undoubtedly be the phrase, but democracy in a peculiarly American sense. It exalts national unity, as, indeed, every civil religion does. On its political side, it means the Constitution. I am reminded of Socrates' deification of the Laws of Athens in the Platonic dialogue, the *Crito*. On its economic side, it means "free enterprise." On its social side, an egalitarianism which, as I have indicated, is not only compatible with, but indeed actually implies, vigorous economic competition and high social mobility. Spiritually, it is best expressed in the very high valuation of religion, and in that special kind of idealism which has come to be recognized as characteristically American. But it is in its vision of America, in its symbols and rituals, in its holidays and its liturgy, in its Saints and its sancta, that it shows itself to be so truly and thoroughly a religion, the common religion of Americans, America's civil religion.

But a word of caution. I have listed a number of aspects of the American Way that do not seem, at first sight, to be religious in a certain narrow sense of the word. But that is exactly the character of a civil religion; it is the religionization of the national life and

national culture. You may be sure that the great annual Panathenaic Procession from the lower agora to
the Acropolis, in which the youths of seventeen or
eighteen received their arms and became adult citizens, entering the Athenian armed forces, would have
seemed to us, accustomed as we are to the idea,
though not to the reality, of the separation of national
life and religion, to be really a political ceremony. But
it was the archaic image of Athena that was carried at
the head of the procession, and the procession moved
on to the Parthenon, the temple of Athena. Do you
want the contemporary equivalent of this symboliza-
tion? Then think back to the presidential inauguration
ceremony of 1973. Who came forward as the intensely
prestigious figures symbolizing this great civil ceremony of ours? The Warrior and the Priest, the soldier
and the clergyman. Here is the perfect synthetic symbol of our civil religion, thoroughly traditional and
immensely potent—and, if I may say so, not altogether
unlike the Panathenaic Procession of ancient Athens.

But let us get back to what I would take to be the
culminating aspects of this account of America's civil
religion—its view of America, its Saints and sancta, its
redemptive history. What is America in the vision of
America's civil religion? Look at the reverse of the
Great Seal of the United States, which is on the dollar
bill. You see an unfinished pyramid, representing the
American national enterprise, and over it the all-seeing
eye of God. Most impressive are the mottoes, in Latin
naturally: "Annuit Coeptis," "He (God) has smiled
upon our beginnings"; and "Novus Ordo Seclorum,"
"A New Order of the Ages." That is America in America's civil religion: a new order, initiated under God,
and flourishing under his benevolent providence.
Could the national and the religious be more combined; is it at all possible to separate the religious and
the national in this civil religion, any more than it was
in ancient Greece or Rome?

It is this vision that gives substance to American

history as redemptive history in America's civil religion. For this we can borrow the felicitous phrase of Oscar Handlin, "Adventure in Freedom." That is how Americans see the ultimate meaning of American history.

A redemptive history has, of course, its messianism. And so does America's civil religion. Over a century ago, in 1850, in an impassioned outburst in *White Jacket*, Herman Melville formulated this messianic vision in these tremendous words:

> God has predestined, mankind expects, great things from our race; and great things we feel in our souls. The rest of the nations must soon be in our rear. We are the pioneers of the world, the advance guard, sent on through the wilderness of untried things to break a new path in the New World that is ours. . . . Long enough have we debated whether, indeed, the political Messiah has come. But he has come in us. . . . And, let us remember that, with ourselves, almost for the first time in history, national selfishness is unbounded philanthropy.

One recalls Pericles' celebrated funeral oration, given by Thucydides.

Similarly Charles Fleischer, at the turn of the twentieth century, observed: "We of America are the 'peculiar people,' consecrated to the mission of realizing Democracy, [which] is potentially a universal spiritual principle, aye, a religion."[3] Or Hugh Miller, in 1948: "America was not created to be supreme among the 'great powers.' It was created to inaugurate the transition of human society to just society. It is a missionary enterprise, propagating a gospel for all men."[4]

With its redemptive history and its messianism, America's civil religion has its liturgy and its liturgical year. The traditional Christian year and the Jewish religious year have been virtually eroded in American popular religion, reduced to Christmas and Easter on the Christian side, and to Passover and the High Holy Days on the Jewish side. But, as W. Lloyd Warner tells us, "all societies, simple or complex, possess some form of ceremonial calendar. . . ."[5] In America it is the ceremonial calendar of America's civil religion, our yearly round of national holidays. Lloyd Warner explains:

> The ceremonial calendar of American society, this yearly round of holidays and holy days, . . . is a symbol system used by all Americans. Christmas, [New Year,] Thanksgiving, Memorial Day, [Washington's and Lincoln's birthdays,] and the Fourth of July are days in our ceremonial calendar which allow Americans to express common sentiments . . . and share their feelings with others on set days pre-established by the society for that very purpose. This [ceremonial] calendar functions to draw all people together, to emphasize their similarities and common heritage, to minimize their differences, and to contribute to their thinking, feeling, and acting alike.[6]

Recall Robin Williams's characterization of civil religion as the common religion of a people that is quoted at the outset of this essay.

America's civil religion, too, has its Saints—preeminently Washington and Lincoln—and its sancta and its shrines—think of Washington, D.C. and Hyde Park. Some examination of the Saints of our civil religion is, I think, in place here. I turn to Lloyd Warner again. He is describing, as an anthropologist would, a Memorial Day service in Yankee City. First, as to the religio-national function of Memorial Day: "The Memorial Day ceremonies and subsidiary rites . . . are rituals which are a sacred symbol system, which functions periodically to integrate the whole community, with its conflicting symbols and its opposing autonomous churches and associations. . . .

Memorial Day is a cult of the dead which organizes and integrates the various faiths, ethnic and class groups into a sacred unity."[7] That is what a civil religion is about. And then he continues, quoting the chief Memorial Day orator at the ceremony he is reporting: " 'No character except the Carpenter of Nazareth,' this orator proclaimed, 'has ever been honored the way Washington and Lincoln have been in New England. Virtue, freedom from sin, and righteousness are qualities possessed by Washington and Lincoln and, in possessing these qualities, both were true Americans. . . .' "[8] It will not escape notice, I hope, that Washington and Lincoln are here raised to superhuman level, as true Saints of America's civil religion. They are equipped with the qualities and virtues that, in traditional Christianity, are attributed to Jesus alone—freedom from sin, for example. And they are endowed with these exalted qualities simply by virtue of the fact that they were—true Americans! I don't know any more impressive illustration of the deeply religious nature of America's civil religion.

What are the sources of America's civil religion? Only in the most general way need we refer to civil religion in the ancient world, or even to the clearly articulated notion of civil religion projected by Jean-Jacques Rousseau as the civil religion of his ideal society so carefully described in his *Social Contract*. First, we must recognize, and I want to repeat, that, in Robin Williams's words, "Every functioning society has, to an important degree, a common religion, . . . a common set of ideas, [ideals,] rituals, and symbols. . . ."[9] And then we have to look to American history and American experience for the sources of the particular form and features of America's civil religion as the American Way of Life. After careful study and scrutiny I have come to the conclusion that the American Way of Life, and therefore America's civil religion, is compounded of the two great religious movements that molded America—the Puritan way, secularized; and the Revivalist way, secularized. The legacy of Puritanism has endowed us with its strenuous, idealistic, moralistic character; but deprived, through pervasive secularization, of the Puritan sense of sin and judgment. The Revivalist legacy has given us its active, pragmatic, what I might term its promotional, character; the slogan "Deeds not creeds!" comes not from John Dewey, but from mid-nineteenth-century revivalism; but again, through drastic secularization it is a pragmatism, a promotionalism, an expansivism no longer "in the cause of Christ."

We do not know how against what earlier background, if any, the civil religion of Athens or Rome emerged into historical times; but we can see the emergence of America's civil religion out of the earlier Protestant Christianity some time toward the middle of the nineteenth century. Here we may be guided by Sidney Mead. "What was not so obvious at the time," Professor Mead writes, referring to the second half of the nineteenth century,

> was that the United States, in effect, had two religions, or at least two different forms of the same religion, and the prevailing Protestant ideology represented a syncretistic mingling of the two. The first was the religion of the [Protestant] denominations. . . . The second was the religion of the American society and nation. This . . . was articulated in terms of the destiny of America, under God, to be fulfilled by perfecting the democratic way of life for the example and betterment of mankind.[10]

In these percipient words, we can recognize the outlines and substance of America's civil religion.

These words suggest that there have been various stages in the emergence of civil religion in America and in the varying relations of this religion to the more conventional religions of Christianity and Judaism. Unfortunately, this aspect of the problem of the development of America's civil religion has not yet received adequate study. Yet we are in a position to distinguish very generally certain phases. There is, first of all, the emerging syncretism to which Mead refers in the passage I have just read. After that, apparently, comes a very explicit and unembarrassed religionization of the American Way. And finally, some time in this century, the explicit exaltation of the American Way, or democracy, as the super-religion, over and above all other religions. Consider these two statements. The first is from J. Paul Williams, a distinguished scholar and professor of religion: "Americans must come to look upon the democratic ideal (not necessarily the practice of it) as the Will of God, or, if they please, of Nature. . . . Americans must be brought to the conviction that democracy is the very Law of Life. . . . The state must be brought into the picture; governmental agencies must teach the democratic idea *as religion*. . . . Primary responsibility for teaching democracy as religion must be given to the public schools."[11] The civil religion as established religion with the public schools as its seminaries. But it is Horace M. Kallen, the well-known philosopher, who has put the matter most clearly and most strikingly. "For the communicants of the democratic faith," Kallen proclaims, "it [democracy] is the religion *of* and *for* religions. . . . [It is] the religion of religions; all may freely come together in it."[12] America's civil religion, democracy, is the overarching faith, in which the particular religions may find their particular place, provided they don't claim any more. Think of the Roman overarching civil religion with its Pantheon, and with the niches in the Pantheon so generously awarded by Rome to the particular ethnic religions, so long as they did not come into collision with the overarching faith of Rome.

How shall we envisage the relation of America's civil religion to the various versions of Christianity and Judaism professed by Americans? This was a problem for the world of classical antiquity as well. Romans and Greeks of those days had at least four different kinds of religion in coexistence: (1) the very ancient Indo-European religion of the high gods, the Olympian deities for the Greeks—the religion of Zeus-Jupiter; (2) the domestic religion, compounded by the cult of ancestors and the household gods, the *lares* and *penates* of Rome; (3) the so-called mystery religions, the personal salvationary cults, largely though not entirely of foreign, oriental origin; and, finally, (4) the great civil religion of the *polis* and the *civitas,* expanded into empire. We know, from unfortunately too fragmentary data, that the relations among these coexisting religions were always uneasy, sometimes hostile. In the Rome of the late republic and early empire, repeated attempts were made to outlaw the oriental salvation cults as incompatible with "true Roman piety," but to no effect. Even when the various bans were lifted or fell into disuse, however, the relations remained far from cordial.

In this country today, there seems to be, for the great mass of Americans, no sense of conflict, or even of tension, between America's civil religion and the traditional religions of Christianity and Judaism professed by almost all Americans. The civil religion is, of course, affirmed as the American Way, but is neither seen nor denominated as a religion by the great mass of Americans; and that makes coexistence all the easier. Yet there are some points of tension, perhaps even of conflict, at the periphery, what I have elsewhere called the "hold-out groups." There are, first, here and there, groups of incompletely enculturated—that is, incompletely Americanized—immigrants; quite naturally they stand on the margins of the American Way, and therefore have not yet come under the coverage of America's civil religion. It would not be difficult to specify names and places, but that is hardly necessary. These groups are very small, and are rapidly diminishing.

Second, there are what are sometimes called the "old-fashioned" churches, churches with a strong creedal or confessional tradition, which tend to look askance at some of the manifestations and expressions of America's civil religion. But this attitude, too, is rapidly eroding, and will not, I think, last very long. Finally, among the "hold-out" groups are the theologians and theologically inclined laymen, a rather small group in this country, but the group from which the various attempts to identify, examine, and criticize America's civil religion have mostly come. All in all, however, these "hold-out groups" comprise a very small proportion of the American people. By and large, the great mass of Americans are not aware of any tension, or friction, or conflict between America's civil religion and their professed faiths, whatever they may be.

I come now to the last, and perhaps most difficult, question that I have set myself in examining this problem of civil religion. And that question is double: how are we to evaluate America's civil religion culturally, on the one hand, and theologically, on the other? Some of my friendly critics, such as Sidney Mead and Andrew Greeley, gently upbraid me for treating America's civil religion too harshly. I plead Not guilty, and I will try to make my case. First, I, of course, regard America's civil religion as a genuine religion; and so was the Athenian civil religion and the Roman—in fact, all the various civil religions of the ancient world. The fact that they were, and America's civil religion is, congruent with the culture is no argument against it; all religions, even the most sectarian, are embedded in, and display some congruence with, some concretion of culture, simply because all religions, in their human dimension (and they all possess a human dimension) must necessarily reflect some aspects of human society and social life. Furthermore, America's civil religion, as it has emerged during the past two centuries, strikes me as a noble religion, celebrating some very noble civic virtues. But so was the Roman civil religion in its best period, and so was Confucianism turnéd into religion in classical China. On its cultural side, I would regard the American Way of Life, which is the social face of America's civil religion, as probably the best way of life yet devised for a mass society—with the proviso that even the best way of life, if it is the way of life of a mass society, will have its grave defects. And, if Abraham Lincoln, for instance, is to be taken as an exemplar of our civil religion, then we can see what a powerful strain of genuine Christian spirituality, in this case Calvinist, has entered into it. So I certainly would not want to disparage America's civil religion in its character as religion.

But, if it is an authentic religion as civil religion, America's civil religion is not, and cannot be seen as, authentic Christianity or Judaism, or even as a special cultural version of either or both. Because they serve a jealous God, these biblical faiths cannot allow any claim to ultimacy and absoluteness on the part of any thing or any idea or any system short of God, even when that claims to be the ultimate locus of ideas, ideals, values, and allegiance is the very finest of human institutions; it is still human, man's own construction, and not God himself. To see America's civil religion as somehow standing above or beyond the biblical religions of Judaism and Christianity, and Islam too, as somehow including them and finding a place for them in its overarching unity, is idolatry, however innocently held and whatever may be the subjective intentions of the believers. But this is theology, which I have discussed elsewhere, and which I have tried to avoid here. In this essay it has been my intention to set down my thinking, and some of the conclusions I have reached, on the nature, sources, purposes, structure, and functioning of America's civil religion, and to call attention to some of the questions that need urgent attention for a clarification of the overall problem. To some degree, I hope, I have con-

tributed to this end, so important for a real understanding of our culture, society, and religion.

Notes

[1] Numa Denis Fustel de Coulanges, *La Cité antique* (1864), chap. VII, *ad finem;* chap. VI, *ad finem.*

[2] Robin Williams, *American Society: A Sociological Interpretation* (New York: Alfred A. Knopf, 1952), p. 312.

[3] Quoted in Arthur Mann, "Charles Fleischer's Religion of Democracy," *Commentary,* June 1954.

[4] Hugh Miller, *An Historical Introduction to Modern Philosophy* (New York, 1948), p. 570.

[5] W. Lloyd Warner, *Structure of American Life* (Edinburgh, 1952), p. 2.

[6] *Ibid.*

[7] *Ibid.,* p. 214.

[8] *Ibid.,* p. 220.

[9] Williams, *op. cit.,* p. 312.

[10] Sidney E. Mead, "American Protestantism since the Civil War: From Denominationalism to Americanism," *The Lively Experiment* (New York, 1963), p. 135.

[11] J. Paul Williams, *What Americans Believe and How They Worship* (New York: Harper & Row, 1951), pp. 71, 78, 368, 374.

[12] H. M. Kallen, "Democracy's True Religion," *Saturday Review of Literature,* July 28, 1951.